The Selling of the
Constitutional Convention

THE SELLING OF THE CONSTITUTIONAL CONVENTION

A History of News Coverage

John K. Alexander

MADISON HOUSE

Madison 1990

For my favorite historian
June Granatir Alexander

LIBRARY OF CONGRESS CATALOGING IN PUBLICATION DATA
Alexander, John K.
The selling of the Constitutional Convention : a history of news
coverage / by John K. Alexander.
p.   cm.
Includes bibliographical references.
ISBN 094561215X
1. United States. Constitutional Convention (1787)—Public
opinion.   2. Public opinion—United States—History—18th century.
3. Press and politics—United States—History—18th century.
4. United States—Politics and government—1783–1789.   I. Title.
JK148.A48   1990
973.3'18—dc20   90-5450
                                                        CIP

ISBN 0-945612-15-X

Printed on acid-free paper

Designed by William Kasdorf

Typeset and Produced for Madison House
by Impressions, Inc., Madison, Wisconsin

Published by
Madison House Publishers, Inc.
P.O. Box 3100, Madison, Wisconsin 53704

FIRST EDITION

Contents

Preface

This work began by chance. Years ago while reading through newspapers for another research project, I became intrigued by how publishers covered the Constitutional Convention. It was obvious that the supposed secrecy of the convention had not stopped the press from offering extensive commentary and speculation on the convention and issues related to it. Although that in itself was hardly surprising, the analysis offered in the newspapers seemed more patterned and more one-sided than might have been expected. It was, of course, possible that the apparent unity would evaporate if an investigation of the country's press, not just a sampling of a few newspapers, were undertaken. I began that investigation by reading the Philadelphia papers and several papers from different sections of the country. As the research progressed, the feasibility of doing a comprehensive inquiry appeared nearly impossible. There were too many newspapers for one scholar to corral, much less read in a systematic and thorough way. Fortunately, the personnel of The Center for the Study of the American Constitution at the University of Wisconsin-Madison were working along parallel lines. For their important Documentary History of the Ratification of the Constitution project, they obtained virtually all the extant press publications and systematically culled them. Even more fortunate, as explained in greater detail in Appendix 2, John P. Kaminski, director of the Center, believes in turning the concept of a scholarly community into reality. John kindly granted me access to the raw files of the Documentary History project. Being able to use those files allowed me to discover what was published and reprinted in 1787 in the press as a whole—not just in a sample of newspapers.

Although this work offers a case study of the late eighteenth-century press in action, it also sheds light on the ongoing debate about bias in the American media of today. The modern media has increasingly come under heavy fire. Critics of various persuasions charge that the media is growing more and more biased. Some analysts account for this by putting special weight on the transformation of the media into corporate big business. In their provocative and perceptive *Manufacturing Consent* (1988), Edward Herman and Noam Chomsky emphasize that numerous variables work as "filters," limiting what the media produces. They stress, however, that the big-business orientation of the media is an especially significant filter. It helps produce what they claim is a dangerous uniformity of view and even news management. Ben Bagdikian, in the latest edition of his *The Media Monopoly* (1990), argues the same theme even more strongly. He offers suggestions to stop what he perceives as the media's ever-quickening march along a path that has already led to dangerous and often subtle shading of news coverage. Intriguingly, Bagdikian's proposals for reform include creating a pattern of diversified media ownership. What he champions closely resembles the situation in the America of 1787. Yet the press of 1787 covered the Constitutional Convention with a stunning single-mindedness as thoroughgoing as the modern media is alleged to employ. Sadly, the evidence from 1787 suggests that independent ownership and operation offer no guarantee of a truly free and informative press. Indeed, it turns out that pervasive "news management" is hardly a modern development. It existed even in what we might like to think of as the most glorious days of the free press in America.

The University of Cincinnati and colleagues at the University helped in the creation of this volume. A one quarter special duty assignment granted by the University of Cincinnati College of Arts and Sciences at an early stage in the work provided valuable research time. The staff of the University's interlibrary-loan department has been unfailingly helpful and efficient. Colleagues and students, who attended a History Department Faculty Seminar devoted to an early outline of the findings, voiced helpful comments.

John Kaminski and Richard Leffler, an associate editor on the Documentary History project, read the work in draft form. Each offered valuable analysis and suggestions. Greg Britton of Madison House did more than shepherd the work into print. Our conversations about the modern media proved stimulating and helpful in focusing my own thoughts on the subject.

Friends who are or have been journalists provided special assistance. Both in word and deed, Ray Horn provided eloquent commentary on the importance of the press. Over the years, John Svicarovich and Joel and Judy Havemann offered thoughtful observations and the gentle encouragement that flows from true friendship.

The debt I owe my historian wife June is almost incalculable. It would require many lengthy paragraphs to recount and praise all that she did and endured to help bring this work to fruition. Truly, there is no adequate way to give her the thanks she deserves. But what it is in my power to give, as another page in this volume makes clear, is given with thanks and with love.

Cincinnati   JKA

Short Titles and Symbols

Brigham, *History*—Clarence S. Brigham, *History and Bibliography of American Newspapers* 1690–1820, 2 vols. (Worcester, 1947).

CC—Designation for documents in *Commentaries on the Constitution*.

CDR—Merrill Jensen, ed., *Constitutional Documents and Records, 1776–1787* (Madison, 1976). This work is Volume 1 of *DHORC*.

COC1—John P. Kaminski and Gaspare J. Saladino, *eds.*, *Commentaries on the Constitution: Public and Private. Volume 1: 21 February to 7 November 1787* (Madison, 1981). This work is Volume 13 of *DHORC*.

COC4—John P. Kaminski and Gaspare J. Saladino, *eds.*, *Commentaries on the Constitution: Public and Private. Volume 4: 1 February to 3 March 1788* (Madison, 1981). This work is Volume 16 of *DHORC*.

DHORC—*The Documentary History of the Ratification of the Constitution*.

Evans—Charles Evans, *American Bibliography*, 12 vols. (Chicago, 1903–1934).

Farrand, *Records*—Max Farrand, ed., *The Records of the Federal Convention of 1787*, rev. ed., 4 vols. (New Haven, 1937).

Hutson, *Supplement*—James H. Hutson, ed. and with the assistance of Leonard Rapport, *Supplement to Max Farrand's The Records of the Federal Convention of 1787* (New Haven, 1987).

WMQ—*The William and Mary Quarterly*, Third Series.

Introduction

The American Revolution did not only pit rebellious colonists against Loyalists and Redcoats. At times, and especially when creating governments, American revolutionary fought American revolutionary. These conflicts could be long, heated, and bitter. Fortunately the political warriors typically fought not with powder, ball, and shot, but with letters, speeches, and the printed word. This last weapon, the printed word, is the subject of this study. The focus is on how newspapers and magazines, which comprised the eighteenth-century news media, covered the Constitutional Convention.

Most American political leaders of the Revolutionary Era quickly divided into two camps on the question of how to structure the central government. Remembering the detested power of Britain's imperial government, one group championed the Articles of Confederation because they incorporated the principle of individual state sovereignty and because the central government did not have the power to tax. These Americans praised the Confederation because it was *not* a strong, national government. The second band of revolutionary leaders, the nationalists, firmly disagreed. Believing the young country *had* to have a vigorous national government, they consistently labored to transform the Articles of Confederation so that the central government would have real power and especially the power to raise revenue on its own.

In the 1780s as nationalists gained strength in Congress, they tried amending the Articles. The Impost of 1781, championed by nationalists, would have given the Confederation government an independent income based on a five percent import duty. In time every state except Rhode Island voted for the plan, but one negative vote was all it took to defeat an amendment. Then the nationalists offered a revised revenue plan that called for a new tariff, the Impost of 1783. Amid political maneuverings, which included conditional passage in Pennsylvania, every state except New York had approved the amendment by mid-1786. At the same time, concern over the Union's unsettled economy spurred Virginia to organize a special convention to discuss America's trade problems and consider drafting legislation empowering Congress to regulate trade. Although only five states attended, the Annapolis Convention of September 1786 took notable action. The delegates urged that the states send representatives to another convention, to be held in May of 1787 in Philadelphia, which would devise reforms enabling the federal government to deal with the Union's problems.

In the fall and winter of 1786–87, discontent flared in various states and burst into civil war in Massachusetts, where disgruntled farmers waged Shays's Rebellion. The conflict reached a violent peak in late January 1787. Then, on February 15, New York's legislature took action that most people believed spelled doom for the Impost of 1783. At the same time, however, the legislature, supporting efforts already undertaken by other states, urged Congress to authorize a convention to correct the Confederation's weaknesses. Congress agreed on February 21 and called for a convention to meet in Philadelphia on May 14. Because delegates were slow in arriving, the Constitutional Convention did not begin its official proceedings until May 25.

Although only authorized to revise the Articles, the delegates seemed willing to scrap them. The Virginia Plan, designed to create a new, strong, national government, was introduced on May 29 and served as the basis for discussion. However, many delegates from less powerful states detested the fact that the Virginia Plan called for representation in the new government's legislature to be based on the wealth or population of the individual states. The tradition had been one state, one vote. To retain that system, the New Jersey or Paterson Plan, which would have amended rather than overthrown the Articles, was proposed on June 15. The delegates voted to reject the Paterson Plan on June 19, but a deadlock quickly developed over retaining or abandoning equality of states in the central government's legislature. As James Madison expressed it, "the great difficulty lies in the affair of Representation; and if this could be adjusted, all others would be surmountable." A special committee was appointed on July 2 to try to resolve the dispute. In part to allow the committee an opportunity to work, the delegates, who had been meeting daily except Sundays, adjourned for two days over the Fourth of July. It took time, but on July 16 the delegates agreed to what is typically called the Great Compromise. Under it, the principle of one state, one vote was retained for the upper house while a form of proportional representation was approved for the lower house. Knotty problems yet remained, but the delegates achieved enough agreement by July 26 to appoint a Committee of Detail to prepare a first draft of what became the Constitution. Again to allow a committee time to function, the delegates adjourned and did not resume deliberations until August 6. A month later they had progressed to the point where they could select a Committee of Style and Arrangement to produce a revised draft of the proposed Constitution; it was adopted on September 15 and signed two days later. After a heated political tussle, those who called themselves "Federalists" finally achieved ratification of the Constitution in 1788.[1]

It has long been recognized that most of the press actively supported the Federalists in the battle over the ratification of the Constitution.[2] But the press entered the political fray even before the Constitution existed. After the fact, John Babcock and Thomas Claxton, the editors of the Lansingburgh, New York, *Northern Centinel*, frankly admitted they had turned their paper into a propaganda instrument during the time the Constitution was being framed. Writing in March 1788, they said they had "conceived it a duty incumbent on them to prepare the minds of their readers for its *reception*."[3]

Although he did not admit it publicly, David Humphreys boasted that he and others had done the same. Writing to George Washington shortly after the Constitutional Convention adjourned, Humphreys spoke of how the press could manipulate public opinion. "Judicious & well-timed publications have," he said, "great efficacy in ripening the judgment of men in this quarter of the Continent."[4] Babcock, Claxton, and Humphreys thus conceded they had functioned as political partisans who had championed the convention.[5]

Politicos and others who did not share the convention boosters' views also believed, and complained, that many editors used their publications as propaganda tools in the spring and summer of 1787.[6] However, even if publishers tried to aid and abet the convention, no way exists to measure accurately the possible influence of their effort. No eighteenth-century equivalents of the opinion poll existed.[7] Nevertheless, examining coverage of the convention and events surrounding it can reveal the extent of the undertaking.[8]

This study offers an analysis of newspaper and magazine coverage of the Constitutional Convention from the time Congress authorized it on February 21, 1787, until the proposed Constitution appeared in print throughout the nation. Although the delegates approved the Constitution on September 17, the document was, of course, printed in some newspapers much later. In Philadelphia, the convention city, the Constitution first appeared in a newspaper either on the evening of September 18 or in the papers printed the next day. The Lexington *Kentucke Gazette*, the last of the extant papers to publish the Constitution, did not print it until October 20.[9]

An impressive number of news media publications was available to cover the convention. In 1787, two biweekly, fifty-eight weekly, eleven semiweekly, and five daily newspapers were published in the United States throughout the year. A new daily appeared in Maryland in August but expired after a run of only a few weeks. The nine weekly newspapers started in 1787 did much better; all were, it appears, still in existence when 1788 dawned. Only two established newspapers in operation when the year began ceased publication in 1787. In addition, two Philadelphia monthly magazines were published throughout the year.[10]

Solid statistical data about circulation is scarce. Clarence S. Brigham, Frank Luther Mott, and Donald H. Stewart all suggest that as late as 1800 the average circulation for a newspaper was something less than seven hundred copies. The two magazines in existence in 1787 probably had only slightly, if at all, larger circulations. However, analysts stress that newspaper circulation figures are misleading because each copy was more widely read than would be the case today. One reason was that inns, taverns, and coffee houses provided copies for their customers.[11] The importance of newspapers to those establishments was well illustrated in 1787 when "Philadelphus" casually noted: "I daily attend the Coffee-Houses, for the purpose, not only of reading the news-papers, but likewise of enquiring into the situation of my country from intelligent persons, and of course making my observations on what I either read, or hear."[12] Equally important, the people of that day, including foreign visitors, firmly believed that newspapers played a vital role in shaping public opinion.[13]

The newspapers published in the United States in 1787 shared many similarities. The numerous signed essays published in their pages, like that by Philadelphus, almost invariably carried a pen name. Because of this practice, a modified form of citation for such works has been used in this study.[14] The newspapers of that day also typically contained material supplied by persons described as correspondents. However, when the editors of 1787 referred to a "correspondent," they were not referring to paid reporters. Using today's terms, they can in many cases perhaps best be compared to someone who contributes to an "op-ed" page or writes a letter to the editor. However, some correspondents served the function of unpaid reporters by providing eyewitness accounts or straightforward "news" accounts.

Most newspapers also looked alike. The great majority had four pages formed by folding a single large sheet. The

first page usually carried advertisements, essays, or official
government documents. Although some news from the Union
might appear on the second page, it was usually devoted to
information from abroad or to essays. The typical third page
contained, in addition to advertising, news from the United
States with one dateline always reserved for the name of the
city where the paper was published. Even that section, however, usually offered very little local news. Advertisements
invariably dominated the last page, but it might also contain
something in a poet's corner or some form of commentary.

Because eighteenth-century newspaper publishing was
often a scissors-and-paste operation, newspapers shared more
than a similar format. As John P. Kaminski and Gaspare J.
Saladino, editors of *Commentaries on the Constitution*, note,
publishers "operated a primitive regional and national news
service."[15] Aided by a tradition allowing them to exchange
their papers free of charge, newspaper publishers had long
had access to what their colleagues produced.[16] And editors
habitually lifted anything from short fillers to long essays from
other publications and reprinted part or all of the material,
often with slight changes. Although newspapers were routinely exchanged, not all publishers saw every newspaper
and magazine published in the country. Unless an item
appeared at some time in a Philadelphia, New York, or Boston source, its chances of being widely reprinted declined
significantly. Moreover, commentary that originated in publications located in the backcountry had very little chance
of being reprinted.[17] In addition, something might be widely
reprinted, but only in one section of the country. While such
points must be kept in mind, the practice of reprinting provides a way to measure the popularity of publications about
the Constitutional Convention. By examining all news media
publications, not just a sample of them, and by tracing how
often and where material appeared, it is possible to assess the
political stance taken by the media.[18]

Tracing reprints is difficult. One problem stems from how
editors went about reprinting. Some, such as John Dunlap
and David C. Claypoole of the *Pennsylvania Packet*, were

generally scrupulous about indicating the source of items they reprinted. Furthermore, Dunlap and Claypoole tended to reprint items exactly or almost exactly as they originally appeared. Unfortunately, many editors were not so careful. Although most cited the date and the city where a reprint item originated, editors also reprinted items without noting that the material came from another source. Many also thought nothing of printing, often without attribution, a portion of an essay. In several cases, editors blended two or three pieces, added a few words of their own, and thus produced "new" items.[19]

Another difficulty in determining number of reprintings stems from the problem of survivability of eighteenth-century newspapers. Although important material appeared slightly before or after these dates, for the current study, the vital period includes late February through September 1787. Using that period as the measure, the problems caused by the failure of some newspapers to survive are clear. For example, even if an item appeared in every state of the Union, that fact would probably go undetected because few issues of Delaware newspapers and even fewer issues of North Carolina newspapers from 1787 have survived. However, except for Delaware and North Carolina, all of the states in the Union and Vermont in 1787 had at least one publication for which there is a complete or nearly complete file available.[20]

Despite such problems, the exact number of reprints is given either in the text or in footnotes. In addition, a measure of reprint popularity has been established based on the maximum number of reprintings that actually occurred. Since any press item printed in ten publications achieved at least twenty percent and realistically closer to twenty-five percent of the reprintings it was possible to attain, it seems logical to say that ten appearances made something a "popular" or "widely" reprinted item.[21] Because the study is designed to assess the media's stance, such extensively reproduced material receives special attention. Indeed, the following rule has been adhered to: if an item about the Constitutional Convention or about issues relevant to it gained "popular" status, the item is cited in this study. Indicating reprint popularity and citing all widely circulated items allow for consideration of all relevant publications without placing undue importance on a well-phrased or extreme, but atypical, piece of literary evidence.

The analysis presented grows out of both political events and news media coverage itself. The first chapter covers the period from late February 1787, when Congress authorized the convention, until May 14, the day it was scheduled to open. Later chapter divisions are based on the press's coverage. For a variety of reasons, Philadelphia was, as noted, a major source of reprint items for American publishers. In addition, because the convention met there, news about the gathering typically first appeared in the Philadelphia press. Such reports probably gained credence because they emanated from the convention city. Thus, it could be critically important if and when something appeared in the Philadelphia press. As the chapters on the period after mid-June make clear, what might reasonably be called the "Philadelphia factor" greatly influenced overall print coverage of the convention.

Because chapters are based on the evolving political situation and press coverage, the significant themes developed in that coverage are not fully drawn together until the conclusion. However, this is a study in history, not a detective story. It is logical therefore to sketch the major points the analysis reveals. Examination of press coverage of the Constitutional Convention provides solid evidence that a campaign was mounted to convince the people to accept whatever the delegates produced short of monarchy. As often happens in political campaigns, the rhetoric grew harsher as the weeks passed. At times the effort to promote the convention went beyond mere editorial writing to include news management. The news media authors of 1787 who wrote on issues surrounding the Constitutional Convention did not focus on abstract or scholarly ideological analyses of political systems such as republicanism. Rather, they emphasized coldly pragmatic and patriotic themes rooted in claims that the Union and its people faced imminent ruin.[22] Overall, the campaign was presented in what people of that day could call a plain-language style.

As the testimonies of Humphreys and Babcock and Claxton reveal, the proconvention effort was in some cases directed by "propaganda editors." Their main interest was proselytizing, not providing news and balanced comment. It is not possible to prove conclusively which or how many editors adopted the strategy outlined by the propaganda editors. One salient point about the press's coverage is, nevertheless, especially revealing: essayists who cast doubt on the convention, its work, or themes developed in the proconvention campaign rarely appeared in print. Perhaps even more important, unless their message was stated circumspectly, these writers seldom got reprinted.

• • •

The news media was thus not merely pro-Constitution once the document existed. From the time the convention was authorized in February, press coverage, taken as a whole, championed it and what it would recommend. Publishers increasingly strove, as David Humphreys said, "to prepare the minds of the Citizens for the favorable reception of *whatever* might be the result."[23] Because of this effort, the press's coverage truly amounted to the selling of the Constitutional Convention.

Notes to Introduction

1. The June 19, 1787 Madison quotation is from Farrand, *Records*, 1: 321. The Farrand, *Records*, with the addition of Hutson, *Supplement*, remains the standard documentary source on the Constitutional Convention. The Annapolis Convention proceedings and report of September 14, 1786 are given in CDR, 181–85. The best short discussion of the workings of the convention is still Max Farrand, *The Framing of the Constitution of the United States* (New Haven, 1913). Useful treatments of varying length and detail on the general developments of the movement for and adoption of the Constitution are: CDR, 176–79; COC1: 3–40; Merrill Jensen, *The New Nation: A History of the United States During the Confederation*

1781-1789 (New York, 1950); idem, *The Articles of Confederation: An Interpretation of the Social-Constitutional History of the American Revolution, 1774-1781* (Madison, 1940), especially 3-15, 107-25, 161-76, 239-45; E. James Ferguson, *The Power of the Purse: A History of American Public Finance, 1776-1790* (Chapel Hill, 1961); William P. Murphy, *The Triumph of Nationalism: State Sovereignty, the Founding Fathers, and the Making of the Constitution* (Chicago, 1967); Robert A. Rutland, *The Ordeal of the Constitution: The Antifederalists and the Ratification Struggle of 1787-1788* (Boston, 1983; originally published 1966); Jackson Turner Main, *The Antifederalists: Critics of the Constitution, 1781-1788* (Chapel Hill, 1961); Richard B. Bernstein, with Kym S. Rice, *Are We to Be A Nation?: The Making of the Constitution* (Cambridge, 1987); Richard B. Morris, *The Forging of the Union, 1781-1789* (New York, 1987). Several collections of essays, especially those spawned by the Bicentennial of the signing of the Constitution, provide valuable comments on the general developments. Included in this group are: Leonard W. Levy and Dennis J. Mahoney, eds., *The Framing and Ratification of the Constitution* (New York, 1987); Richard Beeman, Stephen Botein, and Edwin C. Carter II, eds., *Beyond Confederation: Origins of the Constitution and American National Identity* (Chapel Hill, 1987); Michael A. Gillespie and Michael Lienesch, eds., *Ratifying the Constitution* (Lawrence, 1988); J. Jackson, Leonard W. Levy, and Ken Masugi, eds., *The American Founding: Essays on the Formation of the Constitution* (Westport, 1988); Patrick T. Conley and John P. Kaminski, eds., *The Constitution and the States: The Role of the Original Thirteen in the Framing and Adoption of the Federal Constitution* (Madison, 1988). This last work contains an especially useful piece by Conley on "Posterity Views the Founding: General Published Works Pertaining to the Creation of the Constitution; A Bibliographic Essay" (pp. 295-329). On the misleading nature of the terms "Federalist" and "Antifederalist" and the problems of not using them, see Chapter One, n. 3.

2. See Chapter Five, n. 59.

3. The editors believed that by 1787 the United States had "felt and acknowledged the want of a Constitution that would unite them into *one common band of brothers*; to form which a general Convention convened." Quotations from the Albany *Federal Herald* of March 31, 1788, which was the successor to the *Northern Centinel.* The first line of the statement was rendered in large roman type and the rest in italics which gave the whole piece eye-catching

appeal. John Kaminski kindly drew my attention to this statement. Examples of the partisanship of Babcock and Claxton appear later in this work. Here and elsewhere, unless stated otherwise, all information on names of publishers and newspaper titles comes from Brigham, *History*. Since virtually all newspapers and magazines cited in this study were published in 1787, items printed in 1787 will be cited without the year of publication.

4. See Humphreys to George Washington of September 28, 1787, given in COC1: 261–62 with quotation from p. 261, and see also p. 262, n. 3. Many shared his view on the press's vital role in shaping public opinion. On this, see nn. 11–13 below.

5. Mathew Carey, publisher of the Philadelphia *American Museum*, was accused in October 1787 of only printing material favorable to the new Constitution. Under pressure, he finally allowed some Antifederalist material into his magazine in November 1787. In January 1788, Carey defended his earlier selection policies by saying he was a Federalist. This suggests that he too may have used propagandistic techniques to champion the convention. On Carey's actions, see COC1: xxxiv.

6. See especially "Rusticus," *New York Journal*, September 13, and see also Chapter Five.

7. An example of the problems that can occur when trying to translate public pronouncements into a measure of general attitudes can be seen in Stephen E. Lucas, *Portents of Rebellion: Rhetoric and Revolution in Philadelphia, 1765–76* (Philadelphia, 1976) as analyzed in John K. Alexander, "Urban America in the Revolutionary Era: Studies in the Neglected Period of American Urban History," *Journal of Urban History* 5 (Feb. 1979): 242–43.

8. Although authors of general works on the convention may comment on media coverage, they do not analyze it in a systematic way. A useful example, in which the proconvention press stance is noted in passing while the press is praised for its supposed general honesty, is Clinton Rossiter, *1787: The Grand Convention* (New York, 1966), 35, 138, 168, 180, 203–4, 204n, 206, 222–23. Some analysts who have focused on particular states, publications, or cities have considered newspaper coverage during the convention. In her important *The Eleventh Pillar: New York State and the Federal Constitution* (Ithaca, 1966), Linda G. De Pauw assessed the role of the New York media. Although sensitive to the question of reprinting for items published during the ratification conflict, she unfortunately treated the convention-period items that appeared in New

York papers as if they necessarily originated in those papers; she also missed "antifederal" items published in New York in the spring and summer of 1787. (Cf pp. 69–83, 91–105, and see Chapters Two to Four below.) John P. Kaminski offers valuable analysis in his "New York: The Reluctant Pillar," in *The Reluctant Pillar: New York and the Adoption of the Federal Constitution,* ed. Stephen L. Schechter (Troy, 1985), 48–117, and especially 65–67. Carol S. Humphrey assays material contained in some Philadelphia newspapers that seem directly and obviously related to the Constitutional Convention. Unfortunately, the essay suffers from a narrow geographical base, an apparently narrow definition of what material related to the Constitutional Convention, and some overlooked publications. (See her " 'Little Ado About Something': Philadelphia Newspapers and the Constitutional Convention," *American Journalism* 5 [No. 2, 1988]: 63–80. I wish to thank Richard Leffler, associate editor of *DHORC*, for bringing this article to my attention.) Paul D. Marsella assessed propaganda trends in one newspaper by doing a content analysis of symbols in news stories from every fourth issue of the *Essex Journal and New Hampshire Packet* published from May 1787 to September 1788. He focused most closely on the Constitution once it was printed. In addition, selecting only every fourth issue and examining only "news" items may not give an accurate picture. (See his "Propaganda Trends in the *Essex Journal and New Hampshire Packet,* 1787–1788," Essex Institute *Historical Collections* 114 [July 1978]: 161–78.)

9. The *Gazette,* which printed it in installments, did not complete publication of the proposed Constitution until November 3. The basic source on when newspapers printed the Constitution is Leonard Rapport, "Printing the Constitution: The Convention and Newspaper Imprints, August–November 1787," *Prologue, The Journal of the National Archives* 2 (1970): 69–89. Five Philadelphia newspapers carried the proposed Constitution on September 19. However, in his 1970 essay (pp. 80–81), Rapport suggested that the first paper to publish it may well have been the Philadelphia *Evening Chronicle* of September 18—of which no known copy has survived. He built a good case, and in 1981 the editors of COC (1: 200) said the first newspaper printing did occur in the *Evening Chronicle.* Drawing upon the discovery by Richard Leffler of a printing of the Constitution in Virginia based on a Philadelphia printing dated September 18, Rapport has expanded the case for a September 18 *Evening Chronicle* printing in his "Newspaper Print-

ings of the Constitution: An Unresolved Mystery," *Manuscripts* 39 (1987): 327–36. Nevertheless, as Rapport indicates (pp. 333, 334), it is not yet possible to say conclusively that the *Evening Chronicle* was the first newspaper to publish the Constitution.

10. The weeklies were founded on the following schedule: two in May; one in June; one in July; three in August; two in October. In addition, a New York magazine began operation in December. The two newspapers, both weeklies, that ceased publication were the Charlestown, Massachusetts, *American Recorder* (last issue May 25) and the Boston *Continental Journal* (last issue June 21). Unless otherwise noted, this and all other information given in this study on the number, kind, and status of newspapers and magazines was derived from the information given in Appendix 1.

11. On the magazines, see Lyon N. Richardson, *A History of Early American Magazines 1741–1789* (New York, 1931), 272, 277n, 314–15; Frank L. Mott, *A History of American Magazines 1741–1850* (New York, 1930), 13–14, 100–1. On newspapers, see Clarence S. Brigham, *Journals and Journeymen: A Contribution to the History of Early American Newspapers* (Philadelphia, 1950), 19–21; Frank L. Mott, *American Journalism—A History of Newspapers in the United States through 260 Years: 1690 to 1950*, rev. ed. (New York, 1950), 59, 158–59; Donald H. Stewart, *The Opposition Press of the Federalist Period* (Albany, 1969), 16–17; Edwin Emery and Michael Emery, *The Press and America: An Interpretative History of the Mass Media*, 4th ed. (Englewood Cliffs, 1978), 69; Bernard A. Weisberger, *The American Newspaperman* (Chicago, 1961), 24–25; Alfred M. Lee, *The Daily Newspaper in America* (New York, 1937), 44–47, 258–59; Milton W. Hamilton, *The Country Printer: New York State, 1785–1830* (New York, 1936), 211–14.

12. *Pennsylvania Herald*, 18 April, and cf. Mott, *American Journalism*, 159, 159n. 40.

13. Stewart, *Opposition Press*, 12–19, and see also the other sources on newspapers given in n. 11 above.

14. As indicated by the citation of and reference to "Philadelphus," when material from an item carrying a pen name is first cited in the text, the standard policy of placing the author's pseudonym in quotation marks is followed. However, unless the pen name is a single letter, later references to the pen name in the text are not placed within quotation marks. Thus, the pen name is treated as if it were the author's actual name. This practice has been adopted to enhance readability. The standard citation policy of placing pen

names in quotation marks is, however, retained in footnote references.

15. COC1: xviii.

16. On this practice, which was temporarily interrupted in 1788, see COC4: 540–52.

17. Date of publication combined with distance and what can be called low visibility probably explains why a newsworthy Pennsylvania *Carlisle Gazette* item of September 12 was not reprinted. The piece, an extract of a letter from a "gentleman in Philadelphia," praised the convention and said at least some parts of its work would be made public in about two weeks. Items from the *Carlisle Gazette* typically did not get reprinted even if they were impressive productions. See, e.g., the proconvention effort of "A Citizen" published on August 1 and not reprinted.

18. As noted in the "Preface" and explained in detail in Appendix 2, this study is built on a search of the press as a whole, not merely on a sample of newspapers and magazines.

19. Various examples are given in the body of this study.

20. Delaware had two weekly newspapers in 1787. Only sixteen of their total of sixty-one issues printed from the start of March through the end of September are known to have survived. The situation is worse for the two weekly newspapers published in North Carolina during this period. Only six of the 104 issues published in 1787 have survived. In addition, there are some newspapers from other states for which apparently no issues have survived. See Appendix 1.

21. Thus, throughout this study, number of appearances, as opposed to reprint totals, includes the original publication. Appendix 2 provides further analysis and documentation on the extent of reprinting, additional notations on the sources, and a statement of editorial policies.

22. The media of 1787 add support to those modern analysts who suggest that in seeking to understand the creation of the Constitution too much emphasis has been placed on the role of ideology. For solid and especially relevant commentary on the perhaps too easy use of the idea of Republicanism as a line of analysis, see Issac Kramnick "The 'Great Discussion': The Discourse of Politics in 1787," *WMQ* 45 (1988): 3–32. Peter S. Onuf makes the same point as he emphasizes the importance of giving renewed attention to the events and conditions in the Union of the 1780s. See his "Reflections on the Founding: Constitutional Historiography in

Bicentennial Perspective," *WMQ* 46 (1989): 341–75, and especially 356–60, 374–75.

23. Quotation from COC1: 261 with emphasis added. Henry Knox, in an October 1787 letter to Lafayette about the prospects of the proposed new Constitution, seemed to strike a similar note. He observed that "the minds of the people at large were fully prepared for a change without any particular specification" (COC1: 441–42 with quotation from p. 442). However, taken in context, Knox's comments appear to mean that the people had come to the conclusion that measures must be taken to strengthen the central government rather than that propaganda did the preparing. Of course, and as indicated in the following chapters, some people were not ready or willing to see the central government transformed into the totally new government the Constitution introduced.

1

"We Are No Longer United States":

Looking to the Convention

Extensive news media coverage of the Constitutional Convention began with the publication of the resolution Congress passed on February 21, 1787.[1] Declaring that experience had revealed defects in the Confederation government, Congress asked each state to appoint delegates to meet in convention on May 14 in Philadelphia. The delegates' "sole and express purpose" would be to revise the Articles of Confederation. Their recommendations would be reported to Congress and the state legislatures, all of which had to approve before the Articles could be amended. The goal was to "render the federal Constitution adequate to the exigencies of Government and the preservation of the Union." Obviously this was a major news story: thirty-nine newspapers printed the entire resolution; two others summarized it.[2]

During the next several months, the news media presented a decidedly favorable image of the convention and a bleak view of conditions in America. Many authors of news stories and commentaries who did not even mention the convention implicitly supported it by suggesting that the Confederation government must be strengthened. Those who openly championed the convention developed a variety of themes to prove that the Union was both weak and beleaguered. They said the obvious dangers the country faced and the inability of the Confederation government to handle them justified decisive action. The central government had to be changed, and the convention could be expected to produce admirable results since it was composed of great men. Writers also maintained that "antifederal" types, those who opposed strengthening the federal government, must not be allowed to sabotage the reform effort.[3] Few writers challenged these assertions in the months before the convention opened. Those who did were swamped by press coverage that proclaimed only the convention could save the Union.

• • •

In the preconvention period, writers insisted that the country's problems required prompt action. One important concern was America's ailing economy. Well before Congress authorized the convention, writings bemoaning the hard times confronting America had become a staple press offering. The economic news published in February certainly seemed bleak. A southerner voiced common complaints when he depicted the times as gloomy and lamented that the South's commerce stood on a precarious footing.[4] Northward, things seemed just as bad. A New Yorker grumbled that commercial affairs remained in an embarrassed situation. Shipbuilding had ceased in New York, and most sailors could not get berths. When they did, it was on foreign vessels. Nevertheless, the writer traced economic problems primarily to "that habit of dissipation and idleness which has succeeded economy and frugality."[5] Both accounts, which circulated widely after Congress authorized the convention, reflected the serious complaints about the economy regularly seen in print during the postwar economic downturn.[6]

Linkage between economic issues and the upcoming convention might seem inevitable in the preconvention period. After all, the idea for that gathering sprang from the Annapolis Convention of 1786 which met to deal with the Union's economic problems.[7] Surprisingly, authors rarely tied the work of the upcoming convention to battling economic woes.

However, by emphasizing that the country needed a stronger government to brighten the economic picture, writers implied, and at times not very subtly, that the Confederation government must be overhauled. Their arguments firmly, if silently, supported the convention.

The publisher of the New York *Daily Advertiser* announced his forthcoming edition of John Adams's *A Defence of the Constitutions of Government of the United States of America* by reproducing a section where Adams argued that expanding the central government's powers would improve the economy. Adams, whose comments gained a wide reprinting, appealed to popular authority by observing that Dr. Richard Price and the Abbé de Mably, well-known friends of America, zealously championed expanding Congress's authority. Congress needed full power over all foreign affairs, including foreign commerce. It might even need some authority over interstate commerce. In fact, said Adams, Congress probably also needed "more authority in other things."[8]

Writers who linked economic issues to the question of the central government's power usually stressed the losses incurred and the grave dangers the Union faced because of a weak federal government. Both points were emphasized in mid-March in the most widely reprinted preconvention commentary on the economy.[9] The author described the kinds and number of furs listed for the spring sales in London and proclaimed them worth at least £225,000. That money, he asserted, rightfully belonged in American hands because the vast majority of the pelts the British trapped had come from the United States. Obviously alluding to Congress's inability to compel either Americans or the British to adhere to the terms of the Treaty of Paris, the writer maintained that the travesty occurred because Congress lacked the power needed to fulfill its commitments just as it lacked the ability to force others to keep their commitments.[10]

The loss of a quarter of a million pounds sterling a year was no small matter, but other essayists raised yet more disturbing possibilities as they depicted America confronting a dangerous time of troubles. One author, only reprinted five times, traced a number of problems, including financial difficulties, to a virtually nonexistent federal government. Something had to be done, he warned; otherwise *"the smallest spark may again produce an explosion."* He insisted that the central government had to have more power lest America fall into anarchy and civil war.[11] Another author did gain reprint popularity with a very similar message. He pictured a Congress bedeviled by vexing problems. The commerce of the United States and the failure of many states to pay congressional requisitions stood among those issues requiring quick settlement. He warned that, unless decisive measures were taken, "we shall be annihilated as a Nation."[12]

In early April two writers took a more positive approach. A New Hampshire essayist found little reason to complain about the local situation even though it was true that "times are dull—money is scarce, &c." In a possibly veiled reference to the convention, he proclaimed those economic difficulties would disappear once the states were "united in ONE HEAD."[13] Another story about furs also reflected optimism. A traveler visiting Philadelphia maintained that the Union's unexplored regions could yield extremely valuable Siberian furs. He appealed to a sense of national pride by stressing that economic benefits and political power went hand in hand. Federal power, adequate to protect America's enterprising traders, was needed so they could take over the important commerce "wild Siberians" had monopolized.[14]

These articles on economics, which were linked with the convention through the calls for enhancing the government's power, are suggestive. Economic issues got surprisingly little play in the press and most of the essays on the subject came from New England, an area many perceived as facing especially hard times. When economics were stressed, as in the two items on furs, emphasizing problems proved more popular than heralding the country's great potential.[15] The traveler might dream of unexplored worlds yet unconquered, but only six editors published his thoughts. Three times as many publishers reprinted the story about a whopping £225,000 worth of furs being lost annually.

Whether they dwelt on economic dangers or the potentially rich future, writers who examined economic issues agreed on one essential point: to attain a healthy economy, the United States required a stronger central government. Political reform was paramount. Indeed, the economic stories themselves focused primarily on political issues. As a correspondent of the *United States Chronicle* put it, the Union's sick commerce was but one of the many significant problems confronting Congress. Other momentous issues, such as insuring the right to use the Mississippi River and seeing that the British complied with the terms of the Treaty of Paris, required vigorous action. But again, political considerations were crucial; it was this commentator who said that only speedy action could save the nation from annihilation. Most writers shared this author's foreboding sense of danger because they too believed that grave political difficulties haunted the Union.[16]

Press emphasis on the negative rather than the positive was, in fact, obvious in the often repeated claim that the Union faced possible destruction. Considering the fears naturally engendered by Shays's Rebellion, that was hardly a ludicrous suggestion.[17] In late February 1787, the press still bristled with accounts of the Rebellion as well as commentary on the danger it posed, and the story did not die once the rebels had been suppressed. Even after the convention opened, the press regularly carried accounts of the leaders of the Rebellion and the efforts to hunt them down.[18]

While those leaders remained free, it seemed all too possible that conflict might again erupt. Widely reprinted items emphasized the danger. A letter allegedly written by Eli Parsons, one of the Rebellion leaders, and published on May 2 announced that he and other rebels would renew their fight once spring arrived. A day later, the *Albany Gazette* reported that Shays and other principals in the late uprising were at Crown Point in northern New York preparing for combat. They expected to link up with a large number of men anxious to commence immediate hostilities. Their plan called for an invasion of Massachusetts from both New York and Vermont.

Similar reports and warnings appeared through late May and were widely circulated. The massive rebel attacks did not materialize, but fear of them lingered.[19]

Anxiety about internal rebellion was heightened by concern that the British might aid the rebels or even invade themselves. The *Worcester Magazine* of mid-April, in a widely reprinted piece, assayed the eery possibilities. Reports described the British fortifying their Canadian posts and raising sunken vessels to refit them. British sources claimed that these were defensive actions and that they expected American troops to molest Canada in the summer. This alleged concern about an American invasion was viewed as a smoke screen to hide Britain's own nefarious plans.[20]

Fear of internal rebellion possibly backed by the English gave writers ample opportunity to bewail the weakness of the Confederation government. One correspondent even fabricated evidence to nurture the argument. In early March, "Anti-Party" supplied a Philadelphia paper with what he claimed was a rough draft of a letter found in the marketplace. Allegedly written by an outspoken and ardent British Loyalist, the letter implied that Shays's Rebellion was part of a scheme to destroy the Union. Despite temporary setbacks to that plan, the author believed America would soon disintegrate. He even claimed the upcoming convention could not stop the disintegration, it would merely delay it. Anti-Party argued that the Loyalist's letter should show Americans how their internal dissensions held them up to international derision. "God grant," he pleaded for Americans, "that they may yet become unanimous, and disappoint the wishes of their enemies." His admonition was published in six states.[21]

In mid-March, "Americanus" also linked the British to internal upheavals. He asserted that Shays's Rebellion and similar violence sprang from a fiendish plot to reconquer the United States and subject Americans to a tyrannical government. The British cabinet was, he said, fomenting rebellion through the use of hirelings and spies. The diabolical English even contemplated hiring Indians to help crush American freedom. Although he traced the threat of rebellions to

British intrigue, Americanus candidly admitted that American problems also flowed from America's own failures. An accompanying extract of a letter from a Canadian friend of the Union supported this analysis and proved very popular as a reprint. Writing from Halifax, the Canadian described the joy heard in his country because of "the unsettled, unhinged situation" of the United States. The Union, he said, was being deservedly ridiculed because it lacked a stable, energetic government.[22]

The standard press argument thus held that the Confederation government lacked the power necessary to govern effectively. The author of a widely reprinted essay first published in mid-February actually proclaimed that the feeble Congress was a "useless" mere "shadowy Meeting," not a government.[23] The less extensively reprinted author who warned that a spark could produce an explosion also saw America's crisis as rooted in the federal government's impotence.[24] A popular Philadelphia correspondent warned that defects in the federal compact, hidden during the unity produced by the war, rendered the Confederation government inadequate to preserve the country's sovereignty.[25] A broadly reprinted paragraph from the *Massachusetts Centinel* of April 11 summed up the basic theme: "We are no longer United States, because we are not under any firm and energetic compact." That was the case, the argument went, because the individual states would not acknowledge the supremacy of Congress.[26]

Writers presented a variety of explanations to explain why, as a very popular commentator maintained, the people of some states had persisted in a shameful resistance to strengthening Congress.[27] A Bostonian accounted for it by asserting that the states secretly hated and envied each other and endeavored to thwart one another's interests.[28] Another popular Boston author described how "narrow-soul'd, antifederal politicians" in the various states had "damn'd us [as] a nation."[29] Americanus, who was not widely reprinted, expressed the same view more boldly. He urged his fellow citizens to "hurl from your bosoms, *ye sev-*

eral legislatures, all SYCOPHANTISH members! and those who are swayed by the dangerous principles of SELF-INTEREST, or the interest of any particular state."[30]

Americanus did not name the offending state or states, but others did. In an essay that circulated widely after February 21, a New Englander openly denounced Pennsylvania and New York for dogmatically pursuing their own petty interests. The actions of both states, the author complained, had "long made America the pity or contempt of Europe."[31] In addition, the press in individual states often contained articles deriding the actions of neighboring states.[32] But when it came to fixing blame for the weakness of the Confederation, the American press usually referred to one state above all others—Rhode Island.

Attacks on Rhode Island proved extraordinarily popular in the preconvention period. In fact, the surest way virtually to guarantee that one's comments would be reprinted was to skewer Rhode Island's government. The popular author of a *Salem Mercury* piece actually traced the failure of the Impost, the poverty of the Revolutionary soldiers, high taxes, and the embarrassed state of public finances to Rhode Island's "anti-federal disposition."[33] This shotgun attack was rooted in the state's rejection of the Impost of 1781, its paper money and anticreditor policies, and its refusal to send delegates to the convention.[34] On March 22 the *Newport Herald*, a proconvention newspaper, reported that the Rhode Island Assembly had, by a majority of twenty-three of the seventy-member house, voted against sending delegates. In but thinly veiled editorial comment, the *Herald* writer noted that the ostensible reason for this vote was a concern for the Articles of Confederation. Yet when a legislator advocated paying Rhode Island's share of the congressional requisition, the question was deferred to a future Assembly session. This account, which raked Rhode Island for yet again selfishly opposing the Union's general interests, gained extraordinary popularity. In various forms, it appeared more than forty times and in every state in the Union with the possible exception of North Carolina.[35] Benjamin Russell, editor of the

Massachusetts Centinel, titled his reprinting: "Quintessence of Villainy!"[36]

By late March, Rhode Island was routinely being depicted as *the* haven of "antifederal" mischief. The state many called "Rogue's Island" had become, and would remain, the ready symbol of what ailed the Union. Vilifying Rhode Island had clearly become a popular press sport. Another *Herald* item, extensively reprinted in two versions, revealed the combination of scorn and frustration many felt about the Rhode Island political scene. "Constantius" supplied the history of a fracas between Newport postmaster Jacob Richardson and Governor John Collins. The difficulties started when Richardson refused to accept a letter from Collins because the Governor tried to pay the postage with Rhode Island paper money. This squabble dragged on until the state legislature forced Richardson, a federal official, to apologize. Constantius saw such legislative intervention as a precedent fraught with "serious consequences." More than a dozen editors went even further by proclaiming that such transgressions of power could only occur in Rhode Island or Algiers.[37]

Rhode Island bashing was so fashionable by early May that a 1782 poem republished by the Philadelphia *Columbian Magazine* became extraordinarily popular. The devil, it seemed, had offered Columbia, the mythical symbol of the Union, this exchange: "Give me *one* of your states and the rest shall be free." Knowing she must comply, Columbia shed a tear. But as she thought of how Rhode Island had stopped the Impost of 1781, a smile came to her lips and she handed the state to the devil. Losing Rhode Island to save the other states was, as the poem's title proclaimed, "A Fair Bargain."[38] The reprinting of this poem by more than a score of newspapers illustrates how the press trumpeted the twin themes: selfish Rhode Island caused the Union grave problems and, correspondingly, the Union could well do without the tiny Ocean State. With so many anti–Rhode Island items flowing from the press, it probably came as no surprise when a southern gentleman warned Rhode Islanders that the convention would surely deal with their renegade state. Measures would be taken to create order and good government in Rhode Island, or it would be divided up and the parts annexed to other states. The southerner's thoughts proved very popular indeed.[39]

The symbolism of the press's depiction of the sundry problems associated with the Confederation's purported weaknesses was clear. The convention would put an end to humiliations and failures endured under the Confederation government; the convention could put an end to the time of troubles. Writers also pointedly warned that, unless that government was strengthened, invasion or tyranny would result. A Massachusetts author, asserting that a feeble government actually produced more factions than an oppressive one, plaintively asked: "For what is there now to prevent our subjugation by foreign power, but their contempt of the acquisition?"[40] The correspondent of a Providence paper maintained that "if the people at large have not Virtue enough to govern themselves, as Republicans—they must submit to a different Form of Government which they will have no Choice *but to obey.*"[41]

An essayist's predictions, first published in mid-April and then widely reprinted in early May, sketched a gloom-and-doom scenario. He observed that Vermont, which Americans often castigated as almost another Rhode Island, reportedly shunned the Confederation because of the huge federal debt. Kentucky likely would do the same. Soon these new independent states would be better off than the United States; soon the Union would be divided into the confederated and the unconfederated parts.[42] Looking expectantly toward the opening of the convention, another author of a widely reprinted essay presented a basic summary of the pessimistic view. If it could not create a government able to ensure stability, "this great country" would merely have exchanged "tyranny for anarchy."[43]

Some observers actually claimed the Union could not survive. Writing before Congress authorized the convention and angered by the persistent failure to strengthen Congress, a Massachusetts citizen said the time had come for the New

England states to secede and form a better union. This commentary appeared in a score of papers by early May.[44] In late March and early April, two New Yorkers reached a similar conclusion, and their thoughts were also widely reprinted. "Reason," seconded by "Lycurgus," proclaimed the Articles were beyond repair. Moreover, due to regional differences, one general government was unsuitable for America. The convention should therefore, they said, divide the states into three or four republics, which could then form a permanent defensive alliance.[45]

Recommendations for dismembering the Union probably got wide circulation because of their shock value. In addition, these pronouncements served the proconvention forces by adding support for the often articulated idea of strengthening the central government. The Canadian friend to America, who wished for a stable and energetic government, gained reprint popularity even though he actually dared to say the Union might need a monarch. The vast majority of Americans recoiled at that idea. However, many writers agreed with the author Americanus when he urged: "make your FŒDERAL HEAD adequate to the *requisite* purposes of government."[46] Such observations offered implicit support for holding a convention to tackle the Confederation's difficulties.[47]

Authors and publishers also, as they would throughout the spring and summer of 1787, drew upon the prestige of Revolutionary luminaries to build support for the convention. Samuel Hall, editor of the *Massachusetts Gazette*, used John Adams. In late 1786 while residing in England, Adams had written a preface to his study of American constitutions that seemed to question the structure of the Confederation government. History proved, he asserted, that the people's rights and liberties could only be preserved by a government with a strong executive power separated from the legislature. Adams had also spoken of the possibilities and the glory inherent in America's situation when he proclaimed that "the people in America have now the best opportunity, and the greatest trust, in their hands, that Providence ever committed to so small a number since the transgression of the first pair: if they betray their trust, their guilt will merit even greater punishment than other nations have suffered, and the indignation of Heaven." Although Adams did not know that the convention would be held, Samuel Hall's deft handling of Adams's words made it seem as if Adams was commenting on the importance of the convention. Hall also endorsed that view in his April 20 publication by saying that, "at this important crisis of our public affairs," Adams's words merited the attention of every American, including the convention delegates. More than a score of editors showed their agreement by quickly reprinting the article.[48]

News coverage about selecting the delegates reflected the importance publishers attached to the convention and allowed them to endorse it by praising the Revolutionary heroes who would attend.[49] In December 1786 Virginia's legislature had proposed holding the convention and had elected George Washington as a delegate.[50] Convention promoters naturally attempted to tap his enormous popularity. They often published items that called up the image of the noble Washington. The Marquis de Chastellux's flattering description of him became a very popular reprint after appearing in the *New York Gazetteer*.[51] When it was confirmed in April that Washington would attend the convention, the *Virginia Independent Chronicle* produced another popular item by urging all states to show equal wisdom in selecting their delegates. If that happened, "what happy consequences may not all the true friends to Federal Government promise themselves, from the united Zeal, Policy, and Ability, of so august an assembly."[52] Washington's standing moved "Alexis" to compose a thirty-line poem entitled "On the coming of the AMERICAN FABIUS to the Federal Convention in May next." The leadership of Washington, "the hero," the "great man" of "rigid virtues," would "crown the States with everlasting peace." This poem, first published in Philadelphia on April 9, appeared in seven states.[53]

When Pennsylvania finally added Benjamin Franklin to its convention delegation in late March, the press quickly disseminated the news.[54] Franklin's appointment made it even easier to glorify the convention. When the New York *Independent Journal* reprinted Chastellux's laudatory description of Washington, it seemed natural to add the Marquis' flattering analysis of Franklin. This article also became a popular reprint.[55] One month before the convention was scheduled to open, a Massachusetts writer, in what became a widely reprinted item, projected the majesty of Washington and Franklin onto the convention as a whole. "Much good" could reasonably be expected from the deliberations of "the sages and patriots" who would meet in convention. Indeed, the "union of the abilities of so distinguished a body of men . . . cannot but produce the most salutary measures." In a revealing and perceptive forecast, he prophesied: with the names Franklin and Washington affixed to the Convention's recommendations, "antifederal politicians . . . will not dare to attack, or endeavor to nullify" them.[56]

As the scheduled opening of the convention neared, press support for it became increasingly fervent. In late March a popular author boldly proclaimed: "The political existence of the United States, perhaps, depends on the result of the deliberations of the Convention . . . for the purpose of forming a national government."[57] The *Worcester Magazine* of May 3, in an item quickly reprinted six times, agreed and warned that "it is now the general opinion, that unless some wise plan should be proposed by the federal convention, and adopted by the several states, that our republican governments will speedily terminate,—what will take their place, Heaven only knows."[58]

On May 9, less than a week before the delegates were scheduled to begin work, a *Pennsylvania Herald* author praised the upcoming convention as he worked the "time-of-troubles" theme. His widely reprinted effort symbolized how press coverage had come to link America's destiny with the convention. The obviously inadequate Articles of Confederation, the writer declared, could not preserve America's sovereignty. Unless reform occurred, Americans had "wasted our strength and riches in accomplishing the revolution, merely to furnish another memorable tale for the historian's pen." Patriots were understandably anxious about the convention. The veteran, the statesman, all citizens "must feel that all the glory of the past, and all the fortune of the future, are involved in this momentous undertaking." The fact was that "upon the event of this great council, indeed, depends every thing that can be essential to the dignity and stability of the national character."[59]

Even rather bland news reports suggested the momentousness of the upcoming convention. When the *New York Journal* of March 15 listed the states that would attend the convention and commented on those that had not yet reached a decision, the story quickly became a popular reprint.[60] Lists of delegates began appearing in print in early April.[61] On May 1 the New York *Daily Advertiser* offered what it called the best available roster of the delegates. Ten days later the Philadelphia *Independent Gazetteer* reported that Congress had authorized franking privileges to the convention delegates. The *Daily Advertiser* list and the *Independent Gazetteer* story each appeared in more than a score of papers.[62] The feeling of growing excitement the press conveyed about the convention is also illustrated by the reprint history of the announcements that Connecticut would send delegates. Stories about individual states deciding to attend the convention rarely became popular reprints. However, the account of Connecticut's decision to send delegates, first published the day the convention was to open, eventually appeared in thirty publications.[63]

The growing significance attached to the convention gave Rhode Island a chance to redeem itself. If it sent a delegation, past transgressions might be forgiven. In early May the question came before the state's legislature a second time. Once again, according to the staunchly proconvention *Newport Herald*, the government displayed an "antifederal disposition." The lower house, reportedly bowing to eloquence and reason, reversed its earlier stand and agreed by a two-vote majority to send delegates. Alas, by a four-vote margin, the upper house refused to concur. According to the author, the actions taken right after this branded the legislators as hypocrites. They claimed the vote against attending the convention reflected concern for the Confederation government. Yet when confronted with a congressional request to repeal laws in violation of the Treaty of Paris, the legislators merely denied any conflicts existed. Furthermore, based on the assumption that Congress would not meet during the convention, the legislators decided not to send representatives to Congress. These actions reinforced the state's image as Rogue's Island, and that image was well known: this *Herald* piece was reprinted almost thirty times.[64] Although Rhode Island had in the past expressed some willingness to see the Articles revised, its government was again demonstrating why it had become and remained the symbol of "antifederal" opposition to strengthening the Confederation government.[65]

Rhode Island legislators were not the only citizens who questioned the wisdom of holding the Constitutional Convention. Still, between February 21 and the scheduled May 14 opening, only one newspaper essayist, albeit a bold and prophetic one, directly challenged the idea of holding the convention. "Sidney" issued that challenge in an address to New York legislators printed in the *New York Gazetteer* on April 9. He emphasized that, given their mandate, the convention delegates could recommend any kind of change in the Articles. Raising the specter of an ongoing conspiracy against the political liberties of the people, Sidney claimed the convention would be used to attain the dangerous goals some politicians had pursued since 1780. Those goals included funding and possibly perpetuating a national debt as well as granting Congress an independent revenue. The delegates might even, as some hoped they would, recommend stripping the state legislatures of their principal legislative powers. If this happened, American citizens would be in a worse position than the Irish under the infamous "Poynings' Laws."[66] According to Sidney, the obviously dangerous convention was not even necessary since America's difficulties probably stemmed from "the spurious monarchical principles" of "luxury, extravagance, and dissipation." Events proved that Sidney's fears were not totally unfounded, but his message was hardly heralded throughout the land. Not a single publisher reprinted his essay or even segments of it.[67]

Although the word "convention" did not appear in his commentary, a Philadelphia *Evening Chronicle* correspondent may have shared Sidney's anticonvention view. He observed that in 1775 and 1776 some people had condemned the Revolution, despised its leaders, formed connections with the British Parliament, and laughed at the Whigs. These Tories were, he cautioned, once again politically active. Although there was nothing exceptional in these claims, the correspondent offered them after reminding his readers that Caesar had wanted to subvert the constitution of Rome. If this author aimed to question the convention, he did so indirectly and ineffectively.[68] His essay, like that of Sidney, went unreprinted.

Only one other press item even remotely questioning the wisdom of holding the convention appeared between the time Congress authorized it and its scheduled opening. It surfaced in an extract of a letter from a New York "gentleman" to his friend in Baltimore published by the *Maryland Gazette* on April 24 and subsequently reprinted seven times, but in just three states.[69] The New Yorker remarked that speculation about the upcoming convention swirled about the country. In rather mocking tones, he depicted everyone as constantly examining all past, present, and potential future governments. Then he observed: "America at present appears to me like a vessel of cider newly from the press. It has not yet sufficiently fermented to produce a clear homogeneous palatable body, which time only can effect, if it meet not with some artificial agitations to interrupt the process of nature."[70] He may have been attacking the convention by urging that events be allowed to work themselves out. But if he wanted to undermine the convention, he certainly went about it gingerly.

Virtually all editors obviously found anticonvention comments unacceptable. Sidney went unreprinted; the *Evening Chronicle* author went unreprinted. The New York gentleman did produce an essay that almost achieved reprint popularity, but he voiced his possible opposition to the convention in a most indirect way. Clearly the press was unwilling to feature commentary that challenged the convention. So those who shared the views of Sidney had reason to despair that their views would ever gain prominence in the press. Then, late in the preconvention period, a newsworthy event occurred that raised that possibility.

On May 12 the Connecticut legislature began debating whether delegates should be sent to the proposed convention. The only press account of the debates covered the May 12 session of the Connecticut House of Representatives, and that report was incomplete.[71] Nevertheless, because the arguments came from representatives of the people, the potential influence of press coverage of those proceedings was enormous. Individual commentators, such as the nonreprinted Sidney, might be discounted as silly individuals; however, if elected representatives shared his views, those ideas might gain respectability. In a similar vein, Rhode Island could be dismissed as an insignificant, renegade state. A Connecticut rejection of the convention could not easily be explained away. And if Connecticut refused to attend, it would weaken claims that the Union faced desperate problems only the convention could solve.

Four members of the Connecticut House of Representatives were recorded as opposing the appointment of delegates. They represented the kinds of areas later associated with opposition to the Constitution: each represented a small town located near the Massachusetts border in the landlocked counties of Litchfield or Hartford.[72] All four warned that sending delegates to Philadelphia could endanger liberty. Elisha Fitch argued that the convention might well abridge the people's privileges. Daniel Perkins interjected a note of class conflict when he claimed that Connecticut's delegates would be genteel, affluent men who could not sympathize with the people's problems. That might lead to the ruination of the poor. Abraham Granger announced that he was reflecting the will of his constituents when he opposed sending delegates. Having declared himself the people's spokesman, Granger warned that the convention would probably produce monarchy.

The fourth anticonvention speaker, Hosea Humphrey, took a slightly different tack when contending the convention might subvert the people's liberties. He spoke of protecting Connecticut's right to veto any proposed changes. If the convention met and if a majority of delegates decided to change the Articles, the majority might, he asserted, then force states to accept alterations they opposed. To buttress this point, Humphrey took impolitic action. He praised Rhode Island's refusal to send delegates and said its position was worth imitating. Representative Perkins agreed with Humphrey's general point, but used different logic. He maintained that if Connecticut voted to send delegates, it would be obligated to approve the convention's recommendations.

The anticonvention representatives, at least by implication, rejected the claim that either the Union or Connecticut faced pressing financial or political difficulties. Only Perkins discussed economic issues, and he merely observed that the rich would not be able to understand the plight of the poor. The anticonvention representatives simply ignored issues such as trade and debt payments. Their first speaker, Abraham Granger, even challenged the often printed argument that the political system of the Union had to undergo revision. Congress had, he asserted, been delegated sufficient power and the constitution of Connecticut, in combination with the Articles, could quite adequately serve the state's needs.[73]

Echoes of the unreprinted Sidney could be heard in the words of the anticonvention representatives. They maintained: (1) the Articles did not need alteration; (2) a convention was therefore unnecessary; (3) if held, the convention might recommend dangerous changes and subvert the liberties of the people.

While four representatives spoke against sending delegates, nine spoke in favor of the proposition. Most of the nine represented important commercial areas and thus the kinds of locations whose citizens ultimately voted overwhelmingly in favor of the Constitution. The views these representatives enunciated offered a nearly complete summary of what the press had been printing about supporting the convention and enhancing the central government's power.[74] These men also added new twists. Their unifying theme was that support for the convention was support for a more effective federal government. The proconvention nine steadfastly and emphatically insisted that the well-being of the Union and of Connecticut required a more powerful central government.

Reflecting the dominant theme championed in the press, these men emphasized that the upcoming convention must be supported because the Confederation government was fundamentally defective. The Connecticut House of Representatives and all reasonable people, it was argued, acknowledged that Congress lacked the power even to do what the Articles authorized it to do. An embarrassing example was Connecticut's refusal to comply with Congress's revenue requisition, and Congress could do nothing about it. The sad, simple truth was that the Union faced an alarming crisis. New York, consumed by local interests, had turned "anti-federal." Affairs in Massachusetts, the scene of the late insurrection, remained unsettled. Rhode Island's neighbors justifiably reproached and scorned her. People were deserting the western sections of the established states and venturing to the banks of the Ohio. The Union was so plagued with problems that some Americans openly advocated reuniting with Great Britain.

The proconvention nine held that, unless the Articles were strengthened, the future might be fraught with yet more disturbing occurrences. Various states and localities had different and at times antagonistic interests. Given Congress's impotence, what power would preserve peace among the contentious states? Might not the Union disintegrate? What would happen if the Union were invaded? How would the invasion be repulsed? Considering all this, it was no wonder that Virginia, although located well beyond the currently troubled states, saw the danger and initiated the effort to hold the convention. Connecticut had two choices. She could join her sister states in endorsing a convention that would calmly deal with the problems of continental government. Or, the state's representatives could turn their backs on the convention and let chance and the capriciousness of the people determine the country's fate. John Welton stated the basic theme: "according to present appearances, and unless some alteration takes place, the union will soon be entirely at an end."

Turning to Connecticut's interests, these legislators discounted the claims of the anticonvention four. Using arguments based on the dangers of dismemberment, they ridiculed the assertions about the Union and Connecticut possessing all necessary powers. Failure to validate the convention would, they contended, produce disunion. If that happened, Connecticut's fate as an independent entity would be precarious. The state would neither have nor be able to arrange a treaty or alliance with any other nation. In this condition, a single warship could humiliate the state.

Jedidiah Huntington, who sketched the horrors of an isolated and independent Connecticut, also raised the possibility of the actual destruction of the state unless reform occurred. Connecticut's neighbors—New York, Massachusetts, and Rhode Island—might some day decide to carve up Connecticut. In that event, the state would appeal to the Confederation government; Congress would tell the offending states to stop their outrageous actions; the states might even be ordered to pay an indemnity. All that, he warned, would mean nothing since Congress lacked the power to terminate the actions of the aggressor states. In the end Connecticut, like Poland, would be gobbled up by its neighbors.

After Huntington pictured the disasters Connecticut might experience if it did not back the convention, Representative Wadsworth advanced an argument not yet extensively developed in the press. He emphasized the bright prospects awaiting the people if they supported the convention. Using a straightforward analysis of Connecticut's economic structure, Wadsworth even presented evidence to prove it would gain more from revising the Articles than any other state. Because it possessed excellent land, Connecticut exported large amounts of agricultural produce and imported many foreign manufactures. However, those foreign goods were imported indirectly through either New York City or Boston. When first carried into New York and Massachusetts, the imports were subject to those states' imposts. Accordingly, the ultimate consumers in Connecticut were subsidizing their neighbors' treasuries in the sum of at least $100,000 annually. If state imposts were prohibited and a federal tariff substituted, any tariffs on imported goods would go to the central government for the benefit of all.

In presenting their position, the proconvention nine showed political savvy by carefully nurturing the misleading idea that their ideas were neither new nor radical. Representative Jedidiah Huntington staked out the ground by claiming that the needed reforms could occur by adopting impost plans Connecticut had already approved. Congress could be, Huntington said, empowered to regulate trade for fifteen years and to raise funds via a five percent impost duty. It is essential to note that, although the proconvention speakers developed many arguments, no speaker suggested Congress needed more powers than those described by Huntington. Saying that sent the soothing message that the convention need only find a way to implement what had already been agreed upon.

The proconvention arguments had been so skillfully and fully developed that when Charles Chauncey rose to speak, he claimed there was "little left to be urged on the subject." The reasons for sending delegates were, he said, so numerous and obvious that he need not elaborate on them. He did note that it had long been agreed that Congress needed greater power, and Chauncey also offered the reassuring observation: "we have something to hope and nothing to fear from the convention."[75]

The Connecticut debate suggested that the overwhelming majority of the state's legislators, and by implication its people, advocated holding a convention to strengthen the Confederation government. Only four members spoke against sending delegates, while nine spoke for sending them.[76] This breakdown is not surprising. Most people throughout the Union, as well as the press, believed the Articles required modification. Even much-maligned Rhode Island had endorsed change by voting for the Impost of 1783 and the granting of commercial power to Congress. By popular account, it was New York's legislators who scuttled the 1783 impost. However, they had helped prompt Congress to authorize the Philadelphia convention. So, at one time or another, all thirteen states had voted for increasing the central government's power.[77]

Whatever possible influence Connecticut's anticonvention representatives might have had was probably reduced by an oddity in press coverage. Accounts of the May 12 debate did not appear in print until the *Connecticut Courant* and the *American Mercury* published them on May 21. Yet on May 14 those newspapers reported that Connecticut would be represented at the convention, and fifteen other papers had reprinted the news by May 21. In fact, the proconvention action of Connecticut received quicker and more prominent coverage than the substance of the debate on attending the convention.[78]

Production problems probably account for the seemingly strange timing of the publication of stories about Connecticut and the convention. It took time to formulate the lengthy account of the debate.[79] It required little effort or space to announce that on May 14 Connecticut had officially decided to attend the convention.[80] Nevertheless, those who opposed the convention, some of whom later railed against press bias, might well have shaken their fists in frustration had they known how the press covered the Connecticut debate. The full report of the debate sanctioned the convention and a stronger government by giving disproportionate play to the ideas of the proconvention representatives. They outnumbered the anticonvention representatives by a nine to four margin, yet almost ninety percent of the space in the full account was devoted to the arguments of the proconvention forces.[81] Of course the original full report at least presented some anticonvention views, but only ten newspapers published that account.[82] And when other newspapers reprinted shortened versions of the debate, the coverage was slanted even more decidedly in favor of the convention. Although the Springfield, Massachusetts, *Hampshire Chronicle* account, reprinted three times, devoted much more space to the proconvention arguments, it at least gave an honest summary of the anticonvention arguments.[83] Four other newspapers emphasized the ideas of the proconvention Representatives Huntington and Wadsworth.[84] A correspondent of the *New York Journal* prepared a debate summary, reprinted five times, that totally ignored the anticonvention legislators.[85] Thus, even when they made news, those who questioned holding the convention could not count on their views being reported by the press.

In the preconvention period, and indeed throughout the summer of 1787, those who distrusted the convention for one reason or another got their greatest press coverage from the unquestionably newsworthy Connecticut debate. But elements of the press seemed unwilling, even in news accounts, to give space to those who might denigrate the importance of the upcoming convention. What seemed rather one-sided coverage only got worse once the convention opened. The press continued to emphasize that the convention could, must, and would save the Union. And those who might publicly dispute that idea found it, as they had in the preconvention period, nearly impossible to get their message into a newspaper or magazine.

Notes to Chapter One

1. In important ways press coverage began even before February 21, and some popular items from that earlier period deserve special note. On February 19, John Dunlap and David Claypoole of the *Pennsylvania Packet* published their analysis of the February 15 New York Assembly vote of 36–21 against the Impost of 1783. The editors remarked that "on this important and interesting question Mr. [Alexander] Hamilton went into a large and extensive field of

discussion and with Ciceronian eloquence advocated the measure.—Whether his arguments were irrefragable, and admitted no
reply, those who read the nervous [i.e., strong] oration will judge:
but certain it is, not a word was spoken in opposition to the bill,
yet on calling the question the decision was as above stated." This
call for strengthening the Union, which also carried the vital information that New York had apparently finally scuttled the Impost
of 1783, proved very popular. Between February 21 and March 22,
twenty newspapers reprinted it; it also appeared in the February
issue of the Philadelphia *Columbian Magazine*. On February 26, the
New York *Daily Advertiser* carried Hamilton's lengthy address. It
was reprinted in full by the Poughkeepsie *Country Journal*, March
14, 21, and 28, and in the June issue of the Philadelphia *American
Museum*. Between March 7 and June 15, four newspapers presented extracts of the speech. The timing of the reprinting by the
Pennsylvania Packet (June 5), the *Maryland Journal* (June 15), the
Baltimore *Maryland Gazette* (June 15), and possibly the *Columbian
Magazine*, suggests the reprintings were designed to support the
convention.

2. Resolution from COC1: 45. The thirty-nine printings occurred
between February 24 and March 21; the summary versions appeared
on March 1 and 6.

3. During this period, the term "antifederal" was applied to
those who did not want changes in the Articles of Confederation.
The logic was that the Articles needed revising and therefore to
oppose revision was to oppose the federal system. A good example
of this usage occurs in "Candidus," New York *Daily Advertiser*,
February 6. In a clever political ploy, supporters of the proposed
Constitution of 1787, who were in fact nationalists, adopted the
name "Federalist" and hung the undesirable label "Antifederalist"
on their opponents. Despite the misleading nature of these terms,
their use is long established and, accordingly, they are used in the
traditional way in this study. On these points, see Merrill Jensen,
*The New Nation: A History of the United States during the Confed-
eration 1781–1789* (New York, 1950), xiii-xiv.

4. "Extract of a letter from a gentleman in one of the southern
States," dated January 31, Baltimore *Maryland Gazette*, February
27, with fourteen reprintings between March 3 and April 6.

5. "Extract of a letter from New-York," dated February 15,
Freeman's Journal, February 21, with twelve reprintings between
February 22 and March 19.

6. See, e.g., Jensen, *The New Nation*, 186–93, and the Providence *United States Chronicle*, August 16 discussed in Chapter Four.

7. CDR,177–85.

8. Adams's *Defence* was published in three volumes in London in 1787 and 1788, and American editions followed soon after the originals appeared. Based on his suggestions about the kind of government America needed, Adams became an even more noted, and for some a notorious, figure, and his *Defence* was typically seen as being linked to the work of the convention. A most useful short analysis of John Adams's effort to influence the course of American government through this work and of the response to it is given in COC1: 81–86. The *Daily Advertiser*, May 9, given in COC1: 86–87, with quotation from p. 87, was reprinting material from Letter LIII of the *Defence*. Considering only reprintings before the Constitution appeared, the material cited in the text was reprinted by ten newspapers between May 10 and 31. On Price, see Chapter Two.

9. *Massachusetts Gazette*, March 16; reprinted seventeen times between March 19 and April 19; it also appeared in the April issue of the Philadelphia *American Museum* and in the *Nova Scotia Gazette*, April 10.

10. On these problems, see Jensen, *New Nation*, 14–18, 160–61, 169–71, 265–81; Richard B. Morris, *The Forging of the Union, 1781–1789* (New York, 1987), 194–219; Frederick W. Marks III, *Independence on Trial: Foreign Affairs and the Making of the Constitution*, 2d ed. (Wilmington, 1986).

11. Charlestown *American Recorder*, March 16, given in COC1: 74–75, with reprintings between March 29 and April 26.

12. *United States Chronicle*, March 29, given in COC1: 76, with thirteen reprintings between April 9 and May 17.

13. Given in COC1: 76, with six reprintings between April 12 and May 3. The author also spoke of "their hero" in a way that seemed to refer to George Washington. That too implied his comments referred to the convention.

14. *Pennsylvania Herald*, April 11, with five reprintings between April 12 and May 25.

15. Some positive comment on economic potential occurred. On April 12, the *New Haven Gazette* printed an extract of a letter by a British traveler who chided New Englanders for complaining of hard times. According to him, New England and the United States had "the most natural advantages of any [country] I ever saw."

He asserted that people willing to work, especially farmers, could prosper in America and that average Americans had a real chance to improve their lot. Six newspapers, all located in New England, reprinted this between May 2 and August 17. Comments like these that emphasized America's advantages had appeared in the press for years. (See, e.g., John K. Alexander, *Render Them Submissive: Responses to Poverty in Philadelphia, 1760–1800* [Amherst,1980], 13, 189–90, n. 11.) But when talking about economics and government in 1787, the stress was, as noted, on the negative.

16. For the *United States Chronicle* item, see n. 12 above. A widely reprinted letter, dated at Paris on December 24, 1786, that most readers could easily guess was written by Thomas Jefferson, seemed to downplay the threat from internal disorder. But since his observations were written before the worst incidents of Shays's Rebellion, reprinting Jefferson's words did not undercut the basic "time-of-troubles" theme. See *New Haven Gazette*, April 19, given in COC1: 81, with thirteen reprintings between April 27 and May 29.

17. George R. Minot, *The History of the Insurrections ...* (Worster, 1788; Evans 21259); David P. Szatmary, *Shays' Rebellion: The Making of an Agrarian Insurrection* (Amherst, 1980).

18. In addition to the examples given in the text, see the headnote to section CC18A-G of COC1 (pp. 91–93).

19. The editor took pains to demonstrate the authenticity of the letter. See *Massachusetts Centinel*, May 2, reprinted twelve times between May 5 and 30. For the attribution of the second item to the *Albany Gazette* and for the text, which was reprinted seventeen times by June 30, see COC1: 94. See also Chapter Two below for added examples.

20. *Worcester Magazine*, third week of April, with seventeen reprintings between April 23 and May 21.

21. Despite its wide geographical circulation, "Anti-Party" was only printed a total of seven times. It first appeared in the Philadelphia *Independent Gazetteer*, March 7, and was reprinted six times between March 14 and June 20 in Conn., N.H., N.Y., Mass., and Va.

22. The relationship between the two items is clearly noted in the original source, the *New York Journal*, March 15. Both are given in COC1: 71–74, with quotation from p. 73. "Americanus" was reprinted only three times, quite probably because it was long as well as acerbic and because the letter it introduced was itself rather long. Moreover, the letter was more interesting and

of greater intrinsic news value. Seventeen reprintings of the Halifax letter occurred in ten states between March 16 and May 12.

23. Boston *Independent Chronicle,* February 15, given in COC1: 57; reprinted nineteen times by May 12. As noted, the wide reprinting occurred because the author talked of dismembering the Union. However, as other examples cited in this chapter reveal, the author's attitude about Congress was typical of press comment.

24. Charlestown *American Recorder,* March 16, and see n. 11 above.

25. *Pennsylvania Herald,* May 9, given in COC1: 96–97, with thirteen reprintings by May 31.

26. Given in COC1: 79; reprinted fifteen times in newspapers by May 18 and also in the August issue of the *American Museum* issued on September 1.

27. See n. 23 above.

28. *Massachusetts Centinel,* April 11; see n. 26 above.

29. *Massachusetts Centinel,* April 14, given in COC1: 80, with thirteen reprintings by June 2.

30. See n. 22 above.

31. See n. 23 above. The attack on New York and Pennsylvania probably stemmed primarily from their response to the Impost of 1783. See E. James Ferguson, *The Power of the Purse: A History of American Public Finance, 1776–1790* (Chapel Hill, 1961), 239–41.

32. For example, the Connecticut press carried items that questioned the actions of New York and Massachusetts while the New Jersey press routinely vilified the actions of Pennsylvania and New York.

33. Issue of March 31; reprinted in ten newspapers from April 4 through 18; it also appeared in the April issue of the *American Museum.*

34. On Rhode Island's policies, see Jensen, *New Nation,* 323–25; Irwin H. Polishook, *Rhode Island and the Union 1774–1795* (Evanston, 1969), especially 165–70.

35. Given the fact that very few 1787 North Carolina papers have survived, this popular piece probably did appear in every state.

36. Issue of March 28.

37. "Constantius," *Newport Herald,* March 29; reprinted eight times between April 3 and May 10. In addition, the first two paragraphs were reprinted thirteen times between April 4 and 25; eleven of the publishers added the comment comparing Rhode Island to Algiers. On Algiers, see Chapter Two at n.11.

38. *Columbian Magazine*, April 1787, with twenty-one reprintings between May 5 and August 22.

39. *"Extract of a letter from a gentleman in the Southern States,"* dated April 1, *Newport Herald*, May 12, given in COC1: 80, with thirteen reprintings by June 23.

40. This item, which probably appeared in the March 16 Charlestown *American Recorder* and of which no known copy now exists, comes from the *Pennsylvania Packet*, March 29 reprinting given in COC1: 74–75, with quotation from p. 75. Quite probably because the statements appeared in a lengthy essay, they were only reprinted five times between March 29 and April 26.

41. See n. 12 above.

42. *Pennsylvania Gazette*, April 18. The Baltimore *Maryland Gazette*, May 4, reprinted the excerpt cited here which was itself reprinted ten times by June 1.

43. *Pennsylvania Herald*, May 9, given in COC1: 96–97, with quotation from p. 97; thirteen reprintings occurred by May 31.

44. See n. 23 above. The New York *Daily Advertiser* of February 23 reprinted this item under the heading "Serious Paragraph," and it was reprinted that way in five other newspapers.

45. "Reason," New York *Daily Advertiser*, March 24, given in COC1: 57–58, was reprinted nine times by April 28; "Lycurgus," who was responding to and agreeing with "Reason," appeared in the New York *Daily Advertiser* on April 2, given in COC1: 58–59. "Lycurgus" was reprinted seventeen times by June 9.

46. "Americanus" as cited in n. 22 above.

47. For additional examples of often reprinted items that espoused similar views, see, e.g., *New Hampshire Spy*, April 3 (given in COC1: 76); *Massachusetts Centinel*, April 11 as cited in n. 26 above and the same paper's April 14 comment on Franklin's election to the convention (given in COC1: 80).

48. The article, from the *Massachusetts Gazette* of April 20 and reprinted twenty-seven times by June 9, is given in COC1: 86; on the importance of Adams's views, see n. 8 above. As another popular reprint first published on May 9 made clear, Adams was talking about the state governments rather than about Congress. He maintained Congress was not a legislative or representative body. Because the people had a confederacy and wanted it that way, Congress was "only a diplomatic assembly." "Antifederal" types could have found these comments appealing because Adams said Congress was an "aristocratical body" with a "natural" dispo-

sition to attack the powers of the state. But the logic of Adams's emphasis on independent branches of the legislature and a strong executive quickly convinced "antifederal" types that he represented the opposition. This Adams material, from Letter LIII of his *Defence*, appeared in the *New York Daily Advertiser*, May 9 (given in COC1: 86–87); considering only reprintings before the Constitution was made public, the section cited here was reprinted nine times between May 10 and 31.

49. For a useful example based on one state, see the *Pennsylvania Herald*, March 7, which reported that the governor of South Carolina had told the state legislature that appointing delegates to the convention was "indispensible." Between March 8 and 22, six other papers reprinted this report, and it also appeared in the March issue of the *Columbian Magazine*. The full text of the address by Governor William Moultrie was printed in the *Columbian Herald* on January 29 and then reprinted in Georgia's two papers in February.

50. CDR,196–98.

51. Issue of March 1, with nineteen reprintings between March 3 and May 10.

52. Issue of April 11, given in COC1: 78–79, with quotation from p. 79; reprinted twenty-four times by May 14.

53. *Independent Gazetteer*, April 9, given in COC1: 78; despite the wide geographic distribution, only eight reprintings occurred; they appeared by May 21.

54. The first press report on the appointment was in the Philadelphia *Independent Gazetteer*, March 28. It was reprinted in fourteen papers from April 4 through 30. See also n. 56 below.

55. Issue of March 3, with ten reprints between March 9 and 31.

56. *Massachusetts Centinel*, April 14, given in COC1: 80, with thirteen reprints by June 2. Because it noted that Franklin had been appointed to the convention, this item served as an announcement that he would attend. Excluding the Philadelphia papers, eight of the other eleven papers that reprinted the April 14 item did not reprint the Philadelphia *Independent Gazetteer* announcement of Franklin's appointment. So, Franklin's appointment clearly got wider circulation than is suggested merely by examining reprintings of the first news report carried by the *Gazetteer*.

57. See n. 33 above.

58. The six reprintings occurred between May 5 and 16.

59. Given in COC1: 96–97; thirteen reprintings occurred by May 31.

60. Between March 21 and 31, ten papers reprinted the full story; three more geographically isolated newspapers reprinted the full report between April 4 and May 7. Three other papers reprinted a shorter version of the report that just listed the states that had already appointed delegates.

61. See the Philadelphia *Evening Chronicle*, April 12.

62. The *Advertiser* item was reprinted twenty-four times between May 3 and June 30; the *Gazetteer* piece was reprinted twenty-three times between May 12 and June 6. Such a resolution on postage was, in fact, adopted by Congress.

63. The *Connecticut Courant* and the *Middlesex Gazette* of May 14 printed the same information in slightly different words. Those reports and versions based on them appeared thirty times from May 16 through June 6. By way of comparison, a report on the appointment of Maryland's delegates which first appeared on May 1 had been the most widely reprinted of such items. Counting all printings, the Maryland story appeared in fifteen newspapers between May 1 and June 2.

64. Issue of May 10, with twenty-seven reprints between May 14 and June 14.

65. See also the Philadelphia *Evening Chronicle*, May 10, and the *Worcester Magazine*, fourth week of May (given in COC1: 95), which is described in the following chapter. While the Rhode Island legislature of 1787 appeared decidedly opposed to strengthening the Union, the state had voted for the Impost of 1783 and the 1785 proposal to increase the congressional power to regulate commerce, and it had appointed delegates to the Annapolis Convention. On these points, see Polishook, *Rhode Island*, 110–12, 182–91.

66. "Poynings' Laws" referred to 10 Hen. 7, c. 4 [originally c. 9] (Ire.) passed by the famous Irish Parliament that met between December 1, 1494 and February 1495. It stripped away the idea of an independent local legislature by stating that future Irish Parliaments could meet only with the consent of the king and could not pass acts unless they had already been approved by his council. Chapter 22, originally Chapter 39, was also significant. It declared that English law took precedence over Irish law. Americans and others who were or had been colonials had long depicted such requirements as denying basic rights. See Alfred G. Donaldson, *Some Comparative*

Aspects of Irish Law (London, 1957), 42–48, 75; Art Cosgrove, ed., *A New History of Ireland: Medieval Ireland 1169–1534* (Oxford, 1987), 639–41, 647; J. D. Mackie, *The Earlier Tudors, 1485–1588* (Oxford, 1952), 129ff.

67. "Sidney" was a poor candidate for reprinting for reasons that went beyond his strident attack on the idea of holding the convention. His effort was long, dry, and filled with lengthy quotations. His piece may well, in fact, have been the work that caused an essayist published in the New York *Daily Advertiser* of June 16 to denounce "antifederal" writings as dull, musty productions. In addition, the essay seemed to have a local cast because it was addressed to the New York legislature. On the other hand, New York City newspapers were important sources for items reprinted by publishers in other areas. Also, the author's comments were surely provocative, and he addressed vital national questions. As was done with other items and especially with longer proconvention pieces, snippets could easily have been reprinted. But press editors, who as a group filled their pages with proconvention hype, chose not to reprint any of "Sidney." It is worth noting that the *Journal* became one of the few Antifederalist newspapers once the Constitution was published. See COC1: xxxvii–xxxviii.

68. The *Chronicle* championed the embattled Pennsylvania Constitution of 1776, and so the March 22 essay could have been a commentary on the state constitution. But the wording seems to indicate that the author was indeed not just talking about Pennsylvania.

69. The term "gentleman," which was the standard usage when printing extracts of letters, carried a special connotation at that time. See Alexander, *Render Them Submissive*, 112–13.

70. Text given in COC1: 91. Eight reprints occurred by June 7 in the following states: four in Mass., two in N.Y., and two in Pa.

71. The original and fullest report of the debate appeared in the *Connecticut Courant* and the *American Mercury* on May 21, given in COC1: 104–11. The account ended with the notation that several other legislators had spoken, but their sentiments had not been recorded. See also n. 79 below. The official records offer no extensive information about the debates. See CDR, 216–17 and especially 217, n. 1.

72. Abraham Granger represented Suffield and Daniel Perkins represented Enfield in Hartford County. Hosea Humphrey of Norfolk and Elisha Fitch of Salisbury lived in Litchfield County.

Here and elsewhere information on the legislators comes from the *Connecticut Courant*, May 14. On how geography and economic position seemed to influence the position taken on the Constitution, see Orin G. Libby, *The Geographical Distribution of the Vote of the Thirteen States on the Federal Constitution, 1787-8* (Madison, 1894) and Jackson Turner Main, *The Antifederalists: Critics of the Constitution 1781-1788* (Chapel Hill, 1961), especially 280.

73. The proconvention representative James Davenport proclaimed that the anticonvention gentlemen "say that the articles of confederation need no revision." Davenport's summary was not challenged.

74. Five of the nine came from New Haven or Fairfield, counties that abutted Long Island Sound. Four of the nine represented areas in New Haven County. Charles Chauncey represented New Haven; Jedidiah Huntington represented Norwich; Joseph Hopkins and John Welton represented Waterbury. James Davenport came from Stamford in Fairfield County. Thomas Seymour and Jeremiah Wadsworth represented the city of Hartford in Hartford County. Charles Burrall of Canaan and Benjamin Hinman of Woodbury came from Litchfield County. See also n. 72 above.

75. The debate report ended with the notation that Representative Hinman expressed his approval for sending delegates to the convention.

76. The full vote was not recorded. See CDR, 215–16.

77. See Ferguson, *Power of the Purse*, 111–17, 152–53, 221, 239–40, 242, and nn. 34, 65 above.

78. In all, twenty-eight papers eventually reprinted the story of Connecticut's appointment of convention delegates. See n. 63 above.

79. A comment in the May 21 report that said the compiler had not "been able to collect the purport of their observations" suggests that some representatives might have been queried well after the debate occurred.

80. See CDR, 215–16.

81. The ninety percent figure is based on a line count of the various representatives' comments as reproduced in COC1 that shows the anticonvention representatives with about 28 lines of text and the proconvention representatives with about 219 lines of text.

82. The report was also published in the October issue of the *American Museum*.

83. Issue of May 22. The original is not extant, and so comment on this version is based on the *Massachusetts Centinel* of May 26, which attributed the piece to the *Hampshire Chronicle*. It also appeared in the *New Hampshire Spy*, May 26, and the *Cumberland Gazette*, June 8.

84. The papers that printed such versions were: New York *Daily Advertiser*, June 1; Baltimore *Maryland Gazette*, June 5; *Salem Mercury*, June 12; *Newport Mercury*, June 25.

85. Issue of May 31 with reprintings in: *Northern Centinel*, June 4; Poughkeepsie *Country Journal*, June 6; *Hudson Weekly Gazette*, June 7; *Maryland Chronicle*, June 20; Boston *American Herald*, June 11.

2

"The Collective Wisdom of the Continent":
The Convention Opens

Publishers and authors treated May 14, 1787, the scheduled opening of the Constitutional Convention, as a crucial date. Editors in several states printed major convention pieces, and friends of the convention showed special skill in manipulating when their articles were published. Short, focused pieces remained popular, but lengthy articles containing interrelated arguments appeared far more routinely than before. These carefully crafted publications often reiterated and expanded upon arguments popularized in the preconvention period, especially the idea of the Union bedeviled by problems that might destroy it. Building on this established theme, and occasionally stressing that America had great potential as well as grave problems, many writers intensified their praise of the delegates and proclaimed they should be trusted to do the right thing.

Based on what the media published, the early days of the convention through mid-June belonged to its advocates. Seizing the initiative, they boldly maintained that the American people must do more than just accept the convention as necessary. They also must accept its recommendations. Thus supporting the convention—being proconvention—took on a new meaning. Now to be proconvention meant that one would willingly defer to the delegates. Authors who harbored reservations either about holding the convention or simply deferring to the delegates probably realized they would not get reprinted if they questioned the necessity of holding the convention. Accordingly, most expressed their concerns indirectly by offering general comments on the nature of government that would apply to the delegates' work.

As May gave way to June, it became increasingly obvious that the convention boosters had overwhelmed the potential opposition. The situation suddenly changed in mid-June when news from the convention threw the proconvention forces on the defensive. But from mid-May through mid-June, as the effort to sell the convention shifted into a higher gear, the friends of the convention had little reason to worry about what appeared in the media.

• • •

Ardent convention supporters, eager to see the central government's powers greatly enhanced, displayed a special concern about getting their views into print right as the convention was scheduled to open. For his May 16 issue, Alexander J. Dallas, editor of the *Pennsylvania Herald*, printed three items that read like campaign literature.[1] Two of the three pieces, all of which became popular reprints, originated in the *Herald*. The third, an extract of a letter from Dr. Richard Price of London to Dr. Benjamin Rush dated January 26, merits special attention. Its publication history suggests it was consciously used to champion whatever the convention might produce.

While extracts of letters normally first appeared in a single newspaper, the *Herald* was only one of five Philadelphia papers to publish the Price item on May 16.[2] Rush obviously sought to insure the widest possible dissemination of Price's observations by giving copies to several publishers.[3] It is not clear when the letter reached him, but Rush probably received it well before mid-May.[4] Since its appearance neatly coincided with the scheduled opening of the convention, the timing of its publication probably was not mere chance.

Price's pro-American credentials were firmly established when his extract appeared. Although a citizen of England, he had defended the Revolution in a notable pamphlet of February 1776 and since then had consistently voiced admiration for both America and the ideals of liberty.[5] Considering his renown, one could expect Price's thoughts to be extensively reprinted. They were. Forty-two publications located in nine states eventually carried his letter.[6]

Rush, who hated Pennsylvania's radical constitution and who ardently wanted the country's central government strengthened, had good reason to handle Price's letter as he did.[7] It offered a sobering assessment of America's situation and emphasized the importance of enhancing the powers of the Union's government. Thus a great English friend of America seemed, at least by implication, to endorse holding a convention to strengthen the government. Moreover, in part as Rush arranged it, the press published Price's thoughts at a most opportune time for convention boosters.

Rush did even more to arrange for proconvention material to appear just as the delegates began working. Because most delegates arrived late, they held their first formal proceedings on May 25. On May 26 and May 30, two Philadelphia papers sent that news out to become reprint material.[8] Interest in the convention was likely very high just then, and on May 30 both the *Pennsylvania Gazette* and the *Pennsylvania Journal* carried an important essay Rush probably authored. This lengthy piece, signed "Harrington," advanced all the basic arguments presented in the early period of the convention in favor of strengthening the central government. Rush's very well timed effort was also a very successful effort. In various forms, it amassed more than thirty reprintings, which made it the most widely circulated lengthy commentary on the convention to appear before the Constitution was made public.[9]

These proconvention items, and virtually every other new political commentary published in the month after May 14, emphasized the staple press argument that said the country faced myriad problems, most rooted in the weaknesses of the Confederation government. John Dunlap and David Claypoole, editors of the *Pennsylvania Packet*, featured an economic example, reprinted in six states, of how the government's weakness harmed the Union. French and British agents were in Lisbon negotiating commercial treaties with Portugal, whose trade was of considerable importance to America. Yet the Confederation government did not even have an agent in Lisbon to protect American interests. Frustration oozed from the editors' lament: "To what quarter, indeed, can we direct our attention without finding additional cause to deplore the feeble and disordered state of the continental system."[10]

One of Alexander Dallas's important May 16 political items played upon love of country in a forceful example of how a weak Congress hurt and disgraced America. Proclaiming it a well-known fact that many Americans, captured by pirates, languished as slaves in Algiers, a correspondent asked: "Can anything . . . more feelingly demonstrate the necessity of vesting in Congress the powers requisite to maintain the natural sovereignty, than her present incapacity either to demand or to purchase the freedom of her citizens who languish in Algiers?" More than a score of newspapers reprinted his haunting question.[11]

Shortly after the convention was to have opened, the *Maryland Gazette* of Baltimore carried a lengthy piece that cataloged the government's weaknesses. Although the Articles of Confederation worked during the war, peace and time had, the author said, exposed glaring defects. He offered several solid illustrations of various important functions Congress supposedly had but could not perform. For example, Congress could not compel observance of its treaties or repay borrowed money. The Confederation had become "a loose, incomplete agreement, totally inconsistent with its own principles." The essay became a very popular reprint despite its length.[12]

"Z," published on May 16, offered the most detailed analysis of why Americans believed their country faced a ruinous situation. He forcefully delineated some of the Union's difficulties: America had vast resources, but was impoverished; the people languished in debt and could do nothing about it; industry was stagnant; trade had been destroyed. These and yet more problems revealed discontent at home matched by hatred and insults from abroad.[13] Three days later, a popular *Pennsylvania Herald* author espoused what had become the standard line on the problems of the Confederation government. He maintained that all Americans agreed the central government needed more power and that a strong and efficient executive power must be created somehow, somewhere.[14]

As they had in the preconvention period, authors liked to cite British subjects on the sorry state of Congress. Reading an article from Halifax reprinted by the *Massachusetts Gazette* in early June, one could almost see the sneer on the Canadian's face as he said of America: "Discourd and confusion appear to reign triumphant throughout that once happy land." Because the states could not agree on any general measure, Congress had actually, he laughed, asked Washington to become dictator for six years. Washington refused, but the secret was out.[15] The Dean of Gloucester in England, Dr. Tucker, was also quoted to show the dilapidated state of American politics. He boldly observed that Americans lacked the ability to create an effective government and would forever remain a disunited people.[16] Even Dr. Price, the Union's good English friend, said the weakness of Congress made it a laughing stock not merely in England but throughout Europe.[17]

In stressing how a time of troubles had descended on America in large measure because of its weak government, the authors of widely reprinted pieces often warned that the weight of those problems might crush the Union. The immensely popular Harrington saw America with its underpowered Congress so beset by anarchy that it teetered on the brink of destruction. By late May, speculation about the possible death of America was becoming commonplace.[18] The message even attained popularity in poetic form. The *Massachusetts Centinel* of June 13 offered a moral tale that described how a dying father taught his sons the importance of unity. The father had them attempt to break thirteen sticks bundled together; it could not be done. Once separated however, each stick was easily broken. Although it seemed superfluous, the author asked: "Is not the tale, Columbians clear?" He supplied the obvious answer: " 'UNITE or DIE.' "[19]

Foreign observers were also cited, as they had been in preconvention days, to foster the view that America might disintegrate. The author of the Halifax article maintained that people believed a revolution of some sort would soon occur because Congress could not support its honor or credit. Dr. Price observed that the states' various problems, especially the tumults in New England, allowed the English to gloat about the wretched situation in their former colonies. Europeans had, he said, reached the conclusion that America was crumbling and would soon regret its independence.[20]

In May and early June, extensively reprinted news items about possible insurrections reinforced the dire warnings of the country being torn apart. On May 3 the *Albany Gazette* proclaimed that Shays and his followers planned to invade Massachusetts.[21] Two weeks later the *Massachusetts Centinel* reported that seven to eight hundred rebels would soon strike Massachusetts "to kill, plunder, burn, and destroy whatever comes their way." Accounts depicted Shays and other rebel leaders, supported by men from Sharon, Connecticut, marching to join the marauders. Consequently, the local militia had been ordered to stand ready to repel the invaders. On May 19, the *Centinel* printed the observations of a Springfield gentleman who said Vermont rebels might unite with the Shaysites. More disturbing yet, their leaders were openly enlisting men to serve the King of England. Four days later the *Centinel* published a letter from a Westerfield, Connecticut, writer who also said the rebels were indeed successfully garnering fighters.[22] Reports of mercenary Americans joining the King's service reminded citizens, as they had been reminded since Congress authorized the convention, that the British might help destroy the Union.

In the third week of May, the New England press expressed pleasure at being able to report that decisive action had squelched the immediate danger. Connecticut's legislature had dispatched troops and law enforcement officials to the town of Sharon. Five men described as ringleaders in the planned insurrection had been apprehended. Much to their credit, Vermont authorities had dispersed leaders of the late Rebellion and the approximately two hundred men they had assembled to attack Massachusetts. This reassuring news, like the reports about the threatened invasion, got reprinted throughout the land.[23]

Even as it supplied stories about the effective state action, which also emphasized federal inaction, the press gave wide circulation to accounts of how the danger persisted. In late May, the *New York Journal* carried the chilling news that Shays and a number of his men were being welcomed and supported by the inhabitants of Salem in Washington County.[24] Widely reprinted accounts from the *New Hampshire Spy* of June 9 kept the specter of the malevolent British alive by implying that they might soon invade. Recent information from Canada revealed that its militia was being built into a powerful force that could quickly march to the frontiers. Moreover, another regiment had been assigned to the frontier posts, and five more Irish and English regiments were expected to land at Quebec in the near future. The British had readied a powerful ship for service on the lakes, and other vessels were being fitted out. A popular but less widely reprinted report from the *Spy* directly linked Shays to Canada. Readers learned that, while he reportedly received no encouragement, Shays took a considerable quantity of gunpowder with him when he left Montreal.[25]

In the month after the convention's scheduled opening, the press thus carried a wide variety of commentary and news reinforcing the well-established theme of America and its Union being endangered. Some popular authors presented a variant on the theme. While agreeing that the Union faced perilous times, they voiced an optimism rarely seen in the preconvention period. Echoing the language of *Common Sense*, they emphasized that, with the necessary reforms, a troubled America could yet, as Dr. Price phrased it, become "an example to the world."[26] A Baltimore writer asserted that, bolstered by a stronger central government, America had the potential to enjoy "a glorious independence."[27] Harrington also believed America might attain glory.[28] The link between the time of troubles and the idea of America's great potential also existed in a piece published in two Philadelphia papers on June 5. A correspondent proclaimed that "the present time . . . is a very important one: The eyes of friends and enemies—of all Europe—nay more—of the whole world are upon the United States."[29] At the same time, John Hayes, editor of the Baltimore *Maryland Gazette,* supported the convention and put the best face on the country's situation by quoting Lord Bolingbroke to the effect that any government should occasionally be drawn back "to the first good principles on which it was founded." In a statement reprinted five times in four states, Hayes struck the optimistic note: "If these sentiments of his Lordship are just, we should think it an happiness that we have now an opportunity of taking a political retrospective view of what we have done, in a constitutional way since the revolution. Our grand object should be to secure a permanent foundation to our liberties, and the privilege we now enjoy of doing this is perhaps superior to any thing of the kind that has ever happened since the first formation of Government."[30]

Most authors depicted the convention as the key to solving problems and achieving America's potential. Harrington asserted that only the convention had the ability to quell the disputes that threatened to destroy America. A popular Maryland author declared that "the GRAND CONVENTION" was undoubtedly crucial to the country's political existence and welfare.[31] "Z" voiced the sense of urgency and importance attached to the convention when he said it offered Americans perhaps their last chance to establish a permanent system of continental government. If that opportunity were lost, they might easily fall into "irretrievable confusion."[32] The essential press message on the significance of the convention was put most succinctly by a Massachusetts writer who told Americans that it had been "delegated to work out, if possible, your national salvation."[33]

The press also championed the convention in a self-serving fashion. In late May, a *Pennsylvania Herald* correspondent attacked obstructions to the wide dissemination of newspapers. He cited a proposal to impose new federal postal charges for transporting papers and the Massachusetts stamp act as unreasonable impediments to the press, "that great channel, which serves at once to gratify the curiosity, and to collect the voice of the people." It was, of course, always wrong to restrict the flow of newspapers, but limitations seemed especially repugnant "at this awful moment, when a council is convened, it may justly be said, to decide the fate of the confederation." Ten other editors quickly reprinted this assertion that the significance of the press had increased because of the convention's importance.[34]

During the early convention period, a few writers took the radical stance of voicing approval for the idea that the delegates might exceed Congress's instructions and create a new government. Shortly before the delegates actually began deliberations, editor Dallas of the *Herald* suggested that the Articles of Confederation might not be simply repaired and enlarged. Instead, perhaps "a new and stately building" would be "erected upon the old foundation." That was mere speculation, but it was very extensively reprinted.[35] The immensely popular Harrington expressed a similar thought more boldly. He talked of the delegates creating "a new fœderal government" and urged the states to "throw their sovereignty at the feet of the Convention."[36]

An essayist writing in early June called upon the authority of John Adams to insinuate that the Confederation government needed more than revisions. Prefacing his analysis with examples of how divine intervention aided America at crucial junctures during the War for Independence, he declared that the recent publication of what he called John Adams's brilliant analysis of government in America revealed that divine providence was still promoting the country's welfare. Adams proved, the writer held, that a single-house legislature could not long preserve a people's freedom or happiness. To achieve these worthy goals, a nation needed a system of government with two or three legislative branches and a powerful executive. Adams's arguments could not be refuted, and America's own experience demonstrated the "folly, instability, and tyranny of single legislatures." The author expressed the hope that history and Adams's insights would combine to banish single legislatures from the land. Indeed, the Adams publication was so essential that every elected official, including each convention delegate, should be required to declare he had read it. This endorsement constituted a recommendation for scrapping Congress, a single-house legislature Adams had labeled a mere diplomatic gathering. The essay was fairly lengthy; it offered commentary, not news; its recommendations were rather audacious. Yet it had some appeal. Although the piece appeared in only seven newspapers, reprintings occurred in five states.[37]

In the early days of the convention, the press was obviously willing to reprint allusions to altering the confederation government significantly. However, authors who spoke of what the *Worcester Magazine* had called the horror of a consolidated government were not popular. In early June a self-proclaimed "West-Chester Farmer" actually did advocate creating a "consolidated republic" with a two-house legislature and a president. The states, transformed into mere civil corporations, would be limited to making local ordinances not repugnant to the laws of "the supreme power." With careful accounting based on reducing the size of state government, the Farmer claimed his plan would save New Yorkers £3,000 a year. By late September, the press would accept much of what he said, but in early June it was stunningly radical. The New York *Daily Advertiser* gave these daring thoughts a printing as did the *Virginia Independent Chronicle*, but no other publishers allowed such suggestions to sully their pages.[38]

Although the press essentially ignored the then unsavory proposals of the West-Chester Farmer, its depiction of the delegates worked to give the convention the mandate to foster such bold plans. In the period from mid-May through mid-

June, the press gushed forth praise of the delegates. More stridently than ever before and in innovative ways, writers emphasized that the delegates should be trusted to find the means to save the Union. The dominant press message now explicitly told the people: defer to the delegates; accept what they recommend.

Important modifications in the glorification of the delegates occurred once the convention opened. It could be seen in the treatment of the most revered delegate. Compliments about George Washington were now often tied to daily occurrences and expressed more stridently. Widely reprinted accounts of multitudes braving inclement weather to greet Washington on his arrival in Philadelphia showed how Americans loved him.[39] Popular reprints about his subsequent activities served to remind Americans that the great and beloved former commander-in-chief was enlightened and fair-minded. On May 21 the *Independent Gazetteer* reported that Washington had endured harsh weather to attend a lecture on eloquence given by a lady.[40] Nine days later the *Pennsylvania Herald* noted that Washington and several other delegates attended Mass at a Catholic church.[41] Thus a reader could nod understandingly when perusing accounts of how Washington's attempt to review a militia drill had been interrupted because adoring citizens struggled to glimpse the great man.[42]

Given Washington's stature, it was only natural for editor Dallas of the *Herald* to offer special praise for "our old and faithful commander." According to Dallas, however, the delegates as a group were only slightly less noble than Washington. Indeed, they constituted "the collective wisdom of the Continent." This statement from Dallas's ardently proconvention May 16 issue, which in various forms appeared in thirty publications, illustrates another significant modification in press coverage of the delegates.[43] As the adulation of Washington intensified, it was extended more than ever before to the other delegates. A popular Baltimore writer, published in late May, echoed Dallas's "wisdom-of-the-continent" theme when he spoke of the members of the *"august meeting"* as being "the united wisdom of the continent."[44] Right after the scheduled opening of the convention, the *Pennsylvania Packet* offered a poem of fifteen hefty stanzas in honor of *"the Meeting of the* GRAND CONVENTION." The poet infused all the delegates with the qualities of Washington. Having come forward to ease Columbia's anguish, Washington was, happily, surrounded by "Patriot sages." If they could banish distrust,

> "So shall your country's latest breath
> From grateful hearts declare your worth,
> Your origin divine."

With Washington leading them, the delegates could achieve immortality. The fact that almost a dozen editors printed this lengthy poem demonstrates an eagerness to glorify the members of the convention.[45]

The reverent tone authors usually adopted when discussing the delegates was also clearly evident in a popular New York *Daily Advertiser* story of late May. It informed readers that William Samuel Johnson, a delegate from Connecticut, had been elected President of Columbia College. Francis Childs, the paper's publisher, called this a significant event because it showed that great personages willingly assumed leadership roles in education.[46]

The most flattering composite picture of the delegates, which also appeared in combination with gushing praise of Washington, came from Benjamin Rush's widely reprinted Harrington essay.[47] Rush, even more shamelessly than others, attempted to link the delegates to the Revolution. He claimed, incorrectly, that many convention delegates served in the first Continental Congress.[48] He also maintained, again incorrectly, that many had signed the Declaration of Independence.[49] He asserted, yet again with questionable accuracy, that many delegates had achieved distinction on the battlefield and that some received wounds fighting for independence.[50] Espousing a general view supported by various popular authors, Rush proclaimed that "perhaps no age or country saw more wisdom, patriotism and probity united in a single assembly, than we now behold in the convention of the states."

As Harrington, Rush candidly admitted that his depictions of the men who would create the new central government were designed to beget confidence in and attachment to the new government. And why not? "The immortal WASHINGTON has again quitted his beloved retirement, and obeyed the voice of God and his country, by accepting the chair of this illustrious body of patriots and heroes." It should be obvious to all that the convention would produce a government offering Americans both "safety and blessings."[51]

The essential arguments for trusting the delegates had been sketched by the end of May. Authors were not content, however, to let the glorification of the delegates rest there. In early June, the message was reiterated again and again.[52] "A Watchman" asserted that the convention was devising "wise and proper measures . . . to extricate us from our present difficulties, and to establish order among us."[53] John Hayes of the Baltimore *Maryland Gazette* proclaimed that "the same hands that laid the foundation of the Temple of Liberty, are again employed in this arduous task." Hayes took the even more positive step of prophesying that under the guidance of the convention "we shall keep the chain of friendship bright, and unite as citizens of one respectable and mighty empire."[54] A Massachusetts author, who emphasized that the delegates' knowledge, abilities, and patriotism warranted the confidence of the people, bluntly stated the basic press view. "If ye wish well to your country," he said, "ye will place such confidence in them, as to sanction with your approbation the measures they may recommend, notwithstanding they may, in some small points, militate against your ideas of Right."[55]

One popular item first published on June 6 in the adamantly proconvention New York *Daily Advertiser* neatly presented the case for supporting the magnificent delegates and their recommendations. The author of a letter written at Port Roseway, Nova Scotia, on April 10 reported that accounts from New York indicated "the sentiment of unanimity is daily increasing." Unfortunately for Britain, "the citizens of the late rebellious States are awake to the dangers both of anarchy and its consequent despotism. Such confidence seems to be placed in their posse of patriots and politicians, about to be assembled in Convention at Philadelphia, that every hope of their being once more united to the mother country must *now* die, and their independence and union be considered as *indeed* established." Coming from an avowed enemy, that was high praise both for the American people and for the convention. Perhaps it was too high. The letter could have been authentic; it could have been a fake that publisher Childs accepted as authentic; it could have been concocted for Childs or even by him. Its authenticity cannot now be determined, but it exudes the aroma of a planted item. Whether authentic or planted, the piece effectively summarized how many friends of a stronger national government wanted Americans to view the convention so they would be predisposed to accept the delegates' recommendations.[56]

In urging acceptance of whatever the convention might produce, two widely reprinted Philadelphia writers expressed little faith in the people. They traveled farther along an antidemocratic path than any authors had dared go in the preconvention era. One actually said that, when considering what form of government was best, "fatal experience will instruct us that little can be left to the voluntary disposition of the people." His bold assertion was softened only slightly by the claim that any form of government that did not produce virtuous manners among the people was "a political romance."[57] The even more popular Harrington displayed greater tact. All men could understand the meaning of liberty, he said, but it required special knowledge and abilities to devise a good government. It was therefore indeed fortunate that the members of the convention were experienced and talented men.[58]

News accounts about the convention also illustrate the increasing effort to sell it. The first report on convention activities was short. On Saturday, May 26 the *Evening Chronicle* and the *Independent Gazetteer* each printed the same announcement that seven states were represented at the convention on Friday and, with a quorum finally present, the delegates unanimously elected George Washington president and Major William Jackson secretary. More than thirty publications carried that story.[59] On May 30, the *Herald* told of the election and also indicated that a special committee composed of a delegate from each state would handle communications, gather information, and prepare a report for discussion. Editor Dallas, who believed quick action was required, applauded the plan. Under it, he said, information would be collected from all parts of the Union, and the delegates could proceed without being drawn off into philosophical discussions. This combination of news and editorial comment was swiftly and extensively reprinted.[60]

The response to the delegates' decision to wrap their activities in secrecy demonstrates how the media itself deferred to the convention. The *Herald* broke the story on June 2 when it reported that the delegates found it difficult to communicate with one another because the convention was marked by such circumspection and secrecy. In fact, the concern for secrecy actually caused the delegates to suspend debate if one of their "inferior officers" entered the room. Considering that the convention was indeed news and that the press thrived on filling space with political material, one might expect publishers to have questioned the secrecy rule. That was not the case. Dallas said the secrecy rule would naturally increase the people's anxiety, but he did not contend the proceedings should become public. He merely called for dispatch in remedying the Union's problems. Twenty-six other publishers reprinted his commentary.[61] Thomas Greenleaf, editor of one of the few newspapers that adopted an Antifederalist position once the Constitution appeared, came the closest to suggesting the convention's deliberations should be made public. And Greenleaf merely promised that "no pains shall be spared to procure the debates and resolutions of the Convention for the inspection of the public as soon as any of them transpire." His pronouncement offered in the June 7 *New York Journal* hardly constituted an attack on the right of the delegates to conduct their affairs in secret.

The campaign to sell the convention went beyond publishing commentary and news accounts laced with general praise for the convention and its delegates. Authors also called upon specific groups to support the convention and accept its recommendations. Harrington played the lobbyist by telling interest groups how the convention might benefit them materially. A uniform system of commercial regulations and protection for shipping would help merchants. Those engaged in manufacturing, many of whom were unemployed, read that only a vigorous central government would have the power necessary to encourage their endeavors and exclude foreign competition. Farmers burdened by direct taxation could expect relief from a government able to raise funds through imposts and customs. America's public creditors could expect payment only if an effective government united the country's power and resources. People living on the western frontier menaced by Indians would find protection in the federal government. Those who loved peace must remember that only an energetic government could keep the peace. Thus, Harrington gave virtually everyone who might have a vote a self-interested reason to back the convention's efforts.[62]

The clergy and women also received special appeals. On June 5, a week after Harrington first appeared, two Philadelphia papers published the thoughts of a correspondent who urged the clergy to teach their flocks "the necessity of government." Twenty-one editors found that admonition worth reproducing. The writer's concern with gaining support for the convention was made explicit in a less widely reprinted accompanying paragraph directed to "the American ladies." They had a duty to work for the success of the convention because, he said, the anarchy in America might produce monarchy. In such a world, women, reduced to virtual slavery, would be valued only as the mothers of soldiers. Therefore women must use their influence over husbands, brothers, and sons to make them stop dreaming of liberty under a simple democratic government. Such governments worked against order and decency. For their own sake, women must become active to "preserve the rank—the happiness—the influence, and the character in society, for which God intended them."[63]

The message carried by the press from mid-May to mid-June was clearly and overwhelmingly a proconvention message. Few authors disputed the claim that America was experiencing a time of troubles that had pushed the Union to the brink of disintegration. Few questioned the need to augment the central government's power. Fewer still questioned the value of the convention, and no one challenged the necessity of the convention once the delegates actually began deliberations. Just as important, with only one exception, authors who went against the proconvention thrust of the press were not widely reprinted. Some who rejected the idea of simply trusting the delegates to determine the fate of the Union's government fared better, but they did so only by applauding the need for the convention or by not referring to the convention at all.

An essayist who oppugned the necessity of the convention appeared on May 19 in an unlikely source, the *Independent Gazetteer*. "Dysart" rejected the laudatory and deferential stance writers routinely took when speaking of the convention. Asserting that no one seemed to know exactly what the delegates were to do, he wondered what business they planned and sarcastically suggested it must be of the greatest importance. If the delegates intended to act, he said, the public should be informed prior to the creation of any laws or agreements. This essay appeared before the convention actually opened. So, despite its insulting tone, editors might have reproduced Dysart, if only as a straw man they could pummel with proconvention pieces. But no reprintings have been uncovered.[64] As in preconvention days, editors refused to reprint anything that directly challenged the importance of the convention or the dignity of the delegates.

Dysart's concerns were not totally obliterated. News stories about the Connecticut debate on sending delegates could alert readers to the fact that some legislators outside Rhode Island had actually rejected the idea of holding a convention. However, as noted, those accounts, first published on May 21, made it clear that a solid majority of Connecticut's legislators favored sending delegates. Moreover, some press versions made it seem as if there had been no opposition to the convention.[65]

Except for reports on the Connecticut debate, only one item that seemed to dispute proconvention themes came close to achieving popularity during this period. It was an extract of a May 26 letter from a New Yorker to his Bay State friend. The author, writing before reports of the convention's first proceedings appeared, remarked that the convention had become a hot topic of conversation. Even among respectable men, one heard an astonishing variety of opinions about what alterations the federal system needed. Although the New Yorker did not say so, his analysis suggested that the delegates themselves might harbor differing opinions. In addition, he pessimistically asserted that it would require luck even to convince a reasonable majority of citizens to adopt what the delegates might propose. He also seemed to question the "time-of-troubles" theme and to doubt the necessity of the convention when he asserted: "As we complain of evils which evidently do not exist, I confess, I sometimes almost despair of seeing the day when we shall cease to murmur, and suffer imaginary evils to produce in the end real ones."

The New Yorker's negative analysis was tempered in a number of ways. The convention contained, he observed, many judicious and very respectable men. He softened his apparent questioning of the necessity of the convention by expressing the hope that the delegates could fashion alterations in the Union's constitution that would produce stability and happiness. He further discounted his own questioning of the time-of-trouble arguments by suggesting that the Union's situation would improve if America's governments and people were more established, settled, and steady.[66] He apparently realized what had been a truism since the convention was authorized: circuity must be employed if one wanted to question the glorification of the convention and also get reprinted.

"Z," who like Alexander Dallas and Benjamin Rush understood the importance of timing, thoroughly rejected the anticonvention views advanced by Dysart and hinted at by the New Yorker. Nevertheless, "Z" did want to limit the delegates' freedom to transform the Articles of Confederation. Considering his approach, it seems that more than chance determined when and where his lengthy essay first appeared. It surfaced on May 16, the same day Dallas placed several stridently proconvention items in his *Herald*. It is also significant that the Philadelphia *Freeman's Journal* published the essay. Francis Bailey's paper was one of the few that supported an Antifederalist position after the Constitution was recommended. Equally important, during the convention period, Bailey and Thomas Greenleaf of the *New York Journal* were the only two publishers likely to print original commentary that deviated from the effort to sell the convention.[67] "Z's" essay is thus instructive both as to message and reprint popularity.

Part of "Z's" commentary was tailored to make it popular. No other author writing at the time offered more extensive or varied examples in support of the view that America faced ruin. Moreover, he vociferously maintained that the people naturally hoped the delegates' wisdom would resolve the crisis. The convention was more than important, it was crucial. Although no convention booster could have asked for firmer backing of the convention, "Z" deviated from the standard booster line when he advocated a plan that hardly fit with the theme of deferring to the delegates.

While emphatically asserting that Congress needed augmented powers, "Z" declared that granting Congress the exclusive right to regulate shipping and foreign trade would be sufficient. He clearly advocated limited change and opposed merely accepting whatever the convention might recommend. It is revealing that "Z" mustered only six reprintings.[68] By way of comparison, Harrington's propagandistic essay, which called for a strong federal government and accepting what measures the convention might recommend, appeared in over thirty publications.[69]

Authors who opposed giving the delegates carte blanche achieved their greatest reprint success when they offered general commentary on the nature of government and suggested that Americans should reject certain forms of government, especially monarchy or those that smacked of monarchy. By doing this, the writers could attack the idea of deferring to the delegates without even mentioning the convention or its delegates.

Two essayists took special aim at aristocratic governments. One did it by comparing democracy, aristocracy, and monarchy. He maintained that all political power was derived from the people and that they should limit the power they delegated. A democracy, fortified by a strong and efficient executive branch, offered the best promise of good government. Monarchy and aristocracy were deplorable forms of government, especially for the United States.[70] Aristocratic government also came under attack when six newspapers printed an excerpt from Lord Kames's *Sketches*. He maintained that, while any government that inspired patriotism was a good government, the best government was a commonwealth founded on what he called "rotation of power," where officials worked to merit the approval of their fellow citizens. The essential point was made by asking: "What will our American aristocraticks say to this?"[71]

The attack on aristocracy and monarchy benefited from an interpretation of John Adams's writings that undercut the value of using him to champion the convention. "Biscayanus" detected the putrid whiff of aristocracy and even of monarchy when he reviewed Adams's *A Defence of the Constitutions of Government of the United States of America* for a London newspaper. The *Gazette of the State of Georgia*, the Savannah paper, reprinted the review in late May, and it became popular. Biscayanus viewed the so-called defense of America's constitutions as an attack upon them. The title of the book was, the reviewer charged, purposely designed to mislead Americans into establishing a kingly government based on the English model. Adams reportedly wanted a House of Lords because he believed one branch of the legislature should be composed of "the well-born, or those who are distinguished by their descent from a race of illustrious ancestors." Biscayanus savaged Adams on this point and closed his devastating critique with a few backhanded compliments.[72] The popularity of this review illustrates how unpopular the idea of aristocracy as well as monarchy was.

Another popular author, published in the proconvention *Pennsylvania Herald* on June 2, used the same techniques when he attacked monarchy. Once again the convention was not mentioned; once again the message undoubtedly applied to the convention's work. The writer remarked that various politicians had advanced rather fanciful schemes of continental government. Astonishingly, some serious people were, he said, considering the absurd idea of grafting a monarchy onto America's democratic governmental systems. Yet history showed that popular governments did not give way to monarchies except under force. In his view, Americans would be committing suicide if they willingly embraced monarchy after winning independence in a war against monarchical ambition.[73]

While its author too did not openly refer to the convention, another widely reprinted commentary from this period is especially relevant when considering possible challenges to the idea that the people should defer to the delegates. In late May the *Worcester Magazine* carried a short comment that suggested the people should reject blind deference. The publisher, the well-known and respected Isaiah Thomas, observed that disturbing accounts were circulating throughout the country. People openly talked of creating "one *consolidated* government" to extend from New Hampshire to Georgia. Thomas found that thought repugnant. He expressed the hope that Americans still possessed the virtue needed "to support the free governments her citizens now enjoy."[74] Although short items had an especially good chance of being reprinted, that hardly accounts for the fact that thirteen publishers reprinted the piece by May 30. Its popularity, and the lack of popularity of the West-Chester Farmer, demonstrates press opposition to creating a system that stripped the states of their identity.[75]

Although the *Worcester Magazine* blast against one consolidated government was not an attack on the convention, the argument did attack the idea of giving unlimited trust to whatever the delegates produced. Other publishers concurred by uniformly rejecting the idea of creating a monarchy in America. An aristocratic form of government was also unacceptable. Those were important restrictions. But, except for those limited and hardly surprising constraints, the press maintained its proconvention stance of not questioning calls to trust the delegates. Dysart, the most anticonvention essayist, was published before proceedings actually began, and even he was decidedly less hostile than Sidney. And as with Sidney, Dysart went unreprinted. The New York gentleman's May 26 letter weakly questioned the "time-of-troubles" theme; he did not challenge the convention. "Z" shouted that America's fate depended on the convention and then advocated making only limited changes in the Articles. Those authors who excoriated the idea of creating a monarchy or an aristocratic government did not imply that the convention wanted to produce such governments. Indeed, they did not even mention the convention. Thus, by slashing at monarchy, authors who obliquely challenged the theme of trusting the delegates could produce popular reprints. But if they were not deferentially mindful of the need for the convention, their likelihood of being reprinted declined sharply.

Many writers and editors of this period found even implied criticism of the convention unacceptable. As they had in preconvention days, ardent convention boosters rushed into print to heap ridicule on those who might question the need for the convention to increase the federal government's power. It did not matter that few challenges to proconvention ideals got published. In addition, a new line of attack, the preemptive assault, became visible. Increasingly, authors worked to discredit anyone who dared, or who might dare at some future time, to combat the convention. Such people were depicted as selfish and unpatriotic; some were even accused of actually wishing America harm.

Rhode Island remained a prime target for persons unwilling to brook any possible criticism of the convention. The well-established practice of attacking the tiny state for its supposed failings, especially its "antifederalism," intensified during the early days of the convention. Dr. Price had expressed a common feeling when he denounced "the knavery of the Rhode-Island Legislature."[76] The disdain for Rhode Island was clearly revealed by the popular author who expressed pleasure that every state except Rhode Island was represented at the convention. The Rhode Islanders would have, he said, mortified the other delegates and brought discredit to their proceedings. More important, by refusing to attend, Rhode Island delegates could not undermine the convention's salutary objective.[77]

In early June, three widely reprinted authors further demonstrated the contempt felt for Rhode Island's government. A New York wit spoke of "The University of Rogue Island" conferring a degree on Daniel Shays that Governor Collins would mail just as soon as he could obtain hard cash to pay the postage.[78] The belief that dishonor was a hallmark of Rhode Island's government was evident in a letter, probably an invented bit, purportedly written in Vermont. The author said Shays had been robbed by his followers and the money taken to the "Rogue's Island" treasury. It would be safe there in the hands of people who thought nothing of refusing to pay just debts.[79] A Rhode Islander expressed similar views when he described the state's officials as unprincipled tyrants and also expressed the fervent hope that the convention would take action to rescue his state.[80]

Authors who hammered at Rhode Island did not expect it to reform. That was evident in the state's lack of interest in capturing Shays. According to a *Newport Herald* correspondent, it could also be seen in the monetary ideals of the state's "sons of anarchy." The rascals hoped the recently elected Connecticut and Massachusetts legislatures would emulate Rhode Island and issue paper money.

Reflecting the standard press view, this writer called paper currency an infection that caused an evil plague. The hopes of the "harpies of anarchy" would be dashed, but only after patriotic zeal had been ignited.[81]

Some popular authors who intensified the attack on Rhode Island built upon each other's work. Two days after Price's letter appeared, the *Independent Gazetteer* published an extract of a Rhode Islander's letter. The gentleman reminded his readers that his state had twice voted against attending the convention. He traced the votes to the rural people's desire to ruin the state's commercial areas, a goal they unfortunately were accomplishing. Looking at Rhode Island's actions, he predicted his poor state would be thrown out of the Union.[82] The author of another essay, published the next day in the *Pennsylvania Herald* and then widely reprinted, lamented that Congress lacked the power to control "the selfish interest of a single state, and to compel the sacrifice of partial views, in order to promote the common weal."[83] No reference was made to Rhode Island, but it is unlikely any other state would have come to mind. In the last week of May, the author of a *Worcester Magazine* article leveled the ultimate charge. He observed that the often maligned state of Vermont had worked to apprehend the leaders of Shays's Rebellion. Yet Rhode Island authorities did not care about bringing the rebels to justice. These considerations prompted the blast: "Rhode-Island! Rhode-Island only, as a State, is the only one that has, by its proceedings, encouraged Treason and Rebellion!"[84]

In mid-June, "Black Beard," a classic of the genre, summed up the hatred for Rhode Island and its unwillingness to reform. He did not want the state broken up. No, it should be allowed to leave the Union and to continue along its own selfish path. It would serve a useful purpose by becoming the New World equivalent of the Algerian pirates. Faced with the Rhode Island corsairs, European nations would seek alliances with the twelve states and, to obtain those alliances, the Europeans would grant trading concessions. With mock seriousness, Black Beard hoped that "the fœderal convention will consider this subject fully, and allow Rhode Island to withdraw herself from the union, that the new world, like the old one, may have a band of pirates in the scale of its importance." Although it was lengthy and on a well-worked topic, Black Beard's essay became popular.[85]

Considering the supposed long train of abuses compiled by Rhode Islanders, and given the hostility against Rhode Island, the subscribers of the *Pennsylvania Herald* and the Philadelphia *Evening Chronicle* may not have been surprised to read in their June 9 issues: "We are informed that the Fœderal Convention, among other things has resolved that Rhode-Island should be considered as having virtually withdrawn herself from the union" and that "upon no account shall she be restored to her station in the Union." As part of a report on convention activities, these comments appeared in forty-six newspapers.[86]

The hatred Rhode Island educed was graphically illustrated on May 24 when Thomas Greenleaf, publisher of the *New York Journal*, symbolically made Rhode Island vanish. He proclaimed that "the proceedings of that little, insignificant state" would henceforth be passed over by the *Journal* "in contemptuous silence." Since Greenleaf was already displaying the tendencies that made him an Antifederalist publisher, his comments show that the contempt for Rhode Island was truly widespread and intensifying.

Through early June, Rhode Island remained the obvious and convenient target for persons who opposed "antifederalists." Some authors, however, went further. Beginning a trend that would continue and expand as the summer wore on, several widely reprinted essayists questioned the patriotism of "antifederalists." For example, those who opposed doing what was necessary to save the captives in Algiers, such as strengthening Congress, did not know the value of liberty; they were driven by selfish private interest or they reflected a narrow localist vision.[87] Similar charges came from an author who praised "the GRAND CONVENTION" as the way to reform government. He wondered "what true friend to this country" could object to giving Congress more power.[88]

George J. Osborne, Jr., publisher of the *New Hampshire Spy*, used the same kind of innuendo in denouncing the fact that monetary concerns might cause his state to be unrepresented at the convention. Osborne impugned the honor and competence of state officials and proclaimed he was authorized to say that the state's "true whigs" would carefully inspect and analyze government finances unless New Hampshire sent delegates to the convention.[89]

A Watchman offered bolder pronouncements. His views, published in early June, are especially important because, more than any other writer of the day, he suggested using the threat of physical violence to intimidate. He proclaimed Governor Collins of Rhode Island the Lord Dunmore and Governor Clinton of New York the Thomas Hutchinson of modern times. He advocated unleashing the methods used against Loyalists at the start of the Revolution on "the present breed of tories in America." Isolate them and consider them enemies of the people, A Watchman said. The friends of liberty and government should unite "and bear down all opposition to the wise and proper measures that are now devising to extricate us from our present difficulties, and to establish order among us." Such assertions normally would gain few reprintings because the author named names rather than speaking about people or politicians generally and because he implied that violence should be used. Nevertheless, his comments appeared in nine publications.[90] Although A Watchman almost achieved popularity, his sanctioning of the use of violence against individuals was atypical. Through mid-June, most prochange, proconvention writers were still content to aim their verbal blows primarily at "Rogue's Island." In time that would change.

• • •

Taken as a whole, press coverage in the period from the scheduled opening of the convention through early June worked to build a proconvention momentum. Popular reprints often read like campaign literature. Benjamin Rush played an important role in the developing campaign. He supplied

Price's influential letter to the Philadelphia press just as the convention was scheduled to open. Then, right after the delegates actually began their proceedings, Rush gave the press his Harrington essay. The campaign tone of the general press message on the state of the Union and the convention's role was clearly present in Harrington, the most widely reprinted proconvention essay published before the convention finally ended its work in September. Rush's Harrington essay nicely summed up the essence of press coverage in the month after the scheduled opening of the convention. "Under the present weak, imperfect and distracted government of Congress, anarchy, poverty, infamy, and SLAVERY, await the United States." However, "under such a government as will probably be formed by the present Convention, America may yet enjoy peace, safety, liberty and glory."[91]

The growing power of the proconvention message to defer to the delegates was supported as well by the fact that, over time, the press became less likely to reprint anything that directly undermined the convention or its goals.[92] One potentially strong challenge to the proconvention position fostered by the press did, however, surface in a New York paper about June 4. The full report read: "It is thought by many that the convention will continue to sit some months, and that they will conclude their deliberations by recommending, not an amendment of the old system, but the introduction of one entirely new." Two explosive bits of news rested in this short report. Some authors, who did not claim to possess definite knowledge of the delegates' intentions, had intimated that the convention might recommend fundamental changes in the Confederation's system of government. However, nothing presented to the public had come so close to asserting that the delegates actually planned to scrap the Articles of Confederation. Doing that would, of course, violate Congress's instructions to the delegates. The comment about the convention sitting for months was especially important for two reasons: (1) it buttressed the claim that more than revision of the Articles was occurring; (2) it also undercut the argument that immediate action was required to save the Union.

Two Boston papers, a Virginia paper, and the *Quebec Gazette* quickly reprinted this intriguing and newsworthy item. Yet it was not reprinted anywhere else. The story, which was accurate, may have been given less credence because it did not originate in Philadelphia, the convention city. The fact that some leading New York politicians were seen as "antifederalists" might have raised suspicions about the motives of the person who supplied the report. Nevertheless, New York City was a prime reprint area, as was Boston. The piece also appeared in the *Virginia Independent Chronicle*, a possible gateway to the South. Considering these points, it seems clear that the total of only three reprintings in the United States can be traced to the fact that many editors wanted to squelch the account.[93]

The surprisingly low number of reprints of the story concerning a potential new government certainly aided the convention boosters. The limited reprintings also made it far easier for elements of the press to continue building a proconvention momentum. Then on June 13 a news story appeared that threatened to derail media efforts to sell the convention.

Notes to Chapter Two

1. Those and other items printed with an eye to when the convention started are analyzed later in this chapter. William Spotswood published both the *Herald* and the *Columbian Magazine*, and Dallas was his editor for both. Thus comments attributed here to Dallas may have been approved or even written by Spotswood. On their relationship, see COC1: xxxix.

2. The letter, with slight variations, also appeared the next day in the *Evening Chronicle*, May 17.

3. Rush also sent a copy to David Ramsey, the South Carolina historian.

4. Two other items sent from Price to Rush, one in 1785 and one in 1786, took less than two months in one case and just less than three months in the other to reach Philadelphia. Also, another letter written on April 2, 1787 by Price, but not to Rush, was published in three Philadelphia newspapers on June 20. Based on these

examples, it seems probable that the January 26 letter reached Rush in Philadelphia no later than late April. On the transit time of the letters to Rush, see Lyman H. Butterfield, ed., *The Letters of Benjamin Rush*, 2 vols. (Princeton, 1951), 1: 372, n. 2 and 408; on the other letter, see Chapter Three, n. 30.

5. Price's standing was such that both Federalists and Antifederalists quoted him during the debate over ratification of the Constitution. See headnote to CC22 in COC1: 100–1.

6. As noted in COC1, which gives the letter (p. 101), this piece was at times printed with slight variations and even with sentences missing. The forty-two reprintings occurred between May 17 and June 14.

7. On Rush's political views, see David F. Hawke, *Benjamin Rush: Revolutionary Gadfly* (Indianapolis, 1971); Robert L. Brunhouse, *The Counter-Revolution in Pennsylvania 1776–1790* (Harrisburg, 1942).

8. See nn. 59, 60 below for analysis of these reports.

9. The essay is given in COC1: 116–20 with the attribution to Rush explained in the headnote. The thirty-one newspaper reprintings of some or all of the essay occurred by August 11; another reprinting appeared in the June issue of the Philadelphia *American Museum*. This essay provides the best single example of publishers reprinting parts of essays as individual reprints or blending in bits and snippets of various other publications or writing to produce a "new" item. It also shows that reprintings, even of major segments of long essays, were not always noted as being reprints nor given the identifying pen name. (On these points, see, for example, the reprinting in the *Evening Chronicle*, June 9, and n. 12 below.) The "Harrington" essay was so popular that, even given its great length, seventeen of the thirty-one reprinting newspapers published the full essay.

10. Issue of May 24; reprinted seven times between May 26 and June 9, with reprintings in: Pa., Md., Va., N.H., R.I., and Mass.

11. *Pennsylvania Herald*, May 16, with twenty-two reprintings between May 17 and July 14.

12. Issue of May 22. This essay, given in COC1: 112–13, has a reprinting history complicated by the fact that reprintings included two basic versions, one based on the original and the other on a truncated version. The various reprintings occurred between May 29 and July 7. Eight papers published between May 31 and July 7 reprinted the whole piece; five others gave all but the first para-

graph; three others printed essentially only the first paragraph; two printed the last paragraph, with one of those blending bits of Harrington into a "new" essay. The material and quotation given here were reprinted by fourteen papers. The essential point to note about the complex reprinting history of this lengthy essay is that every part of it attained popular reprint status.

13. This essay from the *Freeman's Journal*, May 16, given in COC1: 98–100 and reprinted six times by June 13, is discussed at length later in this chapter.

14. Issue of May 19, given in COC1: 104–5, with twenty-four reprintings by August 3.

15. Issue of June 5, with the editor probably reprinting from the *Halifax Journal* of May 10. Eight reprintings occurred between June 9 and July 20. Shepard Kollock, editor of the *New Jersey Journal* (July 12), called this a "refugified," that is a Loyalist, paragraph and so did the editor of the *Country Journal*, July 18, who reprinted the Kollock version.

16. His comments, with a counterattack by John Hayes, the paper's editor, appeared in the Baltimore *Maryland Gazette*, June 12. The piece was reprinted in full ten times between June 15 and early July; the *Providence Gazette*, June 30, printed Tucker's comment but not that of Hayes.

17. See n. 6 above.

18. See n. 9 above, and compare the similar gloomy message in "A Watchman," *Independent Gazetteer*, June 4 (reprinted in full five times between June 15 and July 25 and in part three times between June 16 and July 3), and the *Massachusetts Centinel*, June 13 (reprinted by seven newspapers between June 21 and July 4, and in the August issue of the *American Museum*).

19. Poem by "Nestor," *Massachusetts Centinel*, June 13, given in COC1: 132–33. Nine reprintings occurred by September 1.

20. See nn. 6, 15 above.

21. Attribution and text given in COC1: 94; seventeen reprintings occurred by June 30.

22. The first item, from the *Massachusetts Centinel* of May 16, is given in COC1: 94 with twenty-one reprintings by July 7. The May 19 item, an extract of a letter dated May 15, is given in ibid., 94–95. The Springfield gentleman's general report appeared in more than twenty papers; his comments on enlistments occurred in a separate section that was reprinted in more than two dozen papers. The somewhat complicated reprinting history of this letter is given in

ibid., 96, n. 4. On the May 23 item, see following note.

23. The story on the events in Connecticut, reprinted twenty-four times by July 12, first appeared in that state's Litchfield *Weekly Monitor*, May 21. The discussion of events in Vermont comes from the *Worcester Magazine* published in the fourth week of May. Both reports cited here are given in COC1: 95. On May 23 the *Massachusetts Centinel* published a letter from a Westerfield, Connecticut, man who said that the rebels were successfully enlisting fighters and that he expected the authorities would stop the men from doing damage. The reports cited in the text thus robbed this piece of some of its news value. It still became a popular reprint as, in addition to the *Centinel*, ten newspapers printed it between May 29 and June 14.

24. *New York Journal*, May 31, with twelve reprintings between June 2 and July 12. While editor Greenleaf did not say it explicitly, he was apparently referring to New York's Washington County.

25. Twenty-six reprintings occurred between June 13 and August 4; fourteen of them ended with the first section described in the text and thus did not have the comments about Shays and gunpowder.

26. COC1: 101, and see n. 6 above.

27. Baltimore *Maryland Gazette*, May 22, given in COC1: 112–13, with the quotation from p. 112, and reprinted by eleven papers; see n. 12 above.

28. COC1: 120, and see n. 9 above.

29. The papers were the *Independent Gazetteer*, given in COC1: 126, and the *Evening Chronicle*. Twenty-two reprintings occurred by July 25. One writer who just missed gaining reprint popularity also clearly linked the "time-of-troubles" image with the idea of America's potential greatness: "the wide, the unbounded prospect lies before us—but, shadows, clouds, and darkness rest upon it." His piece, given in COC1: 113, appeared in the *New York Journal* on May 24 and was reprinted eight times by June 16. See also a letter from Halifax in which the author spoke of "the indispensible necessity of a general efficient system, for the direction of your government, and [the] respectability of your nation." The letter was printed by the *Pennsylvania Packet*, June 6, with an attribution to a New York paper of May 31, not located. Nine reprintings occurred between June 4 and and July 3.

30. Issue of June 5; the reprintings occurred between June 9 and 30.

31. On "Harrington," see n. 9 above; for the quotation, see Baltimore *Maryland Gazette*, May 22, given in COC1: 112; as indicated in n. 12 above, this material was reprinted eleven times.

32. See COC1: 98 and n. 13 above.

33. *Massachusetts Centinel*, June 13, with seven reprints in newspapers between June 21 and July 4; it also appeared in the August issue of the *American Museum*.

34. *Pennsylvania Herald*, May 26, with ten reprintings between June 4 and 16. In 1785, the Massachusetts government, with a stunning disregard for history, levied a stamp tax of two-thirds of a penny on each newspaper printed. Because of fierce opposition, the act never took effect. However a tax on newspaper advertising was instituted and remained in place until 1788. The obnoxious federal government action stemmed from a proposal, not implemented in 1787, that would have stopped the postal service practice of allowing printers to exchange their newspapers postage free. The federal policy was implemented in January 1788 and caused major controversy. The issue was not settled until 1792 when the basic postage on newspapers was set at one cent each with no charge placed on newspaper exchanges between publishers. On these developments, see Frank L. Mott, *American Journalism—A History of Newspapers in the United States through 260 Years: 1690 to 1950*, rev. ed. (New York, 1950), 143–44, 160–61; COC4: 540–42.

35. *Pennsylvania Herald*, May 19, given in COC1: 104–5 with quotations from p. 104; twenty-four reprintings in nine states occurred by August 3.

36. Quotations from COC1: 118–19, and see n. 9 above.

37. The essay, signed "Sidney," appeared in the Philadelphia *Independent Gazetteer* of June 6, given in COC1: 88. This "Sidney" was not the same person discussed earlier in this chapter who attacked the idea of holding the convention. To avoid confusion, the pen name of the *Gazetteer* "Sidney" is not used in the text. On the importance and role of John Adams's *Defence*, see Chapter One, n. 8.

38. New York *Daily Advertiser*, June 8, given in COC1: 128–130 with quotations from pp. 128, 129. The reprinting occurred on June 27. The "West-Chester Farmer" was obviously conversant with and influenced by John Adams's *Defence*. Cf. COC1: 86–87, 128. On the comment from the *Worcester Magazine*, see n. 74 below.

39. The most extensively circulated of the descriptions of Washington's arrival, all of which were similar, appeared in

the *Pennsylvania Herald*, May 16 (reprinted eight times). The *Pennsylvania Packet* description of May 14 was reprinted four times; the *Pennsylvania Gazette* account of May 16 got three reprintings; five papers reprinted shortened or blended versions of the stories about Washington's arrival.

40. Reprinted six times; a variant, which also appeared in the *Independent Gazetteer* (May 29), was reprinted by four papers, two of which had not reprinted the May 21 piece.

41. Issue of May 30, with eleven reprintings between June 1 and 14.

42. *Pennsylvania Herald* and *Freeman's Journal*, June 6, with seventeen reprintings in other papers by July 9; it also appeared in the June issue of the *Columbian Magazine*.

43. *Pennsylvania Herald*, May 16, with reprintings in twenty-nine papers between May 18 and June 14; it also appeared in the May issue of the *Columbian Magazine*.

44. Quotations from Baltimore *Maryland Gazette*, May 22, given in COC1: 112; as indicated in n. 12 above, this material was reprinted eleven times.

45. *Pennsylvania Packet*, May 17, with ten reprintings from May 19 to June 28.

46. Issue of May 24, with sixteen reprintings between June 1 and the fourth week of June.

47. See n. 9 above.

48. Although there was some question about the representation of New Hampshire in late May, based on the delegates who attended the convention, only seven of the fifty-five (Dickinson, Livingston, Mifflin, Read, Rutledge, Sherman, and Washington) served in the First Continental Congress.

49. Based on the fifty-five delegates who attended the convention, only eight (Clymer, Franklin, Gerry, Morris, Read, Sherman, Wilson, and Wythe) signed the Declaration of Independence, and four of the eight came from Pennsylvania. Moreover, as Merrill Jensen notes, only four of the eight "willingly supported independence." See his *The American Revolution within America* (New York, 1974), 169.

50. Something over half of the fifty-five could claim to have seen military service in the War for Independence, but few had extensive battlefield experience. See the short biographies in James H. Charleton et al., eds., *Framers of the Constitution* (Washington, D.C., 1986).

51. COC1: 120, and see n. 9 above.

52. Only one of the following examples of items published in early June attained popular reprint status. However, taken as a group, the three items appeared a total of twenty-six times and that, when added to the solid popularity of "Harrington," shows that their message was indeed one editors liked.

53. This part of his essay was reprinted seven times; see n. 18 above.

54. Issue of June 12; see n. 16 above.

55. *Massachusetts Centinel,* June 13, with six reprintings in newspapers between June 21 and July 4; it also appeared in the August issue of the *American Museum.*

56. The ten reprintings occurred between June 9 and July 9. According to reports printed in early June, the idea of supporting the convention, and by implication whatever the delegates produced, had already taken hold of some political bodies. An author writing in the New York *Daily Advertiser* of June 8 suggested that recent elections had transformed the state's legislature. He predicted it would "effectually free itself from the odium of being anti-fœderal" in no small part "by adopting the plan of continental government, which will be framed by the wisdom and virtue of the distinguished worthies, who compose the Convention." Perhaps because of its speculative nature about possible local political issues, this item from June 8 was reprinted only twice, in the *Hudson Weekly Gazette* and the *New York Journal* of June 14.

57. *Pennsylvania Herald,* May 19, given in COC1: 104–5, with quotation from p. 105, and see n. 14 above.

58. Quotation from COC1: 116, and see n. 9 above. Prodemocratic statements, such as that in the *Pennsylvania Herald* of June 9 (given in COC1: 130–31, with seven reprintings by July 11), were printed, but they were not nearly as popular as the kinds of comments "Harrington" expressed.

59. The full report appeared in twenty-six other papers between May 26 and June 30; another five papers printed the first paragraph on Washington but not the short paragraph on Jackson's selection as secretary. As reprintings occurred, the form of the story differed over time. Except for omitting the notation that Washington's election was unanimous, the same basic information, as indicated in n. 60 below, also appeared in another paper. Thus, Washington's election was reported in more than forty newspapers.

60. Given in COC1: 122; reprinted in twenty-six papers by July

9 and in the May issue of the *Columbian Magazine*. Some publishers who had already carried the story on the election of Washington and Jackson omitted the first line of this piece, but all the papers carried the segments cited here. Other early reports of convention activities also proved popular and are analyzed below and in Chapter Three.

61. Given in COC1: 122–23; the twenty-six reprintings occurred by July 9. The reprinting in the *Hampshire Chronicle* of June 19 did not carry the line endorsing the secrecy plan.

62. Quotation from COC1: 119, and see n. 9 above.

63. This item appeared in both the *Evening Chronicle* and the *Independent Gazetteer* on June 5. The *Gazetteer* printing is given in COC1: 126–27. The appeal to ministers was reprinted twenty-one times by July 25; the appeal to women got seven reprintings between June 6 and July 9. Six of the reprinting papers carried both sections. Considering prevailing standards, this writer, despite his elitism, voiced a progressive position when he urged women to enter the political fray. Perhaps that is why his appeal to women appeared far fewer times than his appeal to the clergy. On the political role of women, see Mary Beth Norton, *Liberty's Daughters: The Revolutionary Experience of American Women, 1750–1800* (Boston, 1980), especially 157–93 passim; Linda K. Kerber, *Women of the Republic: Intellect and Ideology in Revolutionary America* (Chapel Hill, 1980), especially 7–8, 11–12, 74, 78–80, 85, 279, 281–83; Sara M. Evans, *Born for Liberty: A History of Women in America* (New York, 1989), 45–66.

64. Given the stridently prochange, proconvention attitude of Eleazer Oswald, the publisher of the *Gazetteer*, the only logical explanation for his printing "Dysart" would be to create a straw man. After the Constitution appeared, Oswald did try to be more even-handed; then he became, ironically, an Antifederalist printer. But that transformation was not caused by a philosophical affinity for the ideas of "Dysart." On Oswald's various positions, see COC1: xxxv–xxxvi.

65. See the discussion of the Connecticut debate in Chapter One.

66. *Massachusetts Gazette*, June 5, given in COC1: 127, with seven reprintings by July 12.

67. On Greenleaf, see especially Chapter Five.

68. See n. 13 above. The recommendations offered by "Z" were clearly reminiscent of the so-called Old Colonial System of the Bri-

tish Empire. His publication of "Z" suggests that editor Francis Bailey was for change, but limited change, in the Confederation government. Here one sees an early example of the Antifederalist path Bailey took, just as one sees Federalist leanings among the solidly proconvention publishers.

69. See n. 9 above.

70. *Pennsylvania Herald*, June 9, given in COC1: 130–31, with seven reprintings occurring by July 11.

71. The *Six Sketches on the History of Man* by Henry Home, Lord Kames, the noted Scottish jurist, was published in the United States in 1776. Because that printing gave his name as Lord Kaims, the publishers of 1787 used that incorrect spelling. (See Evans 14801.) The *Massachusetts Centinel* printed the material cited in the text on May 16 and then repeated it on May 23 as part of a longer essay. In the May 16 issue, the editor said the material came from a New York paper of April 16, but that printing has not been located. In any case, it is clear that the *Massachusetts Centinel* was the basic source for the other reprintings that occurred between May 28 and June 14. Editors Dunlap and Claypoole of the *Pennsylvania Packet* (cf. May 28 with June 4) either liked the piece very much or overlooked what they were reprinting; they too reprinted the piece twice in two versions in the space of a week. The reference to six publications includes that in the *Centinel*, but not the unlocated New York printing.

72. As publishers noted, the original came from the London *Public Ledger* of March 16. In addition to this first American reprinting on May 31, the review garnered nine reprintings between June 26 and July 19. Later the Charleston *South Carolina Weekly Chronicle* reprinted it (October 9). On the John Adams work, see also Chapter One, n. 8.

73. *Pennsylvania Herald*, June 2, with fourteen reprintings from June 6 to 20.

74. *Worcester Magazine* for the third week of May, given in COC1: 97.

75. Cf. the discussion of the essay by a "West-Chester Farmer" at n. 38 above.

76. Quotation from COC1: 101, and see n. 6 above.

77. *Massachusetts Centinel*, May 19, with twelve reprintings between May 21 and June 6.

78. New York *Daily Advertiser*, June 5, with thirteen reprintings between June 13 and July 25.

79. Ibid., June 9, with thirteen reprintings between June 13 and August 25.

80. *Independent Gazetteer*, June 6; reprinted in full ten times between June 9 and September 8; two variants appeared on June 19 and 21 in Massachusetts papers.

81. Issue of May 31, with ten reprintings between June 4 and August 25. On the general press hatred of paper money see, e.g., "Paper-Money Bill," *Connecticut Courant*, June 18, with six reprintings.

82. Issue of May 18. The full letter gained fourteen reprintings; parts were reprinted six times between May 19 and July 14.

83. Quotation from COC1: 104, and see n. 14 above.

84. Given in COC1: 95; eighteen reprintings occurred by June 18.

85. *Virginia Independent Chronicle*, June 13. The essay was eventually reprinted ten times, but, perhaps because of the geographic location of the paper that published it, the first reprinting did not occur until mid-August. The ten reprintings, including that in the August issue of the *American Museum*, appeared between August 14 and September 25. It also appeared in the *Pennsylvania Herald* on October 4.

86. Given in COC1: 132; the reprintings occurred by September 8.

87. See the article on Algiers from the *Pennsylvania Herald*, May 16, as discussed in this chapter at n. 11 above.

88. Quotations from Baltimore *Maryland Gazette*, May 22, given in COC1: 112, 113. As indicated in n. 12 above, this portion of the essay was reprinted in fourteen newspapers between May 31 and June 28.

89. *New Hampshire Spy*, May 19, with twelve reprints between May 23 and June 13.

90. That is, including the original publication, this section of "A Watchman" appeared in nine newspapers. See n. 18 above.

91. Quotation from COC1: 120, and see n. 9 above.

92. A suggestive illustration comes from the reprint fate of "Thoughts on the Spirit of Union," first published in the *Pennsylvania Herald* on June 9. In an effort at judicious and conciliatory analysis, the author opined that some challenges to the spirit of Union were acceptable. Naturally, if they arose because of selfishness, they were "dangerous and destructive." But challenges became tolerable if they sprang from honest differences of opinion or if the concerns about the rights and privileges of different ranks

of people were rooted in a concern for the public welfare. Indeed, a republic actually drew strength and thus benefited from these kinds of acceptable "collisions." The author clearly believed that honest differences of opinion about how to achieve the public good could, even should, be tolerated. His arguments were balanced, fair, and thoughtful; he spoke the language of virtue and public good that people of the day supposedly cared about. Moreover, the essayist did not even mention the convention; nor did he say the central government should not be strengthened. The essay did, however, seem to go against the calls for unity of thought so prevalent in the media, and the author's judicious "Thoughts on the Spirit of Union" was reprinted only sparsely. It took over a month for it to be reprinted, and only two reprintings occurred. The reprintings appeared in the *Independent Gazetteer* of July 18, and the *Massachusetts Centinel* of July 28.

93. Quotation from *Massachusetts Gazette*, June 12, given in COC1: 98. Although it has not been located, two points indicate that the item clearly originated in a New York paper around June 4 or 5. First, the *Virginia Independent Chronicle*, which reprinted the piece on June 13, said it was reprinting a New York item of June 4. The *Quebec Gazette*, which reprinted it on July 19, also said the item came from New York, but the *Gazette* dated it as originating in a June 5 paper. Second, the item obviously could not have originated in the *Massachusetts Gazette* of June 12 and also have appeared in the *Virginia Independent Chronicle* the next day. The other paper that reprinted the piece was the Boston *Continental Journal*, June 14, and it did not indicate the source of the item.

3

"We Expect Something Great": Projecting the Image of Unity

June 13, 1787 was a critical date in the news coverage of the Constitutional Convention. On that day a credible report on convention proceedings appeared that threatened to torpedo the effort to sell the convention. Proconvention forces sprang into action. As the pattern of what the press chose to publish reveals, in approximately the last two weeks of June convention boosters created a multifaceted damage-control program. The program was rooted in numerous challenges to the veracity of the June 13 publication. Of course, not all of the commentary produced right after June 13 was part of the damage-control system, but important segments were. The effort included a series of essays that launched preemptive strikes against anyone who would dare challenge the convention or its delegates. Damage control was aided, and at times abetted, by articles that presented and expanded upon established proconvention themes. By the end of June, with the damage-control program apparently having served its purpose, prochange forces relied more on established themes and ways of selling the convention. Their writings typically were, however, brasher than those produced in the preconvention and early convention periods.

Despite the opportunity provided by the June 13 report, people such as Sidney and Dysart did not renew their sorties against the convention. However, in early July, after the end of the damage-control period, people who might be judged as suspicious of the convention ventured into print more than ever before. Their numbers were small, and they did not attempt to use the potentially explosive June 13 report. Indeed, they typically employed circuitous arguments. Still, their presence reflected the increasing acrimony in press coverage of the convention that developed after the bombshell of a story appeared in the *Herald*.

• • •

Based on press comments depicting fervent interest in the convention, reports emanating from behind its closed doors should have been prime reprint material. That certainly proved true when the delegates began work. The first news report on convention proceedings, which announced the election of Washington as president and William Jackson as secretary, got extensively reprinted. The second news account, carried by the *Pennsylvania Herald* on May 3, proved even more popular. In addition to reporting on the election of officers, it added the news that the delegates had created a general communications committee. The third story on convention activities also appeared in the *Herald*. The June 2 issue informed readers about the adoption of a strict secrecy rule. This important news, like the paper's first report on convention activities, rapidly appeared in over two dozen papers.[1]

The *Herald* account of the secrecy rule suggested that, despite the rule, the publisher had a source inside the convention. That possibility seemed even more likely when the next convention account appeared in the *Herald* and the *Evening Chronicle* on June 9. Considering the secrecy pledge, the story was impressively specific. The delegates had agreed, it was said, to boot Rhode Island out of the Union and to keep it out. The troublesome little state would, nevertheless, be forced to pay its proportion of the federal debt. In addition, a mint would be created, and states would draw coin from it in proportion to their contributions to the federal government. The report concluded with the notation that the delegates had sent for the latest statement of the financial accounts between the individual states and the Confederation government. This was, if true, spectacular news, and the account quickly amassed reprintings throughout the land.[2]

It probably did not surprise people when the next news report on the delegates' activities, published on June 13, appeared in the *Pennsylvania Herald*. Once again the story contained spectacular revelations, but it obtained fewer reprintings than *any* of the earlier *Herald* items. While the paper's first and second reports on convention activities each collected twenty-six reprintings and the third got reprinted over forty times, the fourth story accumulated only sixteen reprintings.[3]

The relative lack of interest in reprinting the June 13 *Herald* piece cannot be attributed to a waning concern about the convention.[4] Nor can it be traced to declining respect for the editor's work. When Dallas subsequently offered reports on convention activities, they secured wide circulation.[5] And while the June 13 report collected the lowest number of reprintings of any *Herald* story on the convention's proceedings, just the opposite should have been the case because it contained scintillating news. Clearly the story revealed something many editors chose not to share with their readers.

The article opened with the claim that the particulars of the convention debates were considered secret. Nevertheless, it was possible to report that "a very great diversity of opinion" existed amongst the members who had already given "a wonderful display of wisdom, eloquence and patriotism." The comment about different opinions was new, but the other observation sounded a familiar note. What followed was of a different order: "some schemes, it is said, have been projected which preserve the form, but effectually destroy the spirit of democracy; and others, more bold, which, regarding only the necessity of a strong executive power, have openly rejected even the appearance of a popular constitution." This news undermined the dominant press theme that the illustrious, freedom-loving delegates should be trusted without question.

Dallas's response to this report is revealing. He appeared to try to back away from it by observing that "the people will hardly be induced to make a voluntary surrender of their rights; but they may indeed be deceived, by the flattery of outward shew, into a passive and destructive acquiescence." He was, however, concerned enough to recount a piece of Roman history illustrating that the appearance of freedom could be preserved while "shocking barbarities" occurred. Dallas made it clear that he opposed creating a government that offered the people only an empty show of power.[6]

The press' established point of view explains the cool reception accorded the *Herald* story. With few exceptions, popular authors had advocated strengthening the central government and had ardently supported the convention. Time and again, especially once the convention opened, the press had urged the people to trust the delegates. However, if the June 13 account were accurate, the convention was divided, and some delegates espoused decidedly autocratic views. If reprinted and believed, the story clearly would undermine efforts to build support for the convention. The report's comparatively low reprint popularity thus seems rooted in a desire to suppress unflattering news about the convention that might destroy the effort to portray the delegates as worthy of unquestioning trust.

Editors had ignored other articles that cast doubt on the idea of simply deferring to the delegates, and they would do so again.[7] The report of June 13 could not, however, be ignored; it had to be countered. The pattern of subsequent press coverage suggests proconvention forces reacted by initiating a damage-control program that operated from June 16 through approximately July 1. Contradicting the *Herald* article got high priority. Without mentioning the piece, widely reprinted Philadelphia writers denied that the delegates held diverse or unacceptable political views. The delegates were, the argument went, like-minded. It obviously followed, without even having to be stated, that no delegate embraced antidemocratic thoughts. These pronouncements worked to discredit the *Herald* story and to preempt its use to assail the convention or its work.[8] The fact that some essays built on and, seemingly by design, reinforced each other, also suggests that a coordinated effort at damage control was undertaken.

Eleazer Oswald, an ardent convention booster, published the first damage-control piece.[9] Just three days after the *Herald* story appeared, the *Independent Gazetteer* challenged it in a short, easy-to-reprint item: "We hear that the greatest unanimity subsists in the councils of the Federal Convention. It is to be hoped, says a correspondent, the United States will discover as much wisdom in receiving from them a suitable form of government to preserve the liberties of the people, as they did fortitude in defending them against the arbitrary and wicked attempts of Great-Britain. Nothing but Union and a vigorous Continental Government can save us from destruction." This roundabout convention report, which discredited the June 13 report by trumpeting the supposed unity of the delegates, acquired wide currency because twenty-seven publishers reprinted it.[10]

On June 22 Oswald's *Independent Gazetteer* offered another reason to reject the allegation that division and antidemocratic ideas existed at the convention. A correspondent challenged the veracity of the June 9 *Herald* story about the delegates' plans by saying it was well known that the delegates had observed the greatest secrecy; moreover, absolutely nothing had been officially communicated to the public.[11] Therefore, he concluded, little credit could be given to anything the newspapers had published about the delegates' intentions. These comments obviously applied to the story on divisions and antidemocratic plans and rebutted it without giving it further currency. By mid-July, sixteen publications had reprinted this analysis; three others had emphatically asserted that there was no foundation for saying Rhode Island would be pitched out of the Union.[12] The correspondent's short, harsh second paragraph reinforced the essential message: "The mere idle reports of busy-bodies, and the absurd foolish suggestions of triffling pretenders are not to be viewed and considered as the real and regular proceedings of the Convention."[13]

Although the *Independent Gazetteer* published both the June 16 and 22 items, the commentaries were incompatible. The accuracy of the June 16 piece depended on the author having a source inside the convention. Yet the June 22 story asserted that the delegates refused to discuss their activities with outsiders. One of the accounts had to be wrong. Still, each offered a different way of countering the news contained in the *Herald* of June 13, and the quick, extensive reprinting of both commentaries illustrates damage control in operation.

Even Dallas soon joined in discounting the report carried in his own newspaper. In a strongly worded message of trust published on June 20, he expressed full confidence in the delegates. Whatever they recommended would be, in effect, a revolution in government accomplished by reasoning and deliberation. Saying history offered no example of that ever happening before, Dallas proclaimed that the delegates' achievement would reflect the philosophic and tolerant spirit of the age. His bit of speculative editorial fluff earned a wider reprinting than his crucial June 13 news story achieved.[14]

It is significant that more than a month elapsed before the appearance of the next story possibly based on a source inside the convention. When one finally did surface in the *Pennsylvania Gazette* of July 18, it merely echoed the *Independent Gazetteer* June 16 theme of unity while telling nothing about the delegates' actions. The relevant section maintained that the delegates displayed such unity on all great subjects "that it has been proposed to call the room in which they assemble—UNANIMITY HALL." Within a month, more than two dozen papers had reproduced that observation.[15]

The first articles published after June 13 which were clearly based on insider information did not appear until ten days after the *Gazette* printed its unanimity hall piece.[16] On July 28 the *Independent Gazetteer* and the *Herald* reported that the delegates, after appointing a committee of five to act during the recess, had adjourned until August 1. The *Gazet-*

teer gave the names of the committee members. Although the *Herald* did not supply that information, its report showered praise on the delegates. According to Dallas, these men, distinguished for their wisdom and patriotism, had captured the confidence of all the people. Intriguingly, this editorial report proved significantly more popular as a reprint than the more detailed news story carried by the *Gazetteer*.[17]

Press reports based on convention sources may well have stopped appearing for several weeks because the members of the convention took their pledge of secrecy more seriously in the wake of the *Herald* report. However, that possibility does not explain the stunning transformation in what the press offered the public about the convention. Editors showed no compunction about printing speculation on the convention's activities *before* June 13. But, after turning the June 16 *Independent Gazetteer* speculation and celebration of convention unity into a very popular reprint, editors suddenly stopped printing *anything* that suggested outsiders knew what the delegates might be doing. This dramatic alteration in the pattern of what the press carried suggested the secrecy rule had been followed and thus implicitly discredited the *Herald* report. If they wanted to emphasize the point about secrecy, publishers needed to refrain from publishing material that might have come directly from the convention. Until the explosive power of the June 13 report seemed safely defused, they did just that. In this way, many editors appeared to cooperate in a conspiracy of silence both to promote the convention and to undermine the unsavory *Herald* report about the convention.

The core of the damage-control program was, thus, formed by three interrelated lines of attack against the June 13 convention account. The first important component involved the refusal to reprint the story. Based solely on intrinsic news value, the *Herald* report, like the earlier one about the convention sitting for months and producing a totally new government, was underreprinted. Next, shortly after the June 13 story appeared, Philadelphia authors countered it by proclaiming that the delegates exhibited impressive unity as well as liberty-loving patriotism. Although these widely reprinted items did not mention the *Herald* report, their thrust discredited it. A third vital aspect of the program was also based on popular items first published in Philadelphia. Authors emphasized that the members of the convention were tight-lipped and that no one knew what the delegates were doing. This proved, without even having to say it, that people should discount any report about division and antidemocratic thought haunting the convention. The claims about secrecy gained support when the press changed its publishing pattern and stopped carrying stories about convention activities for more than a month after the *Herald* story broke.[18]

The damage-control program was complex and multifaceted. It contained much more than the core segments. Another vital part of the effort involved stepping up publication of items that deprecated anyone who might mistrust the convention. As with essays that showered ardent praise on the delegates, this kind of essay was not new, but the predatory nature of the items was.

Through mid-June, press attacks on those having qualms about the convention had focused on Rhode Island. Although Rhode Island was still held up to derision, criticism of it declined significantly when the damage-control program was in effect from June 16 to approximately July 1. Five new articles on Rhode Island's alleged political improprieties appeared during those two weeks. Yet only one gained popularity, and it appeared late in the period. It is particularly revealing that a classic Rogue's Island item accusing the state's government of causing almost every evil confronting the Union collected only two reprintings.[19]

The proconvention forces clearly no longer had the luxury of focusing their attacks on the Ocean State. The underlying opposition might be able to sidestep criticisms about Rhode Island while bludgeoning the convention with the *Herald* account of divisions and authoritarianism among the delegates.[20] These possibilities forced convention boosters to develop a more thoroughgoing line of attack against anyone who might use any argument to challenge the convention. Besides contributing to damage control, the boosters' articles, which often gained popularity, amounted to a preemptive strike. Equally important, the arguments they advanced quickly evolved into the standard press defense for allowing the convention to strengthen the government significantly.

The assault against "antifederal" types in general began with two items published in Philadelphia on June 20. The strikingly similar commentaries produced by correspondents of the *Independent Gazetteer* and the *Pennsylvania Gazette*, reprinted in all sixteen times, were probably written by the same person. Both essayists asserted that the opposition to the necessary reforms being devised by the convention would come from selfish government officials or those connected with them. That was a clever touch in a world where virtually all newspaper essayists used pen names and where many accounts were attributed to "correspondents" or "gentlemen." While each piece compared potential convention opponents to the Loyalists, the *Gazette* correspondent also tried his hand at intimidation. He admonished government officials that keeping quiet might allow them to retain their posts while opposing the convention would likely cause them to suffer the fate inflicted on Loyalists at the start of the war.[21]

Other Philadelphia authors embraced these ideas. In fact, the *Gazette* piece begot a similar attack on June 25. While expressing heartfelt hope that everyone would support the good government being framed by the convention, "Civis" seconded the warning that persons moved by local self-interest might oppose the general good. The danger did not end there. The people must vigilantly be ready to check "the malicious insinuations of treacherous and pretended friends to this country, who would rejoice at its downfall, and glory in the idea of our not being able to exist without a King." The convention's potential enemies were, as Civis portrayed them, at best selfish and possibly monarchists or traitors. His analysis, and the *Gazette* essay he praised, won wide reprinting.[22]

The warning Civis offered about false friends became more explicit in a widely reprinted missive published the next day in the staunchly proconvention *Independent Gazetteer*. The undated letter, which may well have been fabricated in Philadelphia, allegedly expressed the views of a concerned Virginian. He claimed his observations flowed from ruminations upon suggestions that Rhode Island and New York might spurn the convention's reforms. As with other pieces then originating in Philadelphia, the author raised general points rather than focusing on those two states. It would not be the delegates' fault if the convention failed to establish an energetic, fair, and effective government. The failure would be "owing to the narrow minds, or selfish views of little politicians, perhaps corrupted by the influence of a foreign power." The point was driven home with the claim that high ranking British officers and members of Parliament visited New York in 1786 and, subsequently, the state voted against the continental impost.[23]

The Virginian's popular commentary reflected the shift in emphasis evident during the period when writers moved to confront any of the convention's potential enemies. He did not employ Rogue's Island examples and mentioned the state just once. Rhode Island was important only as it fit a generic model of unacceptable "antifederal" action. In this author's view, some New Yorkers took preeminence in the ranking of those likely to oppose the convention's efforts. He demonstrated the bolder, more encompassing approach being taken when he implied that any American who opposed the convention's reforms might be in league with enemies of the country.

Damage-control essays aimed at any potential opponent of the convention did not have to originate in Philadelphia. Two commentaries published in the proconvention New York *Daily Advertiser* might well have been penned to counter the June 13 report. On June 18, a *Daily Advertiser* correspondent, reprinted five times, happily claimed that those who opposed the convention and strengthening the central government had fallen silent. He then illustrated what could be done to help

insure that silence continued. As he depicted them, dissenters were fools—or worse. "These men, without consideration
or forethought, have rashly attempted to bring poverty and
shame on their too much afflicted country! Happy would it
be for them, if it had been an error of the head, rather than
that of the heart."[24] A *Daily Advertiser* author published on
June 29 certainly exhibited the increasingly harsh tone evident in damage-control pieces. He leveled the spectacular
charge that an unnamed great New York official had supplied money to Daniel Shays and his followers. Although this
piece appeared in a major city, no reprints have been discovered. The difference between this nonreprinted item and
other preemptive-strike pieces is illustrative. An essayist could
hint at possible liaisons between Americans and the country's
enemies and still be widely reprinted. One could describe, as
Civis did, where and when subversive clandestine meetings
supposedly occurred and still produce a popular reprint. But
it was unacceptable to tread close to naming an important
officeholder and charging him with supporting rebellion and
possibly treason.

Some authors who espoused established themes may
also have been part of the damage-control effort. Indeed,
proconvention commentaries, especially those that originated
in Philadelphia in the month after June 13, often seemed at
least partially designed to discredit the *Herald* story. For example, an unusually large number of new items appeared right
after that story surfaced. In addition, praise for the convention delegates hit new heights. This reflected the fact that,
over time, news analysts of whatever persuasion increasingly
offered more expansive and more vociferous commentary.

During the month after June 13, the press intensified the
most prevalent preconvention themes by reminding citizens
again and again that the Union needed an energetic government and that they should trust the wise and honorable delegates to create it. Three widely reprinted Philadelphia items,
clearly part of the effort to discredit the June 13 report, presented the basic line. The *Independent Gazetteer* analyst of
June 16 who gloried in the convention's unity claimed that

only true unity and a vigorous continental government could save America from destruction.[25] Four days later a *Pennsylvania Gazette* correspondent maintained that everyone agreed the convention was framing a wise and free government.[26] Civis, who lamented the ruinous confusion hanging over America, soon joined the chorus by calling upon the delegates to be the "Saviours of your country."[27]

Authors from outside Philadelphia advanced similar arguments. A New Jerseyite, published in Philadelphia on June 23, bemoaned the nation's economic and political impotency while accentuating the basic point: "we expect something great will be recommended by the Convention."[28] In July two southern authors concurred and said of the delegates, as one put it, that "on their determinations, and our acquiescence, depends our future happiness and prosperity."[29]

Writers offered a variety of specific examples to support their increasingly shrill warnings of doom awaiting the Union unless the people trusted the delegates to create a vigorous government. Measured by number of reprintings, the most influential came from Richard Price. An important second letter from America's great English friend, this one written to William Bingham, surfaced in three Philadelphia newspapers a week after the sensational *Herald* report appeared. Although the timing of its publication may not have been manipulated, Price's letter certainly arrived at a most fortuitous time for those working damage control. Two of the three newspapers published an editorial preface. It praised John Adams's political ideals and implied that an excess of democracy was crippling America. The report described Price as so chastened by the ills various weak governments had produced in America that he was no longer "led away by the airy phantom of a pure democracy." In the reprinted letter, Price did say Adams's *Defence* had convinced him of the impracticality of a unicameral legislature, such as Pennsylvania's. He sorrowed over the Union's problems, especially the possibility of what he called the "internal distresses of wars." He asserted, as he had before, that the ineffective central government must be strengthened. Price thus bolstered those who cautioned that internal discord could flare up again and perhaps rip the Union apart.[30]

A lengthy and widely reprinted letter published the next day in the *Albany Gazette* worked the same antidemocracy theme expressed in the preface to Price's letter. "Where is SHAYS," the essayist provocatively asked. He aimed not so much to warn against possible internal rebellions as to attack the vices of democracy. Daniel Shays himself, the writer said, hardly mattered. The real issue was what he called the general phenomenon of "*Shayism.*" Indeed, "the rage of excessive democracy" would produce another Shays as soon as he disappeared. Shays existed wherever one saw a feeble government, or villainy masquerading as justice, or selfish opposition to the general welfare.[31] This New Yorker brandished the name Shays because it symbolized internal disorder, especially in the backcountry, and because the possibility of internal conflict still haunted America. As had long been the case, commentary and news accounts kept fueling those concerns.

In late June, two widely reprinted *Massachusetts Centinel* pieces continued to remind Americans that Shays and his followers might rise again. One gentleman observed that, shocking as it was to the sensibilities, some of the recently pardoned leaders of the late Rebellion had been seen riding in public carrying sidearms. The other author, a Berkshire County man, voiced the deep frustration felt by those he called the friends of government. Harassed and threatened by night and day, they were exposed to all the evils of a civil war. Proclaiming it was the supporters of good government who had everything to fear, he cried out: "God grant that their fears may not be realized."[32]

The powerful specter of internal disorder was commonly used to back the convention during the damage-control period. The June 26 *Pennsylvania Packet* carried a letter, quickly picked up by four other Philadelphia papers and subsequently reprinted very widely, that claimed Indians enjoyed greater security than many white Americans. The author, a gentleman from one of Virginia's back counties, maintained that more peace, order, and contentment existed in the Cherokee towns than among the Indians' white neighbors.[33] In fact, the whites had felt obliged to hire regulators to crush the vagabonds and thieves who plagued them. Readers, having come to associate backcountry regulation with civil war or rebellion, could not miss the implications.[34] The author forcefully asserted that his information demonstrated the importance of the convention.

On the eve of Independence Day, the *Maryland Journal* carried a series of four letters that supported the convention by presenting the most frightening combination of commentary and news yet published about the situation in the West. The letters, each reprinted more than a dozen times, raised possibilities that would make Shays's Rebellion a minor incident by comparison. Two missives written in Louisville in early December 1786 opened the presentation.[35] The author practiced classic American boosterism by describing the incredible bounty and potential of the West.[36] Unless economic and political reforms occurred, the older states might wither as their citizens flocked west. These observations provided background for his main topic: Congress' controversial proposal to allow the closing of the Mississippi River to American navigation for twenty-five years.[37] Using inflamed rhetoric, he proclaimed that the colonies had fewer grievances against Great Britain than the West had against the eastern states. Westerners were angry. In fact, unless they received greater understanding and support, they would revolt and join other powers, quite possibly Great Britain! If that happened, the United States would in time be destroyed.

The third missive, a circular letter dated 29 March 1787 at Danville, Kentucky, evoked even more disturbing memories of the Revolution. Expressing great alarm over Congress' Mississippi proposal, the authors outlined a series of recommendations. Elections should be held for a body to produce a petition against Congress' plan and to establish committees of correspondence. No reader with a sense of history needed reminding that the march to the American War of Independence began with similar actions. The authors also raised the specter of events that had prefigured the rise of Shays's Rebellion when they stated that, if necessary, a special convention would be called to protect the westerners' "just rights and privileges."[38]

These threats were only partially muted by the fourth Kentucky letter, dated May 3. According to this author, the majority of Kentuckians disagreed with the rebelliousness espoused in the Louisville letters. Kentuckians respected the federal government too much to show such disrespect; only a repetition of injuries could drive them into Britain's arms. He then smoothly requested the earliest possible information about the actions of "the grand convention in Philadelphia." This westerner, like other popular authors, stressed that the convention deserved support and that the federal government needed extensive new powers. He even proclaimed it would be best to remodel and "modernize the whole instrument" of government.[39]

The image of an angry West chafing under Spanish oppression and incensed about Congress and the Mississippi grew more vivid when the *Pennsylvania Packet* printed yet another western letter on July 7. It was probably produced by Hugh Williamson, a member of Congress and of the Constitutional Convention. Writing from Nashville on May 1, 1787, Williamson contended that westerners believed Spain had no legal right to the Mississippi. Only Spain's military power allowed it to steal what rightfully belonged to the westerners. And although Americans living on the Atlantic coast showed little concern, westerners would fight for their rights. The Spanish might then attack the eastern seaboard. In another open bid for support of western aims, Williamson also questioned Spain's title to areas west of the Mississippi. Thus, if easterners vigorously backed the westerners, they could have peace and perhaps even gain more land in the West. If easterners did not offer that backing, they faced the probable devastation of their section of America.[40]

In a popular commentary published on July 12, a correspondent of the *New York Journal* expressed similar concerns as he asserted that the discords in the East only gave the appearance of dying away. He remarked that fears about being denied use of the Mississippi had already produced a frenzy in the West. Indeed, according to reports, westerners could raise twenty thousand militia to defend their rights. The correspondent warned that a united western community would form an alliance and go to war unless it got equality with the original states. For the New Yorker, these horrifying possibilities showed the necessity of immediately creating an efficient federal government. His thoughts obtained a wide reprinting, but only in New York and New England.[41]

Dr. Price had added another dimension to the image of America the endangered when he spoke of the Union's "insignificance and discredit amongst foreign powers." In late June, two New England authors gave dramatic application to that thought. Each pointed out that unless the federal government could control economic issues, foreign countries might use force to collect the debts America owed them. One author specifically looked to the convention for a solution. Although neither commentary gained popularity, they added weight to the argument that the East, especially the seaboard, might feel the sting of foreign invaders—unless the central government became stronger.[42]

As in earlier periods, widely reprinted news stories reinforced speculation about the possibility of insurrection or invasion. A June 23 *Massachusetts Centinel* report on the troublesome western county of Berkshire told how a party of insurgents had entered an official's home in Pittsfield and destroyed writs and other legal papers.[43] In mid-July two Virginia papers relayed the news that incendiaries had torched both the New Kent courthouse and the clerk's office and burnt them to the ground.[44] A week later the Virginia press reported that two men had been arrested for the arson. This reassuring news could not erase the fact that Virginia had experienced antigovernment violence.[45]

The same *Massachusetts Centinel* issue that warned of an invasion by creditor nations provided the news that foreign aggression from another source might already have begun. This widely reprinted story announced that the British had gone beyond merely outfitting ships on Lake Champlain. According to the *Centinel*, the twenty-gun HMS *Maria* had actually captured a United States vessel three miles inside United States territory. The fact that the vessel was described as a smuggler hardly diminished the impact of this warlike threat to American sovereignty.[46]

War did not materialize. Nevertheless, extensive reprinting of news stories and commentaries mentioning possible British threats to peace kept reminding Americans that the central government needed strengthening. A widely reprinted account of a different British threat to America's security reinforced that point. In mid-July a Delaware paper printed an extract of a letter sent by a West Indian merchant to a friend in Wilmington.[47] He reported that England had declared it illegal for British West Indians to trade with the United States.[48] Accordingly, armed vessels would search out smugglers diligently. In any case, English merchants would rush to supply all the islanders needed. The West Indians hated the directives but had neither the spirit nor the unity necessary to fight back. Soon the American-West Indian trade would be confined to two or three minor islands—"if the convention does not impose some severe restrictions." Once again it seemed that Congress' weakness might embroil the Union in a war, only now it was economic war. Once again the popular message averred: look to the Constitutional Convention for salvation.[49]

In the month after the *Herald* report of June 13 appeared, proconvention authors were particularly inclined to accentuate the "time-of-troubles" theme. As publications about navigation of the Mississippi, the foreign debt, and West Indian trade illustrate, economic problems received attention and were portrayed as threatening the Union. But as they had long done, widely reprinted authors emphasized threats of internal violence and war, and now they did so with an unprecedented litany of frightening detail. Discussion of foreign invasion had not occurred so regularly before, nor had the threat been associated so explicitly with the foreign debt or the possible actions of westerners. The solid warnings about western secession represented an especially frightening development. These "time-of-trouble" arguments, which graphically showed that Congress' weakness could trigger war, were presented with a greater intensity and force than ever before. A medical analogy that proved quite popular with editors emphasized the basic points. The short paragraph, first published in late June, offered the wisdom of an eminent surgeon. He advised his apprentice: "Young man probe the sore to the bottom; it is better the patient feel pain at the present, than to have his wound healed in haste, which breaking out again may prove incurable." Correspondingly, "the political operator reasons in the same manner, in regard to the wounds of the State; they should not be skinned over, but cured."[49] This popular analogy clearly urged people to let the experienced and skillful delegates take drastic action to cure the Union.

A variant theme, occasionally hinted at before this period, became more prevalent. Some authors insisted that a disordered America could yet be great—if the people accepted the convention's recommendations. Reflecting the increasing campaign tone of press coverage, the argument was made boldly with graphic examples. Significantly, the three widely reprinted calls to greatness published in the month after June 13 originated in Philadelphia newspapers. Moreover, the most extensively reprinted of the three presented a new, optimistic claim especially useful for damage control. Its author joined those decrying America's governments. Nevertheless, while others saw only danger flashing about, he stressed that, fortunately, the convention was meeting during a time of peace. The illustrious delegates therefore could analyze political systems at their leisure and would have little difficulty creating an effective government for the country. These arguments could, if needed, counter unfriendly queries about why the delegates were taking so long to produce their recommendations.[50]

The other two popular authors who talked about America

achieving greatness described specific possibilities. Having bemoaned the dangers confronting the Union, Civis talked of other countries casting jealous eyes on America's rising greatness. Americans could still have an extensive empire and make their country's name "worthy to be written in letters of gold." This could come to pass if people accepted the beneficial measures being formulated by the convention.[51] A letter allegedly sent by an Irish gentleman to his brother in Philadelphia and published in the *Pennsylvania Herald* of June 23 added "Common Sense" ideas to the mix. The Irishman alleged that men of property, especially Catholic men of property, considered Ireland's legal and political situation abominable. However, the factions, the revolts, and the enfeebled central government of America made the thought of immigrating there especially unnerving. Still, his brother in Philadelphia had placed great hope in "the wisdom of a grand convention." The Irish gentleman implied that, by backing the convention, America could become the asylum for the oppressed.[52]

The effort to prevent damage to the cause obviously benefited from publications that maintained the convention was producing essential reforms. Those claims, however, were impossible to prove since insider accounts disappeared from the press for more than a month after the June 13 report surfaced. This fact did not stop authors from drumming the theme that the noble delegates were doing marvelous things. Commentators, some probably working to counter the June 13 account, lavishly praised the patriotic and unified convention. Although writers had long emphasized the delegates' patriotism and love of liberty, a strident emphasis on *both* unity and noble patriotism was new. As time passed, elements of the press shouted the glories of the convention in ways that, in the parlance of the day, might have brought a blush to the face of a Philadelphia street huckster.[53]

Widely reprinted news stories conveyed a renewed sense of excitement about the convention. Within three days of the appearance of the June 13 *Herald* report, two ardently proconvention Philadelphia papers, the *Independent Gazet-*

teer and the *Packet*, published eye-catching lists of the delegates. Editors found the *Gazetteer* comment that "by this very respectable delegation, ELEVEN States are represented" especially worthy of being reprinted.[54] Later reports that New Hampshire would be represented at "the Grand Federal Convention" and that Governor John Langdon was insuring the state's representation by paying his own way to Philadelphia proved very popular.[55] In early July, as Langdon journeyed south, papers such as the *Essex Journal* reported that "the Honorable and Patriotic John Langdon, Esq." had passed by on his way to "the Grand Convention."[56]

Press coverage made it clear that anyone added to the delegate list would be joining illustrious company. An *Independent Gazetteer* article of June 27 presented this view in innovative ways. The convention was, the author proclaimed, "happily composed of men who are qualified from education, experience and profession for the great business assigned to them." His evidence was, however, rather general. He claimed that delegates who had served as state governors would explain the principles needed to administer the executive duties of government, and merchant delegates would ably analyze and support America's commercial interests. Despite its lack of specificity, this commentary became a most popular reprint.[57]

Fourth-of-July celebrations provided a ready opportunity to praise the delegates. "Regulator," in an essay published on July 4 by the New York *Daily Advertiser*, covered the basics. America's finest had been selected as delegates, and they would unquestionably recommend wise measures to reform and strengthen the federal government.[58] News items describing the traditional thirteen toasts offered at various Independence Day festivities reinforced the message. Both Washington and the convention figured prominently in the toasts, and it was, of course, no insult that Washington typically was saluted before the convention.[59]

Authors, notably during the damage-control period, added a new twist to celebrating the delegates and the convention. Americans read that they were participating in, or at least witnessing, momentous historic achievements. This sense was evident in the New Jersey gentleman's observation, published on June 20, that something great could be expected of the convention.[60] Civis agreed by proclaiming that the eyes of thousands were fixed on the convention "—expecting to see some great and laudable purposes adopted."[61] The Irish gentleman who discussed emigration described all Ireland as enthralled about the convention. It was the topic of conversation at every table; the first toast drunk after dinner was to its success. The gentleman himself was obviously almost consumed with excitement over the delegates' work. He closed his letter with the observation: "I trust in God you will enable me to be the first to carry round the results of their councils."[62]

Writings designed to get people to trust the delegates by conveying a sense of partaking in glorious events continued even after the intense damage-control effort of the last two weeks of June. Just as it provided a ready occasion to praise many of the delegates, the arrival of the Fourth of July also provided a natural occasion for underscoring the convention's historic significance. Regulator expressed the point in his Fourth of July assertion that "the present state of American politics, will form the most important era that ever engaged the pen of the historian." By saying its members had been delegated to reform the Union, he encouraged all citizens to think of themselves as having played a role in the convention. Editor Dallas championed the convention by playing upon the love of country naturally associated with "the auspicious Fourth of July." Americans had a duty, he said, to build upon and perpetuate the happiness, power, and dignity that Independence Day thoughts produced. Fortunately, the means already existed. Dallas urged Americans "to· expect with zeal and confidence" that the convention would produce a government adequate to secure and preserve the rights enunciated in the magnificent Declaration of Independence.[63] A popular July 6 *Independent Gazetteer* essayist declared the convention unique in political history. He also maintained that, while Americans had created various governments over the years, it was still singular to see the delegates, based on free elections, going about the business of reform.[64]

Two southerners, who wrote later in July and who did not quite gain reprint popularity, engaged in demagoguery in order to assert the convention's historic importance. Their emotional pleas linked support for the delegates to honoring and preserving the Revolution. Having described America's many miseries, a correspondent of the Petersburg *Virginia Gazette* asked: "Was it for this, that our fellow-citizens fought and bled in the glorious cause of freedom? Was it for this, that many of our departed heroes triumphant [*sic*] in death, at the pleasing prospect of fixing the glory and happiness of American offspring?—No."[65] A Baltimore gentleman, published in Philadelphia, observed that darkness hung over America's political horizon, "but I hope it will soon break forth into a glorious dawn of light and liberty; otherwise the friends of the Revolution will have laboured and bled in vain!"[66] Both men emphasized that the convention could save America; both implied that only an unpatriotic wretch would oppose the delegates' work.

Probably because the press stopped carrying reports of the delegates' activities, the production of original pieces concerning the convention temporarily declined in July. Still, with the extensive reprinting of proconvention items going on, a sense of anticipation grew. A popular writer in the *New Jersey Journal* of July 19 expressed the feeling. While saying that authentic information about the delegates' activities was unavailable, he observed that the delegates supposedly were working in committees, and "it is not doubted, that, when the committees report, some important resolutions—resolutions which may be big with the *fate* of America—will be adopted and made public."[67]

Damage control, aided by the expanded huckstering for the convention, worked. Only one essay possibly designed to combat the theme of trusting the delegates emerged between June 14 and the start of July. Moreover, although this essay appeared right at the end of the period, it went unreprinted, and part of it actually buttressed proconvention arguments. "Cornelius," published in the Boston *Independent Chronicle* of June 28, maintained that experience had taught citizens that the Confederation government required greater power. Moreover, civil liberty could never be secured under an inefficient government, and, considering the delegates' reputations, the people could expect "solemn" and "wise" recommendations from them. Cornelius, however, stopped considerably short of urging deferential acceptance of whatever the delegates did. He proclaimed that the wisest and most impartial men were subject to the same passions as those at the bottom of society. Furthermore, the natural tendency of people to rush from one extreme to the other raised the danger that America's lethargic government might be replaced by a despotic one. Cornelius also offered suggestions for reforms and called for a careful analysis of the convention's recommendations. Although he did not cite the incriminating *Herald* report, Cornelius rejected much of the convention hype that had appeared in the press. Had his lengthy essay or substantial parts of it been widely reprinted, it might have prompted the kind of discussion the proconvention forces seemed determined to squelch. But his essay, which appeared in a major city, went unreprinted.

By early July, once it seemed clear that the *Herald* report had been safely neutralized, convention boosters eased their strident effort to look past Rhode Island to chasten potential enemies. Soon Rhode Island bashing was again in vogue.[68] Still, the message of the general preemptive-strike articles remained. The essence of that message, including a hint of using violence against opponents, appeared in the widely reprinted *Pennsylvania Gazette* story of July 18 about the delegates being unified. Editors Hall and Sellers proclaimed: "May the enemies of the new Confederation, whether in Rhode-Island or elsewhere, whether secret or open, meet with the fate of the disaffected in the late war."[69]

The convention's potential opponents were not totally silenced, however. As convention boosters continued to fill the press with a torrent of praise for the delegates and arguments for accepting the convention's recommendations, dissenting essays appeared. In July, authors troubled by what the convention might do, or whose words could easily be so interpreted, ventured into print in greater numbers and in a shorter period than ever before.[70] The ardor of the proconvention forces may have sparked the publication of these dissenting essays. The writers may also have believed that rhetoric associated with Independence Day would work to their advantage.

It is revealing that, with one exception, the dissenting essays first appeared in Thomas Greenleaf's *New York Journal*. During the spring and summer of 1787, the *Journal* and Francis Bailey's *Freeman's Journal* of Philadelphia were the only newspapers that came close to publishing regularly what convention boosters would call "antifederal" material. In addition, as with Bailey's paper, Greenleaf's *Journal* became one of the few newspapers that openly championed the Antifederalist position once the Constitution appeared.[71]

The first dissenting piece appeared on July 5 in the *New York Journal* when a writer, probably editor Greenleaf, used the guise of defending Robert Morris, a delegate from Pennsylvania, to attack him. Referring to Morris by his popular title, the author opened by describing how various opinions existed about the American financier general and his credit in Europe. Ominous ramifications might follow because America's credit and Morris's credit were so intertwined. Greenleaf remarked that vague reports, some picturing Morris in a harsh light, had supposedly spawned these rumors. Although he judiciously remarked that the facts awaited investigation, Greenleaf also said that many merchants had hurt America's credit by studiously defrauding their European counterparts. Moreover, reports indicated that some southerners were cheating French merchants. These economic offenders, he asserted, should be prosecuted rather than risk ruining the Union's reputation.

Greenleaf was disingenuous. If rumors about Morris were circulating, they had not become suddenly a matter of press debate; and, there was no reason build a defense for Morris. Moreover, linking questions about his business dealings with charges of improprieties by unnamed merchants did not defend Morris; it attacked him. By claiming that Morris's honor and honesty were being questioned, the *Journal* author certainly deviated from the press' standard exaltation of the convention delegates. The article mustered just four reprintings; intriguingly, none occurred in Pennsylvania, where interest in material about Morris should have been strongest.[72]

The camouflaged assault on Morris did not directly attack the convention, but one author did. His work appeared on July 7 in the New York *Daily Advertiser*, a paper that typically published ardently proconvention material. Employing the language of classical republicanism, "Sylvester" talked of how the people should protect their rights and warned about the dangerous influence of wealthy and commercial men. Saying they should consider any person's recommendations, Sylvester asked the delegates to ban paper money. What seemed like a call to strengthen the government then took on a different cast. Sylvester boldly asserted that "our *notables*, or notable attornies and politicians, who are called the *wisdom* of the western world" would do more good by inquiring into financiers and contractors than by attempting political transformations. Disrespect surfaced again when he theorized that barring paper money and creating economic investigatory tribunals would give the world a better example of the delegates' political wisdom than "forming speculative [political] systems which look beautiful and perfect in the recess of the state-house, but vanish when exposed to the touch of the people." Sylvester marched well past disrespect when, in an apparent reference to the delegates, he satirized "that *dignity* which is always in the mouth of those political *upstarts*." If Sylvester's mordant remarks were designed to make people question the work of the convention, they had little chance of succeeding. Only Bailey's *Freeman's Journal* reprinted Sylvester, and not until August 1.[73]

No author who directly challenged the convention, or who even seemed to do so, attained reprint popularity from mid-

June through late July. However an essayist who faulted the press for hyping what were standard proconvention themes did become popular, although only north of Pennsylvania. His commentary appeared on July 12 in a logical place, Greenleaf's *New York Journal*. The writer emphasized that the East as well as the West teemed with danger and therefore an efficient federal government must be created immediately. "Consequently, to blow the trumpet, and sound the alarm, is," he said, "incumbent on every public printer." These comments may explain why the essay accumulated nine reprintings by August 2. The positive approach emulated the one that had earned "Z," which appeared in Bailey's *Freeman's Journal*, a few reprintings in the early convention days. But like "Z," the New Yorker added basic qualifications that indirectly challenged the convention. He sharply questioned the methods some newspaper authors and publishers adopted when calling for an efficient government. While stressing that real grievances should be analyzed carefully in the press, he groused: "to suffer pieces, which are studiously calculated to alarm the community (and which perhaps originate with our internal enemies) to circulate unanswered and undetected, is *criminal* negligence, and the height of *impolicy*." This commentator obviously believed the Union needed a stronger federal government; he in no way implied that the convention was unnecessary or the delegates unworthy. However, he rebuked at least the tone of much of what the press had published about the convention and its task. In time, the New Yorker's complaint about press bias became a standard "antifederal" argument.[74]

Although some "antifederal" pieces appeared, the general inactivity of those who might have pursued the *Herald* story seems surprising. Of course, few publishers would have printed or reprinted their essays, but since Cornelius and Sylvester got published, some effort to use the June 13 story could have been undertaken. A perceptive, although not widely reprinted, article in the New York *Daily Advertiser* of June 18 helps explain why that did not happen. The author found it remarkable that the men who had ransacked their brains and political treatises to produce long, tedious essays in support of withholding necessary powers from the Union "should all at once be fairly silenced." Despite his obvious partisanship, the reasons he proffered for why that silence occurred had merit. He wondered whether the forces opposed to change had suddenly realized it was wrong to contest the strengthening of Congress. Based on the resolution authorizing the convention and what people read in the press, he was right to contend that the idea of augmenting the federal government's power appeared to enjoy overwhelming support. Indeed, most writers who opposed giving Congress great power argued, as "Z" did, that some reform must occur. The *Daily Advertiser* author also wondered if the delegates' wisdom and dignity awestruck their potential adversaries or made them "apprehensive that their sinister policy will be crushed." His comment about the respect accorded the delegates clearly hit the mark. Even discounting the misleading puffery offered by Harrington and others, the convention was principally made up of leading lights headed by the honored and truly beloved Washington. Unless one knew what the convention was proposing, how could one directly challenge it and not demean Washington, Franklin, and other noted Revolutionary leaders? To have attacked the convention without knowing what was happening behind its closed doors would have opened anyone to ridicule.[75]

The New Yorker offered valuable insights, but he did not exhaust the possibilities. He could also have justifiably observed that the stance taken by the press made it difficult to question the convention. If editors had groused about the convention's secrecy rule, it would have been far easier to challenge the workings of the convention. The news media, however, embraced secrecy. Equally important, significant elements of the press worked to neutralize the *Herald* report about divisions and antidemocratic thought in the convention. In addition, the press did not reprint essays that seemed in any way critical of the convention. In so doing, many editors ignored the ideals stated in a widely reprinted pronouncement about the vital role of the press in a free society. On June 20 the *Independent Gazetteer* carried the thoughts of "Numa," who assessed what it took to spread and preserve good government in any country. Three of his four points concerned religion, language, and roads. The fourth, listed as second in importance after religion, stressed "the regular, punctual, and free diffusion of knowledge by means of *newspapers*."[76] When it came to extensive reprinting and commentary on the newsworthy account of divisions and antidemocratic thought in the convention, much of the press seemed more concerned with squelching the possible implications of the story than with diffusing knowledge.

• • •

By late June, the initial printing blitz growing out of the June 13 *Herald* report had subsided. Based on what the press offered readers, it almost seemed as if the *Pennsylvania Herald* report never existed. In July, articles and news stories associated with the Fourth of July and press items in general once again presented a proconvention image that looked virtually unassailable. Then in the the third week of July, three spectacular newspaper accounts appeared that again threatened to sabotage the selling of the Constitutional Convention.

Notes to Chapter Three

1. See the discussion in Chapter Two.

2. The *Herald* version is given in COC1: 132. Neither editor claimed to have a source in the convention, and each report merely began with the formal opening: "We are informed." The *Evening Chronicle* editor may have obtained his information from the *Herald* of the same date. Thirty-six of the piece's total of forty-six appearances occurred by the end of June; the eight reprintings from July through September 8 appeared in more geographically isolated newspapers.

3. Given in COC1: 123, with fifteen of the sixteen reprints appearing between June 15 and July 9; the other occurred in the *Georgia State Gazette*, August 25. (The total of sixteen includes the items noted in COC1: 126, n. 3 and the reprinting in the *Massachusetts Centinel*, June 20.) No Philadelphia paper reprinted

this item, but that was normal. Two papers reprinted the May 30 *Herald* item; one reprinted the June 2 story; one reprinted the July 28 piece. Otherwise, the Philadelphia press did not reprint the various *Herald* convention reports. It seems likely that the other Philadelphia papers did not want to appear dependent on the *Herald* for information concerning the convention.

4. For example, on June 19 the Baltimore *Maryland Gazette* printed an extract of a letter written by a Philadelphian who commented on the convention without offering any information not already in *Herald* reports. Rhode Island came in for nasty words, but that too was standard fare. Only one point might have made the letter of special interest. The author maintained that representation in Congress should be based on the population and wealth of the individual states. This piece, which took almost the identical space to print as did the *Herald* report of June 13 and which is given in COC1: 123–24, was reprinted fifteen times by July 26. In addition, a short paragraph on the convention from the Philadelphia *Independent Gazetteer* of June 16 that could not even claim to be based on the delegates' activities was nevertheless picked up by twenty-seven newspapers. This extract of a letter is given in COC1: 124; on the reprintings, which occurred by July 28, see ibid., 126, n. 5.

5. On June 20 editor Dallas offered a short laudatory comment on the convention that hinted at the possibility that a new government might be created (given in COC1: 135). Although he did not claim to be reporting convention proceedings, seventeen publishers opted to print his article with the reprintings occurring by July 23. Almost a month passed before the *Herald* again carried a story that seemed to come from inside the convention. However, as indicated, after the June 13 article appeared, and possibly in part because of it, the number of printed items supposedly based on direct reports from the convention declined sharply in all papers, not just in the *Herald*. On July 25, when the paper again offered convention news, it proved very popular. Dallas reported that the convention would sit about a month longer and then give the public a suitable plan of government; his speculation found its way into twenty other publications by August 21. (See COC1: 98.) On July 28 the *Herald* once again contained a story, given in COC1: 125, allegedly based on direct knowledge of convention actions, and it was reprinted thirty times within a three-week period. The work was eventually reprinted thirty-five times with the last reprinting appearing on September 8.

6. Given in COC1: 123, and see n. 3 above.

7. The same kind of limited reprinting had occurred with the potentially damaging June 4 story about the convention sitting for months and creating a totally new government. See the discussion in Chapter Two.

8. All of the points made about the aspects of damage control in response to the June 13 *Herald* item would also hold for the shockingly underreported June 4 story mentioned in n. 7. Although the media printed a great deal of proconvention speculation, it would have been most difficult to attack the convention unless one could claim to know what the delegates were doing. The *Herald* report provided the means to do that because it obviously seemed based on knowledge of convention proceedings.

9. It is not clear if any correlation exists between the damage-control effort and the popular reprint letter, dated at Philadelphia on June 15 that the Baltimore *Maryland Gazette* printed on June 19, given in COC1: 123–24, with fifteen reprintings by July 26. The writer noted there was great interest in the convention's actions; he gave information on how the convention was organized but noted that nothing had yet transpired. He mentioned neither the *Herald* story about division and antidemocratic thought nor the report about Rhode Island being kicked out of the Union. The author may not have known about these points; or, he could have suppressed them. In either case, his report supported the kinds of points developed in the damage-control articles described in the text.

10. Issue of June 16, given in COC1: 124; reprinted twenty-seven times by July 28.

11. Editor Dallas had himself, of course, reported on the rule of secrecy supposedly being firmly observed by the delegates.

12. *Independent Gazetteer*, June 22, given in COC1: 132; the sixteen reprintings occurred by July 16. The other report appeared in the *New Haven Gazette*, June 28; reprintings occurred in the *Hudson Weekly Gazette*, July 5, and the *Gazette of the State of Georgia*, August 2. A similar kind of argument originating in the *New York Journal* of August 23 was reprinted six times between August 27 and September 13.

13. Given in COC1: 132 and reprinted by all the publications that reprinted the first paragraph (see n. 12 above), with the exception that it did not appear in the July 11 New Bern *North Carolina Gazette*.

14. See n. 5 above. The way Babcock and Claxton, the "propaganda" editors of the *Northern Centinel*, handled such material from the *Herald* is suggestive. They did not reprint any of the first four *Herald* convention reports, but they did reprint the June 20 item on July 2. On August 6 they also reprinted a July 28 *Herald* piece that was an endorsement of the convention.

15. Given in COC1: 124; the twenty-four reprintings appeared by August 11.

16. Some reports which might have been based on delegate comment did appear outside the Philadelphia press between July 18 and 28. In its July 21 issue, the *Georgia State Gazette* printed a story saying the publisher had heard that the convention was "doing business." He noted: "among the many important matters to be taken under consideration by that august body, the following are said to be the principles [*sic*]. . . ." He then listed three rather drastic possibilities from breaking up the Union, to having Congress revise state laws to bring them into conformity, to having the executive power of the Congress enlarged. No reprints of the story have been discovered. All these possibilities had been raised outside the convention. Still the article might possibly have been considered by some as an insider report. However, the report was either not seen as vital, or publishers did not want to reproduce it. On July 26 the *Gazette of the State of Georgia*, citing a July 18 Charleston source, not located, said it had been learned that the convention was expected to break up about the end of the month. On July 25 the Poughkeepsie *Country Journal* announced it had been informed that the convention had adjourned for a few days and that it was said delegates Hamilton and Yates were in New York City. Even taken at face value, this piece did not claim nor need to be based on insider information.

17. Both items are given in COC1: 125. The *Gazetteer* report was reprinted seventeen times by August 20; the *Herald* version was reprinted thirty-six times by September 8.

18. Although the next report unquestionably based on convention sources did not appear until July 28, as indicated in n. 16 above, some reports printed outside Philadelphia between July 18 and 28 at least hinted at having inside information.

19. The one popular reprint, which described "Rhode-Island Faith" as having become a standard term of reproach when one violated agreements, appeared in the *Newport Herald* of June 28; it was reprinted thirteen times between July 2 and August 1. The

harsh anti-Rhode Island government piece about the third vote on sending delegates appeared in the *Newport Herald* on June 21; it was reprinted in *Providence Gazette*, June 30, and *Pennsylvania Packet*, July 12. Similarly, a superb bit of Rhode Island bashing contained in letter from that state dated June 11 and printed by the *Independent Gazetteer* on June 23 achieved only two reprintings, on June 29 and July 4. A June 18 *Gazetteer* item that had a Rhode Islander describe the convention as the only thing that could save his state from destruction was reprinted in three other Philadelphia papers and in four New York papers between June 20 and 27. A Rhode Islander's call for his fellow citizens to use the Fourth of July to show they were not totally antifederal appeared in the *United States Chronicle*, June 28, and was reprinted five times between July 5 and 23. Scornful comments about Rhode Island first published on June 19 in Baltimore did become popular, but only as part of a longer essay that covered a number of points rather than focusing on the Ocean State. See n. 4 above.

20. The opposition might also have tried to attack on the basis that the convention planned to undermine the Articles. However, in contrast to the early convention period, few items published in this post-June 13 period suggested the delegates were formulating a new government. The closest any popular author came to emphasizing that possibility occurred in the *Pennsylvania Herald* item of June 20 cited in n. 5 above. See also following note.

21. The *Gazetteer* piece was reprinted six times between June 26 and July 10. Three of the reprintings cut the comment about a "new" federal government coming. A desire to avoid giving anticonvention types possible ammunition may have prompted that omission. The *Gazette* item, reprinted ten times by July 28, is given in COC1: 135–36. As printed, the two correspondent essays were different. However, the writers were not directly quoted, and, as rendered, both said very similar things. Therefore, the two items probably sprang from one source. Among the papers that reprinted either of these items, only the *Pennsylvania Packet* carried both of them. On the theme of keeping quiet, see the similar comments of a New Yorker cited at n. 24 below.

22. "Civis," *Pennsylvania Packet*, June 25, given in COC1: 144–45. "Civis" was reprinted eleven times by September 6.

23. This extract from the June 26 issue is given in COC1: 145–47; seventeen reprintings occurred by August 8. (This letter also illustrates the decline in traditional Rhode Island bashing.

Although the attack on local interests and pettiness certainly would apply to Rhode Island, it was mentioned by name only once.) A *Massachusetts Centinel* correspondent picked up the same theme in a June 30 publication. He began by fervently asserting that "the united wisdom of the Convention" would produce a plan to create the stronger government the United States desperately required. He closed with a warning about those who might counsel rejection of the convention's recommendations. The people must be "on guard against those pretended friends but real enemies, who may perhaps approach them with the mask of gravity and popular zeal, and enkindle jealousy and faction to the ruin of our fairest prospects." Although he voiced views being widely reprinted, this commentary only gained five reprintings. Perhaps the low number of reprintings stemmed in part from the fact that this item did not originate in Philadelphia. The article is given in COC1: 148–49, with quotations from p. 149; five reprintings occurred by August 2.

    24. Given in COC1: 133, with five reprintings by July 11; see also n. 75 below.

    25. See n. 10 above.

    26. See n. 21 above.

    27. See n. 22. above.

    28. This extract of a letter dated June 20 from the *Independent Gazetteer*, June 23, was reprinted seven times between June 25 and July 23. The reprintings might have been kept down in part because the writer was not sanguine about the state legislatures accepting what the convention recommended.

    29. Quotation from issue of July 26, as based on *Pennsylvania Packet* reprinting of August 4, given in COC1: 178–79. Counting the appearance in the *Packet*, seven reprintings occurred between August 4 and 27. This item was written before the author could have seen the vital July 25 items analyzed in Chapter Four. The author quite possibly also had not seen the other significant piece, that of July 21, described in Chapter Four. The second item was an extract of a letter of July 20 from a Baltimore gentleman printed in the *Independent Gazetteer*, July 27, given in COC1: 180, with nine reprintings by September 13. This author also wrote before he could have seen any of the vital items mentioned above.

    30. The letter first appeared in the June 20 issues of the *Gazetteer*, the *Packet*, and the *Gazette*. The *Packet* editors omitted the introduction. The text of the letter, based on the *Gazetteer* printing, is given in COC1: 133–34. Twenty-two reprintings occurred by July

12. As indicated in the *Packet,* the letter was dated April 2. This suggests it may, unlike Price's letter to Rush, have been reprinted as soon as it arrived in America.

31. The extract of a letter from a gentleman in Washington County, presumably in New York, to his friend in Albany probably appeared in the June issue 21. Fourteen reprintings occurred between June 28 and July 19. Due to its length, some incomplete reprintings appeared. However, all the papers reprinted the sections cited here. For the attribution to the *Gazette* and the text of the letter, see COC1: 141–44.

32. Both items appeared in the June 30 issue. The first piece was reprinted thirteen times between July 2 and 26; the Berkshire item was reprinted fourteen times between July 3 and 26, with a delayed reprinting due to geographic isolation on August 13 in the *State Gazette of South Carolina.*

33. The only date given for the letter was in the rather standard form of "a letter of a late date." The four Philadelphia papers reprinted the letter the day after the *Packet* published it, and within a month nearly twenty more papers carried the Virginian's message. Since this item appeared in the damage-control period and covered themes typical of damage-control pieces, the item may well have been invented. All but one of the twenty-three reprintings occurred by July 23; almost surely due to travel time, the *Georgia State Gazette* did not carry it until August 8.

34. See, e.g., Elisha P. Douglass, *Rebels and Democrats: The Struggle for Equal Political Rights and Majority Rule During the American Revolution* (Chapel Hill, 1955), 4, 71, 85–108 passim; Richard M. Brown, *Strain of Violence: Historical Studies of American Violence and Vigilantism* (New York, 1975), 41–90; COC1: 91–93.

35. These letters from the *Maryland Journal* , July 3, each reprinted fifteen times, are given in COC1: 152–54. As analyzed in ibid., 158, n. 1, Thomas Green probably wrote the Louisville letters.

36. On the genre see, e.g., Daniel J. Boorstin, ed., *An American Primer* (Chicago, 1966), 31–47; Richard C. Wade, *The Urban Frontier: Pioneer Life in Early Pittsburgh, Cincinnati, Lexington, Louisville, and St. Louis* (Chicago, 1964; originally published 1959), 322–25.

37. A useful introduction to the issues involved in the conflict over the possible closing of the Mississippi River to American com-

merce is given in COC1: 149–52; see also Richard B. Morris, *The Forging of the Union, 1781–1789* (New York, 1987), 232–44.

38. This *Maryland Journal* item of July 3 was reprinted sixteen times between July 7 and August 8. On the conventions held in Massachusetts and elsewhere and their relation to Shays's Rebellion, see David P. Szatmary, *Shays' Rebellion: The Making of an Agrarian Insurrection* (Amherst, 1980), 37–44.

39. This *Maryland Journal* item of July 3, given in COC1: 154–55, was reprinted eighteen times by September 8. The author added suggestions (ibid., 155) that he conceded might well be called "Utopian schemes" designed to make states about the same size.

40. Extract of letter given in COC1: 155–57. For the attribution to Williamson, see ibid., 158, n. 3. The piece was extraordinarily lengthy, which probably explains why it was only reprinted eight times. Seven reprintings occurred by July 30; the *Georgia State Gazette* reprinted it on October 20.

41. Given in COC1: 157–58; nine reprintings appeared by August 2; five of them occurred in Massachusetts where, due to Shays's Rebellion, people were naturally sensitive on the issue.

42. See *Massachusetts Centinel*, June 30, given in COC1: 148–49; five reprintings of these comments, which were part of a long essay, occurred by August 2. See also, "A Friend to this State," *Newport Herald*, June 21. It too was rather long, which may help account for why it was reprinted only twice by July 12. On Price's comment, see n. 30 above.

43. Reprinted eighteen times between June 26 and August 2. During the Revolution, the inhabitants of Berkshire County acquired a reputation for taking vigorous action against state policies they opposed. See Ronald M. Peters, Jr., *The Massachusetts Constitution of 1780: A Social Compact* (Amherst, 1978), 19–20, 69, 96, 98–103, 130–31, 158–59; Douglass, *Rebels and Democrats*, 150, 151, 154, 187–88, 211.

44. The more detailed of the two reports appeared in the *Virginia Gazette and Weekly Advertiser*, July 19, given in COC1: 96; eleven reprintings occurred between July 26 and September 15. The other account, from the *Virginia Independent Chronicle* of July 18, was reprinted five times between July 26 and August 9. Since no paper carried both versions, total appearances include all newspapers that published either version.

45. The original from the Petersburg *Virginia Gazette* of July 26 has not been located. For the text and attribution, see *Pennsylvania*

Packet, August 4. In all, eight papers reprinted this between August 4 and 28.

46. Issue of June 30; reprinted nineteen times between July 2 and 30. The piece silently but clearly built upon the widely reprinted account of British military activity carried in the *New Hampshire Spy* of June 9, and discussed in Chapter Two. Apparently drawing upon the *New Hampshire Spy* report, nine editors added a paragraph about the Canadian militia being put on a ready footing, about the arrival of six regiments, or about both. It may not have been mere coincidence that Russell, the publisher of the *Centinel*, chose June 30 as the day to print the correspondent who looked to the convention and said "it would be better to embrace almost any expedient rather than to remain as we are." This went too far; his views were only reprinted five times. The item is given in COC1: 149; the reprintings occurred by August 2. The issue of June 30 also carried the dire comments on the possible renewal of Shays's Rebellion.

47. The original printing of the letter, dated June 25, was in a Wilmington, Delaware paper of July 18, presumably the *Delaware Gazette*, not found; attribution based on the *Pennsylvania Packet* reprinting of July 23 from which the material given in the text is taken. Counting the appearance in the *Packet*, ten reprintings occurred between July 23 and August 16. On July 21 the *Packet* had carried the rather similar thoughts of a writer "on the present times" who did not, however, draw the clear link to the work of the convention. He urged people to work hard, to stop complaining about exaggerated evils, and to obey the laws. "Seek the redress of real grievances, if any such you have," he said, "in a constitutional way, but not by mobs and riots." These thoughts were reprinted six times between August 1 and 18 in N.J., S.C., Mass., Conn., R.I., and, Vt. Later reprintings occurred in the *New Hampshire Gazette*, September 22, and the *Albany Gazette*, November 8.

48. Confirmation of this action was given by a letter dated June 25 in Dominica published in the *Pennsylvania Packet* , July 23, and reprinted eight times between July 25 and August 13. The writer claimed that the British government intended to open "channels" for trade with all nations except the United States.

49. *Pennsylvania Herald*, June 27, with thirteen reprintings between June 28 and August 23. The editors of the *Pennsylvania Packet* actually reprinted it twice, on June 28 and again on August 13.

50. *Independent Gazetteer*, June 27, given in COC1: 147–48; reprinted twenty-three times by July 19.

51. Quotation from COC1: 145, and see n. 23 above. The passage could possibly be read as meaning that the convention would be worthy of having its name written in gold. The exact text, following a comment praising the work of the convention, is: "and raise to this country a name worthy to be written in letters of gold."

52. *Pennsylvania Herald*, June 23, with eleven reprintings between June 27 and July 23. If the letter did originate in the Old World, it arrived at an opportune time for the proconvention forces.

53. On this comparison and image, see, e.g., Philadelphia *Evening Chronicle*, July 14.

54. The June 16 *Gazetteer* list, which indicated that the missing states were Rhode Island and New Hampshire, was reprinted ten times between June 20 and July 28. The more elaborate *Packet* list of June 15 was reprinted three times between June 16 and July 2. The separate *Gazetteer* comment about the nature of the delegation was carried by over two dozen papers.

55. The *New Hampshire Spy* item of June 26 on two men being elected to represent New Hampshire, from which the quotation is taken, was reprinted twenty times between June 30 and August 2. The July 5 *New Hampshire Mercury* report on Langdon attending was reprinted eighteen times between July 7 and August 13.

56. Issue of July 11; reprinted eight times between July 19 and August 2. Cf. the Langdon travel report in the *Connecticut Courant*, July 16, which was reprinted six times between July 20 and 30.

57. Given in COC1: 147–48; reprinted twenty-three times by July 19.

58. This was the ninth essay in a series by "Regulator." The relevant section of the July 4 essay became a reprint item after an excerpt appeared in the Baltimore *Maryland Gazette* on July 13. In that form, it was reprinted six times between July 19 and August 30. Thus, the item appeared eight times in all. In a similar way, a Philadelphian quoted in the Charleston *Columbian Herald* of July 5 singled out Washington and Franklin for special praise. He was careful however to stress that the people considered the convention an "illustrious assembly" and that the delegates had gained the "confidence" of Philadelphians. The letter, dated June 1, is given in COC1: 167. The first reprinting did not occur until August 1; the twelve reprintings appeared by August 16.

59. Although editors typically reported on the local or state celebrations of Independence Day, the coverage of celebrations that occurred outside their own state varied considerably from paper to paper. The best overall coverage, and upon which the comments in the text are based, is in the *Pennsylvania Packet*, July 6 through August 18 passim.

60. See n. 28 above.

61. Quotation from COC1: 144, and see n. 22 above.

62. See n. 52 above.

63. See n. 58 above and the *Pennsylvania Herald*, July 14, given in COC1: 165, with eight reprintings by July 25.

64. Given in COC1: 168, with nine reprintings by July 26.

65. Issue of July 26; see n. 29 above.

66. Extract of July 20 letter from the *Independent Gazetteer*, July 27, given in COC1: 180. Reprinted nine times by September 13. See also n. 29 above.

67. Fifteen reprintings appeared between July 23 and August 6.

68. The Baltimore *Maryland Gazette* of July 10 carried a piece, reprinted ten times between July 16 and August 4, whose author blamed Rhode Island for the loss of the impost amendment and suggested that the little state be expelled rather than let it stop efforts to strengthen the Union. On July 16 an *Independent Gazetteer* correspondent described Rhode Island as being run by "a set of ignorant countrymen" who were held in such disrepute that the governor of New Jersey had ordered only twelve cannon fired on Independence Day. This account was reprinted in full fourteen times between July 18 and August 2; a section ridiculing the governor of Rhode Island was reprinted in an additional four papers between July 28 and August 8.

69. See n. 15 above.

70. The thoughts of a "grouchy" author published in the *Norwich Packet* on July 5, given in COC1: 167, defy categorization. Still, his piece got ten reprintings by September 3, and some of his points were relevant for the convention's work. In staccato fashion, the author listed what he called the "orthodox sentiments of the day upon political subjects, especially for Connecticut." He did not attribute any of the sentiments to convention delegates, but the list included sentiments that could be construed as hostile to the convention and to strengthening the central government in the lines: "the confederation must be strengthened—Democracy should be seasoned at least, with Aristocracy, if not with Mon-

archy." The author also noted, however, that "All attempt to be politicians—Genuine liberty terminates in licentiousness—Lawyers must be Esquires, legeslatores." This litany ended with "in short the reigning politics of the times *ever* was, *is* and *shall* be right." This enigmatic ending, like the whole piece, seemed to suggest real displeasure with the political world or with what others thought, but the Connecticut writer did not assault the convention.

71. Additional examples are given at various points in this study, and see also COC1: xix.

72. Reprinted four times between July 11 and 24.

73. The close of the last line, deleted above, is not clear; it reads: ". . . those political *upstarts*, who have no real claim to public or private." It is surprising that Francis Childs, a proconvention editor, published this. Perhaps the piece was designed as a straw man or to let Childs claim he was open to various points of view.

74. See n. 41 above and Chapter Five.

75. See n. 24 above on the *Journal* piece, and see also n. 25 above.

76. Ten reprintings occurred between June 21 and the second week in August.

4

"Prepared To Receive With Respect": Selling the Unknown

News media coverage of the convention had reached a holding stage by mid-July. The burst of printing activity that followed the appearance of the June 13 *Herald* report had run its course, and fresh items based on insider information had disappeared. This relatively tranquil state ended in the third week of July when, in the space of five days, three accounts appeared that threatened the proconvention consensus depicted in the press. Once again, the news coverage offered to the public revealed that a desire to champion the convention often governed what publishers reprinted. Once again, as with the June 13 report, proconvention forces adroitly maneuvered to neutralize the potentially damaging information.

Coverage of the convention from late July through August was also influenced by the fact that analysts believed the delegates' recommendations would be forthcoming near the end of August. A widely reprinted August 8 *Pennsylvania Herald* news story seemed to confirm that timetable. The report indicated the delegates had begun debating the individual paragraphs of the plan they would submit to the public.[1] By mid-August, it was openly suggested that the delegates were creating a new national government. In anticipation of its unveiling, editors increased publication of pieces about the convention, and writers injected more passion into their writing. Persons who might question the delegates' actions came under increasingly vicious attack as the call to trust the delegates received even greater emphasis. Other established arguments, such as the Union confronting a time of troubles, were not merely reiterated, they were expanded. Important modifications, such as proconvention writers focusing more on economic issues, also occurred. As had been the case, convention boosters continued their dominance. However, near the end of August, persons labeled "antifederal" displayed a new feistiness, and they also began adopting techniques that improved the chances of getting their message before the public.

• • •

The first of the three significant July articles that could have ignited controversy about the convention appeared in the New York *Daily Advertiser* on July 21. In a lengthy unsigned essay, Alexander Hamilton charged that Governor George Clinton had publicly decried holding the convention and had "predicted a mischievous issue of that measure." The Governor allegedly argued that the existing Confederation government did not need changing. The convention had been called merely "to impress people with the idea of evils which do not exist." Clinton supposedly believed the Philadelphia meeting was actually dangerous: the public would "despair" if the convention failed to act, or if its recommendations were rejected. Considering all this, the convention probably "would only serve to throw the community into confusion." Having laid this groundwork, Hamilton ripped into Clinton. In nine numbered segments and a closing paragraph, Hamilton defended calling the convention, applauded its work, and proclaimed that Clinton and others who harbored anticonvention views could not be trusted.[2]

Hamilton's attack seems ill-timed. Clinton did question the value of the convention, and he had already received convention reports from his political allies, delegates John

Lansing, Jr., and Robert Yates, who last attended the convention on July 10. However, they had not publicly breached the convention's vow of silence; nor had Clinton, despite what Hamilton claimed, publicly denounced the convention. Thus there was no apparent need to discredit Clinton; moreover, Hamilton's attack undercut the idea that the convention enjoyed overwhelming support throughout the Union—with of course the possible exception of that pariah, Rogue's Island. Tiny Rhode Island could be dismissed as an aberration that would not be allowed to halt needed reform, but if the popular governor of the crucial state of New York questioned the convention's efforts, others could logically do so as well. In that case, it might prove impossible to correct the central government's deficiencies.

Hamilton may have believed his essay made political sense as a preemptive strike against anyone who might question the work of the convention. It seemed certain that Clinton would oppose the delegates' recommendations once they became public and accordingly would become a target for the nationalist forces. Hamilton may have ventured into print out of a fear that the Governor, or Lansing and Yates at Clinton's urging, might soon deface the flattering picture of the convention being developed in the press. Hamilton might also have reasoned that a preemptive attack would silence them and other potential opponents, at least for a while.[3]

Although apparently ill-timed, Hamilton's lengthy essay was brilliantly fashioned to force Clinton into backing the convention. The Governor reportedly worried that the Union would face grave dangers if the convention did not act or if the people rejected its results. It followed that, even if one had opposed holding the convention, the delegates' work must be supported.[4] Whether or not Clinton subscribed to the views attributed to him, the force of the statements Hamilton advanced about the concerns of the people could not easily be dismissed.

From the convention booster's point of view, Hamilton's attack on Clinton cut both ways. It skillfully undermined potential opposition to the convention, yet it also undermined the claim that the convention's work would not be challenged. A crucial press report that surfaced four days later seemed to cut one way only, and that way was potentially devastating for the proconvention forces. On July 25, the Connecticut *Fairfield Gazette* printed an extract of a letter purportedly written in Philadelphia on June 19. It expressed the views of a Loyalist who laughed at the ineptitude of American government and chortled over the Union's trying times. He even asserted that, given the Union's desperate situation, three out of four Americans would, if given the opportunity, vote to sanction establishing a monarchy. The Loyalist advanced a plan to achieve that end. The Bishop of Osnaburg, the second son of George III, should be made king of America. The writer prophesied that, to achieve this, the British would form an alliance with the United States and throw in parts of Canada and forty ships of the line for good measure.[5]

Normally such musings might have been dismissed as the prattlings of a fool. What made this letter potentially so damaging was the author's claim that "the convention we understand have the subject [of forming a monarchy] in their deliberation, and are harmonious in their opinions; the means only of accomplishing so great an event, appears principally to occupy their counsels." Indeed, "the scheme ripens fast."[6] Although the writer did not say so, his account would explain the convention's lengthy deliberations and its secrecy. Obviously it would take time to conduct overseas negotiations with Britain, and those delicate negotiations would require the utmost secrecy. This letter could have been an invented antimonarchy piece ineptly designed to garner support for strengthening the government. Still, if even a small percentage of people accepted it at face value, it could shatter confidence in the convention.

The third significant press item from late July virtually guaranteed that commentary on the convention would heat up no matter what happened with the *Fairfield Gazette* letter or Hamilton's anti-Clinton blast. On July 25 editor Dallas of the *Pennsylvania Herald*, who had surely established a reputation for knowing something about what the delegates were doing, told his readers the convention would complete its work in about a month. Then the delegates would present a plan of government "adapted to the circumstances and habits of the people, without regard to the fine-spun systems of elementary writers."[7]

The situation obviously changed with the nearly simultaneous publication of the attack on Clinton, the letter on monarchy, and the report that the convention would probably announce its recommendations in late August. The potential for extensive and possibly fierce debates dramatically escalated almost overnight. The reprint history and the responses to these three vital publications are, thus, most instructive.

Only one newspaper reprinted the *Fairfield Gazette* monarchy letter, and that hardly mattered since it occurred in Vermont on September 17.[8] Although the lengthy letter appeared in a minor paper located away from the major reprint centers, the lack of reprintings of this sensational report seems surprising. As happened with other repugnant missives, the letter or part of it could have been reproduced with a notation that its importance prompted the reprinting. Alternatively, it could have been reprinted and its author savaged to prove that dangerous, if deluded, royalist thought yet existed. In addition, the information contained in the *Fairfield Gazette* became known despite the lack of reprints. Hamilton learned of it in New York and was concerned.[9] Had newspaper editors not had another agenda, the report should have gotten wide circulation. Proconvention editors, however, apparently refused to reprint anything that suggested the delegates contemplated establishing a monarchy. This interpretation is supported by what the press did publish about monarchy in the weeks right after the monarchy letter surfaced and also by what editors printed when rumors about the delegates possibly thinking of creating a monarchy surfaced.

The press cleverly used the threat of monarchy contained in the *Fairfield Gazette* letter as yet another reason to sanction the delegates' work. On August 2 the *New Haven Gazette* reported that a circular letter supporting the idea of making the Bishop of Osnaburg the king of America "gains friends and partisans rapidly."[10] The publishers, Josiah Meigs and Eleutheros Dana, transformed this news into a sweeping convention endorsement. They asserted that "the Federal Convention may save us from this worst of all curses (A ROYAL GOVERNMENT) if we are only wise enough to adopt their recommendations when they shall be communicated to us." Although the *Fairfield Gazette* report gained only one reprinting, the *New Haven Gazette* "spin control" piece garnered twenty-eight reprintings.[11]

The suggestion that the delegates supported creating a monarchy also brought an explicit denial. In the only direct statement attributed to delegates in the period before the Constitution was made public, on August 18 Dallas of the *Pennsylvania Herald* reported: "We are well informed, that many letters have been written to the members of the federal convention from different quarters, respecting the reports idly circulating, that it is intended to establish a monarchical government, to send for the Bishop of Osnaburgh, &c. &c.—to which it has been uniformly answered, 'tho' we cannot, affirmatively, tell you what we are doing; we can, negatively, tell you what we are not doing—we never once thought of a king.' " This pronouncement, which silently but firmly branded the allegations in the *Fairfield Gazette* as lies, appeared in more than thirty newspapers in less than a month.[12]

The press's response to Hamilton's lambasting of Clinton is also revealing. The essay originated in New York City, a prime reprint source area, and in the *Daily Advertiser*, a proconvention paper from which editors often lifted material.[13] The July 21 issue probably reached Philadelphia by July 23 or 24, and the *Pennsylvania Packet* reprinted Hamilton's essay on July 26. The next reprinting did not occur until August 2 when the *Hudson Weekly Gazette* of New York carried it. The third reprinting, in the Baltimore *Maryland Gazette*, appeared eight days later. Only after that, when it was increasingly expected the delegates would soon recommend a new national government, did the anti-Clinton diatribe become popular. From August 11 through the end of the month, eleven papers reproduced Hamilton's piece or versions of it. Three more publishers reprinted it during September.[14]

The general delay in reprinting the attack on Governor Clinton cannot be attributed solely to geography: the essay appeared in New York on July 21 and in Philadelphia five days later. It easily could have been reprinted by more than two other papers before August 10. The slow reprinting process suggests some editors delayed publication until they believed it would do the convention more good than harm. It certainly made sense to print Hamilton's item at some point because his powerful essay contained most of the basic proconvention arguments advanced in the wake of reports that the delegates' proposals would appear in late August.

The history of the press response to the July 25 *Herald* report about the expected completion of the convention is intertwined with that of two other press accounts. The story gained confirmation three days later when Eleazer Oswald of the *Independent Gazetteer* informed his readers that "the Honorable convention" had adjourned on July 26 and would reconvene on August 6. Oswald reported that five delegates, whose names he listed, would serve as a committee during the recess.[15] With one important exception, the July 28 issue of the *Herald* carried the same information. Editor Dallas did not provide the names of the committee members. He did, however, proclaim that "the public curiosity will soon be gratified," and he added a glowing endorsement of the convention and its noble delegates.[16]

Each of the three news stories became a popular reprint, and together they spread the word across the land that the delegates were nearing the end of their labors. Despite the popularity of each article, telling differences occurred in the number of reprintings. The account that contained the most actual news, the *Gazetteer* report, amassed seventeen reprintings. The first *Herald* item got reproduced twenty times. The *Herald* endorsement report of July 28, although it did not give the names of the committee, was reprinted a total of three dozen times.[17] Given the choice of a shorter but more newsworthy report on convention activities or a convention endorsement statement, many editors preferred endorsement to news.[18]

The press's penchant for handling newsworthy material in a blatantly proconvention manner is also illustrated by what happened to a significant news story published on July 26 by the *New Haven Gazette*. Editors Meigs and Dana reported that Roger Sherman, a convention delegate, had arrived in New Haven the previous Sunday. Mindful of the great secrecy purportedly observed by the delegates, the publishers dutifully asserted that Sherman had not given them any particulars concerning the proceedings of "that illustrious assembly." Still, they declared that "a happy and auspicious unanimity" prevailed at the convention and that the delegates would probably complete their work in early September. Here was a solid news report from the best possible source, a delegate whose name could be given. If any news merited extensive republishing, it was Sherman's judgment that the convention would not complete its business until sometime in September. The account did appear in the major reprint centers of New York City and Boston. Yet the *Gazette* story got reprinted only seven times, and nowhere south of New York.[19]

Convention boosters had two basic reasons to pass over the Sherman article. First, by late July editors were again willing to print and reprint accounts of what the convention was allegedly doing. Nevertheless, many editors apparently opposed publishing anything directly attributable to a specific delegate since it would brand the convention's vaunted secrecy rule a lie, and, notwithstanding their disclaimer, Meigs and Dana clearly had obtained information from delegate Sherman.[20] Second, and perhaps even more important, saying the convention would drag on into September raised troublesome possibilities. The press had carefully nurtured the idea that the delegates were—as Sherman described them—unified. But the longer they met, the more people might credit claims that division and perhaps even disharmony stalked the convention.

Despite its great distance from the convention city, the *Columbian Herald* of Charleston, South Carolina, published several vital news reports and commentaries about purported convention activities. They merit close analysis both for their content and how their reprinting again illustrates press bias. On July 26 the *Herald* published a significant letter written by a Philadelphia gentleman on July 4 to a friend in Charleston. The author said he was writing in response to his friend's request for information about commerce and politics in general. Most of the lengthy letter covered convention actions, and the Philadelphian asserted that, although the delegates had agreed upon secrecy, some of the most important men in the city concurred about the major points the delegates were considering.

With impressive specificity, the Philadelphian commented upon a wide variety of issues ranging from use of the Mississippi River, to personal debts, to the probable disposition of federal troops in each state. The federal government would be retained, and the state of Vermont would join the Union. The revised Articles of Confederation would authorize a five percent import duty on all goods for a twenty-one-year period; the income would be used to pay the foreign and domestic debt. A 2.5 percent duty on some exports would provide the funds necessary for maintaining a small army and navy. In a unique direct reference to what, if anything, the convention might do about slavery, the author proclaimed: "Have just heard from undoubted authority, that a member of the Convention will propose this week, that no slave whatever be imported into any of the states for the term of twenty-five years."[21]

Although it was somewhat dated when published in late July and although the first reprinting did not occur until August 13, the letter covered central issues in detail. In addition, the description made sense.[22] It fit well with the delegates' charge to revise the Articles, the proposed Imposts of 1781 and 1783, and what the press had proclaimed as the vital issues confronting the Union and the convention. The letter also offered reassurance to those who wanted only what Congress specifically authorized—modification of the Articles. The missive was a natural for reprint popularity, which it gained easily. Of course, the Philadelphian's claims proved incorrect, but most people, including publishers, did not know that at the time.[23]

In immediately succeeding editions, the *Columbian Herald* offered other significant reports about convention activities. The next weekly issue, that of August 2, also carried an extract of a letter from a Philadelphia gentleman. This time it was an undated letter to a friend in Wilmington. Parts of the missive fit nicely with the themes prevailing in the press. The writer emphasized that, although he knew that various committees had recently presented their reports, secrecy prevailed at the convention. He described how passersby reacted when they saw delegates in the streets. People anxiously scrutinized the delegates' every look and listened to their every word. The resultant conjectures were, he suggested, "doubtless often very wide of the truth, and cannot fail to amuse those in the secret." The rest of the letter diverged from mainstream press coverage of the convention. The author said that the delegates' deliberations had really just begun. More pointedly, he noted that the most general remark convention watchers made was that the delegates "seem very dull, from which some conclude that they are not unanimous in their opinions." He also added that many delegates reportedly disliked the secrecy rule because it stopped them from gaining the advice their intelligent friends might furnish. Based on its news value, this *Herald* report logically should have been reprinted widely, yet it was reprinted only once.[24]

The *Columbian Herald* of August 9 offered yet another extract of a letter from Philadelphia that, again if judged solely on newsworthiness, should have guaranteed it wide circulation. The complete extract, written on July 21, reported: "It is expected the Convention will adjourn in September: Their proceedings are still kept secret—Three plans have been submitted to their consideration; one by Colonel Hamilton; another by Mr. Patterson, late Chief Justice of Jersey, and a third by the late Governor of Virginia. They are now going on with the last, and I believe, with a few alterations, it will be pretty unanimously agreed to." This *was* news. No other publication had reported on the number of plans being considered or named the delegates who proposed them. This solid report, which stressed unity even as it mentioned different plans, should have been very widely circulated, but instead it was reprinted only once.[25]

All three *Columbian Herald* convention items described here, and another relevant one from the July 5 issue, were extracts of letters from Philadelphians.[26] That may explain why no Philadelphia newspaper reprinted them; the Philadelphia press rarely printed letters from Philadelphia first published elsewhere.[27] However, two of the four *Columbian Herald* items became at least moderately successful as reprints. The letter published on July 5 that offered glowing praise of the convention but few specifics was first reprinted by the *Massachusetts Centinel* on August 1. Then, in just over two weeks, another dozen papers published it. Eventually the letter appeared in Rhode Island, Connecticut, and Georgia as well as in South Carolina and Massachusetts.[28] The July 26 story that offered a detailed list of issues purportedly before the convention proved even more popular and is, thus, more useful for comparisons on reprinting. The first reprinting occurred in the New York *Daily Advertiser* on August 13. Once having appeared in a major reprint center, the letter soon gained popularity; it appeared in over a dozen more press publications by the end of August and then three more times in September.[29]

The reprinting history of these *Columbian Herald* pieces again illustrates a press effort to sell the convention. Although available to editors, the two *Columbian Herald* items that went against the general tone of press coverage almost vanished. The reports of August 2 on possible divisions among the delegates and of August 9 on three plans being considered by the convention each achieved only one reprinting. In both cases it was the *Gazette of the State of Georgia* that opted to reproduce the articles.[30] In sharp contrast, the two *Columbian Herald* missives that upheld the standard proconvention press interpretation became popular reprints.

The press did not always ignore news stories that might question proconvention themes. On August 15, when it was expected that the delegates would soon complete their work, editor Dallas reported that the delegates had met until five o'clock on August 13 debating "the most important question" considered since the convention assembled. This account, which seemed to concede that the delegates might not be unified, was very widely reprinted.[31] Nevertheless, the great bulk of evidence from late July through August shows that major segments of the press typically selected reprints based on whether or not the material supported proconvention themes. Reporting newsworthy material was, at best, a secondary consideration.

By early August there was a new and particularly strong reason for editors to intensify their partisanship. Once it seemed clear that the convention would complete its work in late August, the sporadic hints about the delegates transforming the Articles gave way to a deluge of popular items suggesting that the convention was creating a whole new government.[32] By late August, widely reprinted essays from the Philadelphia press treated that point as an open secret. For example, the *Independent Gazetteer* of August 22, a blatant convention-booster issue, contained the thoughts of two very popular essayists who asserted that the delegates would give America a "new" government. One writer even spoke of "the national government to be elected under the new constitution."[33] On the same day, a popular *Pennsylvania Gazette* correspondent actually said he hoped the name Congress would be put aside in the new federal government the convention was producing.[34]

A week later, just when the delegates were expected to reveal their plan, two *Gazette* correspondents talked about the convention's new government. One spoke matter-of-factly about the convention producing a "new" federal government; the other discussed the "national" government the convention would recommend.[35] In August, writers increasingly used the word "national" when discussing the convention.[36] But one _Gazette_ correspondent employed that term exclusively; the word "federal" did not once appear in his comments. Such an omission was unheard of before late August.[37] The correspondent spoke boldly of the goals of a national government, of a national system of commercial regulation, of a national taxation system, of a national force to protect against Indians. Indeed, "our august national Convention" would, he said, produce "an enlightened and stable national government." This celebration of things national became quite popular.[38]

Press coverage thus urged readers to assume that the delegates were producing a new, and in important ways, national government. Of course the exact details could not be known. Still, as August drew to a close, readers would not have been surprised if informed that the delegates had done more than revise the Articles. The increasing use of "national" as opposed to "federal" is especially revealing. In late May a popular essayist had decried the fact that people talked of creating one consolidated government for New Hampshire through Georgia.[39] By late August, that thought was more in vogue. As they applauded the delegates for creating a vigorous government, popular authors often castigated various state governments and spoke openly of the glories of a new national government with national powers.

Once it was anticipated that the delegates would soon complete their work, probably by late August, the press naturally increased publication of items about the convention and issues related to it. In justifying why Americans should accept what the convention proposed, authors typically reiterated staple themes. However, important variations materialized. Authors employed increasingly dramatic prose to justify supporting whatever the convention might recommend short of monarchy, and some commentators even omitted that qualification.[40] In mid-August a _New York Journal_ correspondent asserted that the delegates would give the American states "their lawful, and in every sense, legitimate _offspring_, generated by a _whole empire_, and brought forth from the chaste body of their *delegated wisdom*."[41] The New Yorker's pronouncement illustrates another aspect of the August effort to sell the convention. A *Pennsylvania Gazette* author had good reason to speak about the minds of the people being "well prepared" to accept the delegates' plan.[42] As the anticipated time for its unveiling drew near, authors labored mightily to coax people into accepting what the convention recommended.

From late July through August, the flattering coverage accorded the delegates was reminiscent of the exaltations printed when the convention opened in May. Once again George Washington's movements were carefully noted and widely reported. In early August, Philadelphia newspapers reverently told of the former commander-in-chief visiting Valley Forge during a convention recess. The *Packet* reported on his visit to an iron furnace—which reminded people that the southern planter was a friend to manufacturing.[43] One extraordinarily popular author even made it sound as if Washington had been elected to the convention in a Union-wide election. He asked: "How great . . . must be the satisfaction of our late worthy Commander in Chief, to be called upon a second time, by the suffrages of three millions of people, to save his sinking country?" The country's editors promoted that bit of electoral fiction by reprinting it more than thirty times in just over three weeks.[44]

Although glorification of Washington was hardly new, it intensified when it was assumed the delegates' recommendations would soon be made public. In similar fashion, the effort to infuse the other delegates with Washington's nobleness was also increased. Authors reinforced, and at times sped past, Alexander Dallas's May 16 claim that the delegates represented the collective wisdom of the continent.[45] The following composite picture of the convention, based on popular reprint material drawn from half-a-dozen items published between July 27 and August 28, illustrates how extensive and vociferous the escalating glorification of the delegates was. "The Honorable the CONVENTION of the United States" was an "august" gathering.[46] "The Grand Federal Convention" was composed of "men distinguished for their wisdom and patriotism" who, when it came to creating governments, were "our great MASTER-BUILDERS."[47] "Such a body of enlightened and honest men [had] perhaps never before met for political purposes, in any country upon the face of the earth." Lucky was the Union to have such "a chosen band of patriots and heroes, arresting the progress of American anarchy."[48] It was thus little wonder that a Massachusetts writer lionized these "ILLUSTRIOUS SAGES!" as "a band of Patriots and Philosophers, who would have adorned the history of Greece and Rome, in their most brilliant æras."[49]

The delegates were, then, enlightened, patriotic philosophers. Equally important, according to commentators, they were *unified*. That message, which elaborated upon the theme developed in the damage-control period of late June, was presented with greater regularity and force from July through August. On July 26, while carefully noting that delegate Roger Sherman did not give them particulars about the convention's proceedings, the publishers of the *New Haven Gazette* clearly implied that Sherman had told them that remarkable "unanimity" prevailed at the convention.[50] Quickly thereafter what was probably a single report on unanimity became three different and widely reprinted stories. "An American," published in the *Massachusetts Centinel* on August 4, claimed that the delegates had "unanimously agreed on a system for the future government of the United States—which will speedily be laid before the several legislatures for their acceptance and ratification."[51] Three days later, the *Salem Mercury* reprinted the same statement almost verbatim but without attribution.[52] Then on August 28, the Springfield, Massachusetts, *Hampshire Chronicle* also printed virtually the same thing and attributed it to convention delegate Caleb Strong of Massachusetts.[53] Perhaps all three reports flowed from Strong's words. The important point is: the claim that the delegates had unanimously agreed to a plan of government appeared in forty-seven publications between August 4 and the time the Constitution was made public.[54]

The idea that unanimity prevailed in the convention was supported as well by the popular account that said the delegates had never once thought of introducing a monarchy and by the fact that authors often used phrases such as "the united wisdom" of the delegates. On August 6, Edward Powars, publisher of the Boston *American Herald*, formulated a new way to support the unity claim. He asserted that "the profound secrecy" the delegates had assiduously followed was "a happy omen." "It demonstrates," he maintained, "that the spirit of party, on any great and essential point, cannot have arisen to any height."[55]

Convention boosters continued to urge the people to trust the delegates. As the anticipated completion of the convention drew near, the number and ardor of such pieces increased, and the message changed. Now, trusting the delegates became the patriotic thing to do. Early in the period, on July 25, editor Dallas of the *Pennsylvania Herald* made the point by proclaiming that the convention's plan would be well suited to the needs of the people.[56] Three days later, he presented what soon became a basic press theme. He expressed his hope that, because of "the universal confidence" Americans had in the delegates, "the minds of the people throughout the United States are prepared to receive with respect, and to try with a fortitude and perseverance, the plan which will be offered to them by men distinguished for their wisdom and patriotism." Dallas's endorsement proved extraordinarily popular with other editors.[57]

In early August, the press continued to bristle with widely reprinted appeals to act patriotically by trusting the delegates. A New Yorker, published in Philadelphia, said his state had placed its hopes in the convention to check the evils of anarchy and division.[58] The writer An American noted that the people did not yet know what the convention would recommend. Still, considering the delegates, there could be no doubt that their proposed government would be "founded on justice and equity—in which the rights of the citizens, and of the rulers, would be properly *ballanced*."[59]

Proconvention rhetoric escalated to the point where very widely reprinted authors moved from insisting the people *should* support the delegates' recommendations to saying they *did* support them. A *Pennsylvania Gazette* author used this approach in an August 8 essay which, unintentionally no doubt, demonstrated real insight into the selling of the convention. He claimed the American people were not *"half so well prepared"* to accept the 1775 resolutions of Congress or the Declaration of Independence in 1776 "as they are *now* for a vigorous fœderal government."[60] In his stridently proconvention issue of August 22, Oswald claimed that letters and private accounts from most of Pennsylvania's counties revealed that the people of all political parties were "prepared and disposed to receive" the convention's new government. The people it seemed mirrored the delegates; they were unified in support of what Oswald called "the national government to be elected under the new constitution."[61] An even more widely reprinted writer, published in the similarly ardent proconvention *Pennsylvania Gazette* issue of August 22, expected the delegates' recommendations to receive a cordial reception on an even wider front, and for that the American people could take a bow. What the writer described as "the general determination" of all classes to accept the government that the convention was then framing indicated "the degrees of order and good sense in the Americans, that have seldom appeared in other countries." This praise of Americans also, and not incidentally, championed the idea of trusting the delegates.[62]

As they intensified their glorification of the delegates and their calls for accepting what the delegates produced, authors also stressed the many dangers confronting the Union. Continuing what had long been its pattern, the press emphasized that the greatest danger lay in the possibilities of internal division and violence, particularly in frontier regions. The fear of foreign, especially British, involvement was stated explicitly or lurked between the lines. Yet in this period some writers broke new ground by suggesting that the potential for internal dissension was decreasing.

A New York paper of July 26 reported that robberies perpetrated by Shays's followers had destroyed his popularity.[63] On August 6, a Massachusetts editor observed that almost perfect peace had been restored in the state that had spawned Shays's Rebellion.[64] Soon thereafter the *Worcester Magazine* implied that Shays had abandoned the idea of renewing his rebellion.[65] Another reassuring item appeared in mid-August when a writer claimed that the spirit of Shaysism was rapidly subsiding in the East and that Shays himself had virtually no companions.[66] Press authors, however, were not discarding the claim that internal division and violence might inflict mortal wounds on the Union, they merely shifted their focus. By late July, writers were highlighting the potentially lethal problems stemming from foreign intrigue and the concerns of the remote frontier areas.

The desire to emphasize the danger of foreign intrigues led some elements of the press to inventive chicanery. In early August Baltimore's *Palladium of Freedom* carried an item any discriminating reader would have branded a fabrication. Publishers Maurice Murphy and Richard Bowen printed a letter supposedly written in late June at Halifax, Nova Scotia. It came from a person who wanted to foster Canadian, not American, interests. He confirmed that, as previously reported, the Canadian garrisons were being reinforced. Moreover, thousands of British troops mustered out in Canada at the end of the Revolutionary War found working their poor lands so uninviting that they ardently sought combat. Unless quick action occurred, these forces would obliterate America. Lest anyone miss how all this related to the convention, the author chuckled at the weakness of America's federal government but also said: "by the first opportunity, let me know what your Grand Convention are about." Although the writer admonished his correspondent to safeguard the letter, it purportedly came to the editors by way of a person who just happened to find it lying on "Cheapside Wharf." Despite being an obvious invention, the warning about Canadians thirsting after American land became a popular reprint.[67]

Murphy and Bowen's "Cheapside Wharf" missive probably did not convince many readers that violence would be visited upon the Union unless reform occurred. They and many others were, however, soon confronted with a very widely reprinted letter that appeared authentic and starkly described frightful possibilities. The letter, written by John Sullivan from the frontier of the Creek Nation in Georgia, was addressed to the Spanish minister in New York. Identifying himself as a former captain in the American army, Sullivan spoke ominously of a new drama in the West in which he would play a leading part. He claimed he could raise an army of fifty thousand Americans because westerners were so determined to defend their right to use the Mississippi River. These Americans would become a part of Spain or create a new western nation if that was required to guarantee use of the Mississippi. Sullivan's letter sounded a theme heard in the early convention days, but now it was put less ambiguously: if the Union could not secure the navigation of the Mississippi for the West, the West would secede.[68] Although Sullivan may have been engaging in self-serving puffery, the threats he articulated could not be dismissed as the isolated thoughts of a bold adventurer.[69]

A related account, a widely reprinted letter that appeared in the Charleston *Morning Post* in early August, described the situation in the West as having reached an important crisis. Quite possibly referring to Sullivan's comments, the writer talked of a well-known former Continental army officer now employed by various western governments. He was in Charleston buying large quantities of arms and ammunition. There was, the writer speculated, "certainly something a-brewing," quite possibly "a daring enterprise against New-Orleans." This author feared that westerners were ready to make war and would simply disregard any agreements between Congress and Spain if the arrangements denied them use of the Mississippi.[70]

These fresh pieces on the established themes of possible armed conflict or even secession gained additional force from the continued reprinting of earlier messages about other dangers that might destroy the Union. Thus, while some authors reported that Shaysism was dying out in its birthplace, other writers emphasized that the Union was yet in peril and that only a stronger government could save it.

Over time, the general press coverage had described economic woes as another reason why the Union needed a more energetic government. Here too the theme was modified. Commentary on economic problems typically had appeared in general discussions of political issues. But when writers referred to economic issues in late July and August, they were more likely to infuse them with calls for patriotism and assertions that glory awaited America if the people embraced the proper reforms. Given the Union's needs *and* opportunities, according to the new standard message, it was imperative to accept what the sagacious delegates of the convention recommended—even though one did not yet know exactly what those recommendations would be. This message was presented repeatedly, often with little pretense at subtlety.

Alexander Dallas, in a July 28 piece that did not mention the convention, was clearly talking about issues pertinent to it when he gave a rather upbeat assessment of America's economy and government. Having observed that many European governments liked to laugh about the numerous vexing problems confronting the United States and its citizens, Dallas retorted by producing solid examples showing that the governments and citizens of France, Russia, Portugal, Great Britain, and Holland had their own problems. This led him to ask: "Which then, of these nations can boast superior happiness?" Americans should, in fact, be pleased with what they had accomplished. More important, let Americans "anticipate the future, and they will find that their prosperity and honor depend upon themselves." Dallas, who regularly advocated strengthening the Confederation government, clearly struck a responsive chord when he defended America against the ridicule of the haughty Europeans. Twenty publishers decided to share his analysis with their readers.[71]

As August opened and moved toward the anticipated disclosure of the convention's plan, buoyant and campaign-like comments about a potentially bright future appeared frequently in widely reprinted pieces. Publications that

appeared during the first week of August revealed the tendencies. A *Pennsylvania Gazette* correspondent proclaimed
that "all our hopes and wishes of national glory and prosperity" were nearer fulfillment than ever before—provided
America adopted the means of obtaining them. He declared
that only an efficient federal government could stop oppressive taxation and fulfill those hopes and wishes.[72] While con-
ceding that the Union faced problems, another author maintained the country had "every advantage that nature can
bestow to make it Great." All that the people need do to
claim greatness was to accept the delegates' recommendations. A Boston *American Herald* author concurred. If the
people accepted the convention's proposals, America would
find "power, glory, peace and safety."[73]

During the middle two weeks of August, authors who
stressed America's potential as well as its problems amplified
their efforts to promote the convention's as yet unpublished
proposals. A correspondent of the *New York Journal* created
a typesetter's nightmare when he gushed about "the important epocha from which the several states will be dated; this
[is] the *trying season* for PATRIOTISM; this the time of *new birth*
to GLORY and EMPIRE, or of *ignominious death* to SLAVERY and
her vital companion, NATIONAL INFAMY." America could attain
"the gift of HONORABLE EMPIRE!" Indeed, "should *patriotism* and *unanimity* reign triumphant, 'the wilderness would
blossom like the rose, and deserts become fruitful fields;' justice would run down our streets like a river, and judgment
as a mighty stream."[74] A popular Philadelphia author put the
issue more succinctly. Once the Union adopted the new federal government that the convention would offer, "America
will be the delight of her friends and citizens, and the envy,
admiration and example of the whole world."[75]

In mid-August a very widely reprinted *Pennsylvania
Gazette* correspondent presented a religious analogy to
assert that the future could be bright, if past errors were
recognized. Even though the convention was never mentioned, the analogy nurtured the idea of accepting the delegates' plan. Comparing the individual states to the prodigal

son, the writer saw them returning, sick and indebted, to their father's house. Most readers, it seems sure, caught the reference to Washington in the statement: "Their Father no sooner beheld signs of distress and contrition among them, than he opened his arms, to take them a second time under his protection." The support for the convention was implicit when the author expressed his hope that joy would soon resound throughout the land "since the States that were lost and dead are now found and made alive, in a vigorous, efficient, national government."[76]

The argument that the convention could both redeem America and somehow unleash its great potential had appeared in the press before. Calls to support the convention by tapping a sense of patriotism had also been expressed before. But increasingly from late July through August, hyperbolic essays carried these points to new heights. The feeling that a time of decision was drawing near permeates the articles; they evoke a sense of excitement two centuries after the fact. The increasingly ardent stress on deferring to the delegates' wisdom was accompanied by direct appeals to specific groups to embrace the stronger government it seemed certain the convention was producing. This occasionally had been done before, as in the widely reprinted Harrington essay, but in late August, with the convention about to complete its work, a spate of these appeals appeared. Their authors emphasized economic considerations more than at any time since the convention had been authorized.

Several widely reprinted efforts gave special attention to manufacturing and shipbuilding. A writer who proclaimed that agriculture and manufacturing provided the means to attain national wealth, happiness, and independence also said those two branches of the economy needed an effective government to prosper. The description of Washington's interest in iron furnaces implied that manufacturers could expect the convention's proposed government to demonstrate sensitivity to their needs. Alexander Dallas offered another practical reason to support change when he reported that America's shipbuilding industry was in a state of decay and especially so in New York, where only one small hull was on the stocks. Dallas clearly alluded to the convention as he expressed hope that shipbuilding and all manufacturing would soon be revived by an efficient central government.[77]

The *Pennsylvania Gazette* of August 8 presented a writer who also focused on economic matters, and he employed a tone and arguments that mocked the states. Railing against the cost of the "little army of rulers" who occupied state executive and legislative offices, he advocated adopting what he claimed would be the frugal government recommended by the convention. Turning to the question of political talent and sound laws, he asserted that the folly of some constitutions and laws could be traced to America having two thousand state legislators. Having so many legislators caused problems because "their wisdom decreases in proportion as their numbers increase." Accepting what he called "the simple, frugal and wise" government the delegates were constructing thus made sense on several counts. It would reduce the cost of government while giving America greater world stature. Embracing the convention's proposals would allow America to pay its debts by imposts and excises without having to resort to unequal and oppressive land taxes that were so injurious to agriculture. Moreover, adopting the delegates' recommendations "will extinguish state parties, which are so detrimental to social happiness." How all this would come about was not explained. What was made clear was that these and the other specific benefits would come only with acceptance of the government framed by the convention. The fact that the essay amounted to little more than wild speculation did not stop editors from reprinting it widely.[78]

The two popular *Independent Gazetteer* authors of August 22 who stressed that the delegates were creating a new government specified the benefits that would accrue when the change occurred. They too reflected the increased emphasis being placed on economic considerations. One author focused on the knotty problem of debts and maintained that paying the national debt would be one of the new national government's first actions. There was no attempt at indirection or subtlety in the pure campaign-style appeal: "Every holder of a public security of any kind is, therefore, deeply interested in the cordial reception, and speedy establishment of a vigorous continental government." This political hard-sell artist also evinced state pride with the questionable observation that "it is remarkable that Pennsylvania has in every great measure, set an example of a federal disposition to all the states."[79] The other writer, described as a correspondent, claimed private letters from Europe revealed that thousands of Europeans would immediately embark for America—if the United States adopted the new federal government. These would be desirable immigrants: rich merchants from Holland and whole colonies of German and Irish farmers would come; industrious English and Scottish artisans and manufacturers would fill America's towns and cities.[80] Nothing less than "the liberties, safety, population, and glory of our country" rested on the adoption of a national government.[81]

On August 29, the *Pennsylvania Gazette* published two popular essays that provided an appropriate close to the month of anxiously awaiting presentation of the delegates' plan. One author focused on practical economic benefits. He dramatically proclaimed that "the pulse of industry, ingenuity and enterprise, in every art and occupation of man, now stands still in the United States" in anticipation of receiving the convention's work. Every hope and wish was with "the present august national Convention." As with other convention boosters, he did not let a minor thing like ignorance of the delegates' plans stop him from heaping speculation upon speculation as he implied that accepting the convention's recommendations would shower benefits on various interest groups. He predicted that a new national government would assist the states in building roads and canals as well as making other needed improvements. Merchants and manufacturers would get uniform national commercial regulations. The emission of paper money would stop. Public creditors had reason to hope that an enlightened and stable national government would save them. A national system of taxation would be better and fairer. Under that system, wealthy farmers could buy land without fear that state taxes might destroy them. Poor farmers and tenants who wanted to seek their fortune on the frontier would gain a national military force to protect them from Indians. In sum, the convention's national government would offer solid material benefits to all free white men.[82]

The second *Gazette* author took a different tack. Although he too emphasized that the Union required a new effective central government, he focused on social rather than economic issues. In his view, America's weak governments had produced idleness and licentiousness that, like a deluge, threatened "to wash away all the remaining religion and morality of our country." To stem that flood, just and free governments that favored morality must be upheld. Good men had a duty to submit to such governments and therefore ministers of the Gospel had a duty "to inculcate submission to the powers which are to arise out of ourselves." On the issue of supporting the delegates, this author obviously did not believe in the separation of church and state.[83]

In late July and especially in August, press coverage of the convention thus often resembled campaign literature designed to prepare the people to accept whatever the delegates recommended. It became easier to advance that argument once reports indicated the delegates shunned the very thought of a king. Increasingly as it seemed the delegates' plan would appear any day, essayists said the people, the masses, *were* indeed prepared to support the new government soon to be unveiled. It was not that simple. As Alexander Hamilton's attack on Governor Clinton made clear, some Americans would oppose the convention's proposals. Still, what another New Yorker said in mid-June remained true: those who might question the need for a more vigorous government or the work of the convention essentially had fallen silent. Considering items first published from the last week in July through mid-August, one looks in vain for direct challenges to the convention's rumored efforts to produce a strong new government.[84] When authors finally voiced such thoughts, they rarely were reprinted. That was not surprising. As the fate of the *Columbian Herald* items illustrates, publishers at times even refused to reprint newsworthy items that might depict the convention unfavorably.

The closest any authors came in August to questioning the need for a stronger government occurred in denunciations of John Adams's *Defence of the Constitutions.* Here too the language sharpened as older themes underwent refinement. However, authors typically plied the safe course of attacking aristocratic and monarchical ideas without mentioning the convention. After the people read that the delegates had never even thought of creating a monarchy, writers who attacked Adams probably were not seen as threats to the delegates. Thus, the work of such authors could be reprinted safely by the staunchest prochange, proconvention publishers. On August 15 a Virginia writer, in what became a popular reprint, warned Americans that Adams's ideas could "prove an eternal ulcer on the body politic of this country."[85] Two weeks later in an item reprinted seven times, a Marylander savaged Adams's reference to the wellborn. Four mordant paragraphs suggested that, when Adams talked of the wellborn, he bowed, scraped, and paid homage to "the shrivelled, tasteless fruit of an old genealogical tree."[86] Such arguments urged people to oppose any government that reflected the ideas advanced in the *Defence.* The anti-Adams writers, however, did not reject the call for a stronger government, nor did they claim that the delegates shared Adams's views.

Only after mid-August did any writers express even limited anxiety about simply accepting the delegates' work. The author of an offbeat, yet popular, essay printed in the staunchly proconvention *Pennsylvania Gazette* went as far as anyone in openly qualifying the idea of trusting the delegates. He hoped they would not lessen the dignity or usefulness of their government "by any imprudent accommodation to the present temper or prejudices of the uninformed part of the community." Only the wise and good could be depended upon to support the convention's efforts. Accordingly, those men "ought to be pleased—their principles ought to be consulted—or they cannot concur in establishing the new government." This author obviously wanted a vigorous government, but his observations challenged the well-developed image that all good, wise, and patriotic people would support the convention's plan. Nevertheless, his thoughts got reprinted almost a dozen times by early September.[87]

The first sustained effort to dampen convention-booster hype also came after mid-August. The antibooster writers, whose work exhibited the growing intensity common to articles written in August, at first railed against the press's slanted coverage. Then, late in the month, when the convention's recommendations were expected daily, significant efforts to challenge the convention appeared. As had long been the case, however, gaining wide circulation for those thoughts required skillful subtlety.

The author of an August 16 *United States Chronicle* essay opened the endeavor by denigrating press coverage of issues related to the delegates' work. He began by summarizing the basic points advanced in the press for strengthening the government and backing the convention. Newspapers from New Hampshire to Georgia, he argued, had been filled with subversive paragraphs about evils supposedly arising from America's republican forms of government. The author then described what an intelligent foreigner would conclude about the United States if he relied only on newspapers published in the preceding two years. "He would conceive us to be a poor, miserable, distracted People, distressed and suffering almost of the Necessaries of Life—without Order or Government—in Anarchy and Confusion." But that was, said the author, manifestly untrue. The alleged evils either did not exist or were caused by something other than the nature of republican government. The writer pleaded with the press to correct misconceptions and to exercise better judgment about what it printed. Scurrilous pieces, filled with personal invective, should no longer find a publisher. Editors should, in addition, accentuate the good in America; they should reject essays that brought America into contempt. The essayist did not mention the convention and, as a Rhode Islander, he could be accused of focusing on press comment about his state. Nevertheless, he spoke of the situation throughout the Union, and he unflinchingly said the press's depiction of a dangerous time of troubles created a false image. Moreover, his words could easily be construed as saying that a major overhaul of government was unnecessary. This challenge to the selling of the convention managed to get republished twice in Boston and once in Philadelphia, major reprint centers. Despite that fact, it was not reprinted anywhere else in the Union. Virtually all editors wanted nothing to do with an essay that criticized their coverage and that might, even if indirectly, challenge the notion of accepting whatever the convention recommended.[88]

A *Pennsylvania Packet* essayist who openly attacked the press fared better on the reprint circuit, probably because he combined a moderate tone with phrasing that called forth vaunted American revolutionary principles. Yes, he said, in a pure republican government all power flowed from the people; however, the necessary purposes of government required that some men be vested with power and authority. Still, considering the frailty of human nature, the people must strictly guard and limit the power they bequeathed. Indeed, the failure to place essential checks and restraints on governors explained why the vast majority of people lived as "tyrants or slaves, oppressors or oppressed." Echoing established ideals championed in the struggle for independence, in words perhaps none would dare doubt publicly, the author proclaimed: "Let America for ever boast, that her subjects freely and fully enjoy liberty and property and all those natural rights which God and nature assigned to them." The word "convention" did not appear in the essay, and in many ways it reflected views commonly enunciated by convention boosters.[89] But, the emphasis on the danger from rulers, not weak government, challenged the effort to convince people to approve anything the convention recommended short of monarchy. This essayist, who foreshadowed arguments Antifederalists used, demonstrated that the proconvention forces did not have a monopoly on clever penmen. His piece was short and first appeared in a major newspaper from which editors often borrowed material. These attributes significantly increased its chances for reprinting. Although the essay did not gain popularity, it proved relatively successful. Two other Philadelphia papers, both outlets for those championing democratic ideals, published it as did two New York and two Virginia papers.[90]

On August 17 Eleazer Oswald published "Meanwell," either a misguided proconvention piece or, more likely, a crafty dissenter effort. Meanwell praised the delegates effusively and proclaimed that all honest men agreed that America's future depended on them. He also recommended that, rather than dissolve the convention once it issued its proposals, the delegates should "adjourn to meet again, if need be, at some future period." By doing this, the delegates could reconvene quickly if any state proved so silly as to reject their recommendations. A good foundation would then exist, said Meanwell, for uniting the states that had approved the recommendations into a confederation with George Washington at its head. In that event, states that had rejected the convention's proposals might reconsider and join the new confederation. Meanwell claimed, but did not explain how, other advantages would flow from adopting the adjournment strategy. In an important way, his observations fit neatly with a view often articulated in the press: Rhode Island should be cast aside rather than be allowed to scuttle reform. However, merely adjourning the convention went against the strategy touted in the press, which said the delegates' recommendations must be accepted. By adjourning rather than dissolving the convention, the delegates would signal that they expected to have to revise their handiwork. This subversive idea slipped past editor Oswald, but it did the dissenters little good. Only the publisher of the New York *Daily Advertiser* chose to reprint Meanwell.[91]

"Z" came at the convention more directly in his *Freeman's Journal* essay published on August 22, a popular day for convention pieces.[92] While agreeing that Americans eagerly looked to the convention for relief from the embarrassing distress confronting them, he denounced what he called the local junto that was so committed to its own narrow political program that it had appointed a non-Pennsylvanian, while keeping Benjamin Franklin off the Pennsylvania delegation.[93] The belated addition of Franklin as a delegate only partially alleviated what "Z" described as the insult to "this country" of Pennsylvania. He then sarcastically observed that, if the delegates recommended something "a little unpalatable," the good people of Pennsylvania would surely not mind once they thought about how fully they had been represented at the convention. This biting essay was rather lengthy, much of it had a local focus, and it went against the typical proconvention publications that dominated the press. Not surprisingly, it also went unreprinted.

In contrast to "Z," a correspondent whose essay appeared in the next issue of the *Freeman's Journal* showed what could be done when qualms were carefully packaged. This August 29 production is the one challenge to the convention published in the period that became a popular reprint.[94] "It is laughable," the author began, "to observe the strange whims and ideas of people in respect to the Grand Convention and their proceedings. It is taken for granted by the generality that something is accidentally wrong with our political machine, which a little skill and contrivance may at once put to right by the magic of a few resolves upon paper." But "the evils and confusions we experience have originated in great measure with the people themselves, and by them only can be eventually rectified." The heart of the piece elaborated on what individuals had to do to reform. They must eschew foreign luxuries and be frugal; they must give close attention to agriculture while supporting home manufacturing; only by embracing "a spirit of union and national sobriety" could they place America "in the respectable rank of rich and flourishing nations." The author added that, while all Americans panted for that result, few seemed willing to pursue it actively. Blaming the people for bringing troubles upon themselves and combining that criticism with a call for personal reformation was a popular literary form.[95] Questioning the ability of the convention to reform government was not. The suggestion that the Union's political system might be basically sound was equally unfashionable and anathema to many in the press. Thus, the author's use of the established jeremiad genre and his surreptitious phrasing probably account for the author's popularity.

Convention boosters were horrified. Because the *Freeman's Journal* author adroitly undermined important points developed in the selling of the convention and because his essay was being reprinted, reaction came swiftly. In early September, three writers attacked him because, in their estimation, he denigrated the need for an effective new federal government. They also alerted proconvention editors to the danger of reprinting the piece.[96]

Considering widely reprinted material, the August press coverage belonged to the proconvention forces. Nevertheless, as in the past, convention boosters still took no chances. They worked diligently to silence potential opponents. Part of their endeavor included developing a rather uniform picture of those who might undermine the convention's efforts to strengthen the Union. The following description of those who were supposedly "antifederal" comes from articles published during the first three weeks of August. The popularity of the assessments is demonstrated by the fact that each one got reprinted at least fifteen times. Those who would reject the work of the convention were portrayed as "enemies to the prosperity of our infant empire" who would create "a painful anticipation of anarchy and confusion."[97] It was the "timid, or perhaps *interested* politicians," men moved by "self-interest and faction," who would comprise the opposition to the delegates' good efforts. The factions would consist of "salary and perquisite men" from the state governments.[98] Driven by "selfish or party purposes," these evil men were greater enemies to America than monarchists like Thomas Hutchinson or traitors like Benedict Arnold.[99] An immensely popular August 22 *Pennsylvania Gazette* author summed up the basic view: only "tyrants and official pensioners" would criticize the convention's plan for governmental reform.[100] These unflattering depictions contained a significant admission. More than ever before, numerous authors conceded and even emphasized that the delegates' recommendations would come under fire. As a *Pennsylvania Gazette* correspondent phrased it on August 29, it would not be surprising "if a few ignorant people, headed by interested and designing men should oppose the new federal government."[101]

Convention boosters did more than describe the enemy. Some urged "antifederal" thinkers to change their minds or at least to keep their thoughts to themselves. A New Yorker, whose thoughts appeared in the *Pennsylvania Herald* on August 1, illustrated the fundamental message when he addressed "anti-fœderal" people. At this critical moment, dogmatic commitments must, he argued, yield "to the passions and exigencies of the country." Anyone who would speak against accepting the delegates' proposals did not understand the needs or feelings of Americans. Those with influence, therefore, should be cautious about what they thought and said.[102] On August 6 a writer in the Boston *American Herald* also warned "antifederal" thinkers to keep quiet. They had to realize that the new constitution the national convention would soon present simply must be accepted. Denouncing "the little, mean jealousy" that had plagued America, the writer threatened that anyone who tried to stop necessary reforms "shall be stigmatized and dishonoured by the united execrations of the whole people."[103]

Barrages against those who might question the convention's work did not stop with admonishing the potential opposition to remain silent. Authors also typically exhorted Americans to oppose the selfish politicos and their minions who failed to heed the advice given by the proconvention forces. In his very popular August 4 essay, An American employed what had become the standard approach. He maintained that all ranks of citizens, except those steadfastly opposed to the prosperity of America's infant empire, backed the convention. The people should be on their guard because those enemies would, "under the mask of patriotism," artfully try to destroy America.[104] An American was harsh, but not as harsh as those who came after him.

As August progressed, the threats against anyone who might scorn the convention's recommendations became more prevalent and less circumspect. On August 7 a popular *New Hampshire Spy* author flatly asserted that some influential Rhode Islanders and New Yorkers opposed the convention and would employ every trick to overthrow the great plan being generated by the united wisdom of the delegates. Although he did not mention names, the writer asserted that those who uniformly had opposed reforming the government were well known. Mincing no words, he threatened: "It would be well for them to desist from their nefarious schemes. The united force of America is against them—The bolts of vengeance are forging—tremble ye workers of iniquity, and no longer oppose the *salvation* of your country, lest *speedy destruction* come upon you, and you fall into the pit which *your own hands* have digged."[105]

As a natural corollary of the August effort to denigrate and intimidate the "antifederal" opposition, writers kept hammering states that might reject what the delegates offered. The *Pennsylvania Herald* and *New Hampshire Spy* writers demonstrated that New York was being raked more than ever before.[106] However, Rhode Island retained top billing as the state truly opposed to strengthening the government and supporting the convention, and consequently it came under increasingly vicious attack. Of course, thrusts directed at the Ocean State cut at all who shared the Rogue's Islander view of government and reform.[107]

The assaults on Rhode Island mirrored the intensification of feeling displayed in August. Commentators had been saying that Rhode Island's intransigence would be overcome somehow, perhaps even by throwing it out of the Union. In August, those thoughts gave way to pronouncements that said, at least metaphorically, the state would die if it rejected the delegates' recommendations. Various essayists made the point ever more graphically as the anticipated unveiling of the convention's plans drew nearer. On August 2 a South Carolina author joked about Rhode Island being sold to the highest bidder to pay off the national debt. The punch line revealed the state's scant importance: a Georgia rice planter had discovered that his holdings were probably worth more than all of Rhode Island. This commentary got only six reprintings. When another southern gentleman slashed Rhode Island even more viciously in a piece published by the *Independent Gazetteer* on August 7, more than a score of publishers expeditiously reproduced his work.[108] Displaying a reverent excitement, the southerner announced that "the eyes of the whole continent are now cast on that respectable body, the Convention. The heart of every American, good or bad, must be interested in the result of their deliberations. It will either form a glorious epocha in the history of America, or, by doing nothing, leave the disease to the violent remedy of curing itself." It was, he declared, necessary to stop Rhode Island from blocking implementation of the delegates' proposals. In fact, whenever he thought of "that petty state," he contemplated having men with shovels and pickaxes rip it up and cast it into the sea. Apparently sure of the answer, he asked: "Do you think by such a measure the Union would suffer?" As the popularity of his message demonstrates, the southerner did not misjudge his audience.

A widely reprinted moral tale first published in two proconvention Philadelphia newspapers on August 22 went even further in predicting Rhode Island's doom if it resisted the delegates' plans. No names were used, but names were not necessary. The tale concerned a husband, his wife, and their thirteen sons. Upon arriving in America, they lived well in one large home until each son decided to build his own cabin. Troubles soon beset each son, and, in time, twelve of them petitioned the father and asked to return to the homestead. The father happily agreed. After first working together to repair and fortify the old house, the twelve returned home, and the reunited family enjoyed happiness and prosperity. The thirteenth son refused to rejoin the family. After living miserably by himself for three years in the woods, he "was found *hanging* by his garter to the limb of a tree near his cabin." The moral was clear.[109]

In the combative atmosphere of August, few publishers

showed reservations about reprinting items that implied Rhode Island would commit political suicide or be destroyed if it did not join the proconvention team.[110] Most editors, however, clearly put limits on how specific and how inflammatory essays could be. On August 8 the *Independent Gazetteer* carried a derogatory story about two Pennsylvania politicians, George Bryan and Jonathan Bayard Smith. They were well-known leaders of Pennsylvania's Constitutional Society, so named for its staunch support of the state's radically democratic constitution of 1776. The author charged Bryan and Smith with holding meetings at their homes to organize the distribution of prejudicial pamphlets designed to stop the adoption of the new federal government. Why would they do that? Well, said the writer, each man held a lucrative political office: Smith's yielded £2,000 a year; Bryan, who was related to Smith by marriage, received £600. They constituted, in sum, a "pampered, official family."[111] The author predicted their pamphleteering efforts, fortunately, would prove futile because most people who belonged to the Constitutional Society were "friendly to the present Convention, especially to its worthy and excellent head." This piece meshed nicely with general themes often seen in the press. As the author described it, here were state politicians opposing the convention for selfish reasons. Their little minds, he claimed, had become so clouded that they could not see that a majority of their own party supported the convention. Yet the piece got reprinted only once. John E. Smith, who sought to publish all shades of opinion, put it in his *Gazette of the State of Georgia* on September 13.

A ruder attack on a person accused of "antifederalism" appeared on August 18 when the *Massachusetts Centinel* published a short bit of poetry under the heading "Impromptu." The poet claimed that reading about Governor Clinton's *"insurgency* and *anti-federalism"* moved him to write. Why was it, he asked, that Clinton had lately moved to save a state by opposing Shays: because Clinton "hop'd . . . HIMSELF to wreck the *whole* THIRTEEN, Without *a partner* in the *Treason*." Only one newspaper reprinted this. On September 3 it graced the pages of Babcock and Claxton's avowedly proconvention *Northern Centinel*. As with the attack on Bryan and Smith, editors typically rejected authors who named names when they pilloried suspected "antifederalists."

Eleazer Oswald did not. It was no accident that unreprinted or minimally reprinted diatribes against possible opponents of the convention often first appeared in his *Independent Gazetteer*. It was one of the most virulently proconvention papers in the Union. Original material Oswald published about the convention was often reprinted. However, editors shunned some essays he printed in August. On August 16 Oswald published an author who said his comments stemmed from the report on Bryan and Smith. Wondering how men could oppose what they had not yet seen, he urged them to think about the fate of crown officers and Loyalists in the Revolution and bluntly warned them to stop opposing the convention. "Let us hear no more from you gentlemen on this head, or you may expect to wear a coat of TAR and FEATHERS." On August 23 the stridently proconvention New York *Daily Advertiser* became the only newspaper to reprint this chilling piece. The press would reprint items about Rhode Island's demise. It would reprint items about the united vengeance of the continent being directed against "antifederalists." It would even warn such people about being treated as the Loyalists had been. But, as illustrated by this and yet another Oswald publication, openly threatening specific individuals went too far.

On August 28 a correspondent, possibly the author of "Tar and Feathers," sent Oswald an essay that he published two days later. In scathing language, the correspondent denounced the essay by "Z" published in the *Freeman's Journal* on August 22. "Z" was charged with assaulting the convention and abusing some of its members in an effort to begin a campaign in Pennsylvania against the new government. He and his kind allegedly disapproved because they feared losing their lucrative offices when a less expensive government was introduced. The author menacingly warned that if they worked against reform, they would be acting "treasonably" and might live to regret it. "The spirit of the people is up, and if a coat of *tar and feathers* will not deter them from their seditious practices, they very possibly may meet with a HALTER." This climax to the increasingly hot rhetoric of August was also reprinted but once, and as with the "Tar and Feathers" piece, it appeared in Francis Childs's New York *Daily Advertiser*.[112] He was thus the only other editor who joined Oswald in openly sanctioning violence to sustain the delegates' work.

• • •

The press did not have to embrace violence to neutralize two of the three July articles that threatened the proconvention impression created by publishers. Alexander Hamilton's assault on Governor Clinton was not extensively reprinted until it seemed that the delegates' recommendations would soon appear. The *Fairfield Gazette* monarchy letter achieved only one reprinting. Moreover, the press countered the letter by depicting the convention as the instrument that could save America from the horrors of monarchy. When reports indicated the delegates would finish their work by late August, the press responded with an outpouring of proconvention material. In effect, the press geared up in anticipation of the release of the delegates' proposals. One could see it, especially in the newspapers issued in the last ten days of August.

When the convention failed to produce its recommendations as expected, tension increased as autumn approached. Convention boosters increasingly tightened that tension by employing ever more strident rhetoric as the press once again engaged in the kind of proconvention build up that made the August coverage so intense. But September was different because those dubbed "antifederal" became more combative and lashed out against the selling of the convention.

Notes to Chapter Four

1. The August 8 item, given in COC1: 125, was reprinted twenty-nine times by August 30.

2. Given in COC1: 136–38, with quotations from p. 136 and attribution to Hamilton (p. 141, n. 2) based on Harold C. Syrett, ed., *The Papers of Alexander Hamilton,* 27 vols. (New York: 1961–1987), 4: 248–49, n. 1. On reprintings, see n. 14 below.

3. To an extent, that may be what happened. Whether because of Hamilton's efforts or not, Clinton and his allies did not venture into print with strident defenses of Clinton or attacks on the proconvention arguments until early September when it was clear that those called "antifederalists" had to fight more vigorously or quit the field. See Chapter Five. Linda De Pauw, who emphasizes that Clinton did not take a public stand against the convention, presents a similar analysis of Hamilton's motives for producing the July 21 piece in her *The Eleventh Pillar: New York and the Federal Constitution* (Ithaca, 1966), 72–78.

4. This line of argument vindicates the Connecticut legislators who had maintained that sending delegates to the convention would become an argument for accepting what the convention did. See Chapter One.

5. Given in COC1: 172–74. On the Bishop of Osnaburg, see ibid., 171.

6. Quotations from COC1: 173, 173–74.

7. Given in COC1: 98; on reprintings, see n. 17 below.

8. The *Vermont Gazette* reprinting contained only very minor differences.

9. See COC1: CC51D–F.

10. From the context, it is not clear if the *Gazette* publishers were talking about the local area, the state, or a large section of New England.

11. Given in COC1: 174 as CC51B; twenty-eight reprintings occurred by September 22; another reprinting appeared in the December issue of the *American Museum.*

12. Given in COC1: 174 as CC51C; thirty-three reprintings appeared by September 22.

13. See the various COC1 reprintings of *Daily Advertiser* items.

14. The delay in the September printings was in at least two and possibly all three cases due to geographic location. Those reprintings occurred in the *Pittsburgh Gazette,* the *Vermont Gazette,* and the *New Hampshire Recorder.* There were eighteen reprintings in whole or part. Full reprintings occurred in the *Packet,* the *Hudson Weekly Gazette,* the *Maryland Gazette* cited above, and in seven other

papers published between August 11 and 29. Three papers published between August 21 and September 8 printed only the first three paragraphs, which means they omitted the numbered portions of the piece. The *Vermont Gazette* gave a significantly shortened version on September 3. The *Northern Centinel*, August 27, and the *New Hampshire Recorder*, September 11, blended parts of Hamilton's essay with a *Pennsylvania Herald* item of August 1 from a New Yorker given in COC1: 138.

15. Issue of July 28, given in COC1: 125, with seventeen reprintings by August 20. The names of the members of the Committee of Detail were reported, but their duties were not described.

16. *Pennsylvania Herald*, July 28, with quotation from COC1: 125, and see nn. 17, 57 below.

17. Twenty reprintings of the July 25 *Herald* report appeared by August 21. The *Independent Gazetteer* item was reprinted seventeen times by August 20. The July 28 *Herald* piece was reprinted thirty-six times by September 8.

18. As indicated by the many printings from them given in COC1, both the *Independent Gazetteer* and the *Herald* were popular sources of reprints. (For the period ending when the Philadelphia press published the Constitution, fourteen *Gazetteer* items and seventeen *Herald* items are reproduced in COC1.) Moreover, both the *Gazetteer* and the *Herald* were published in Philadelphia on the same day; therefore, most editors probably had their choice of which item to reprint.

19. Reprintings occurred in: *Connecticut Courant*, July 30; *Massachusetts Centinel* and Poughkeepsie *Country Journal*, August 1; New York *Daily Advertiser*, August 4; *Newport Mercury*, August 6; Portland, Maine, *Cumberland Gazette* and *United States Chronicle*, August 9. Thus, the information appeared in the following states: Conn. (2), N.Y. (2), R.I. (2), Mass. (2).

20. This interpretation is supported by how the press handled other reports of convention activities that could be traced directly to specific convention delegates. See n. 54 below.

21. Given in COC1: 179–80, with quotations from p. 179. The first reprinting occurred in the New York *Daily Advertiser*, August 13; seventeen reprintings appeared by September 12. All but one were full reprintings; the *Northern Centinel* cut the last section on limiting the importation of slaves. The omission is suggestive. All other commentators on the convention avoided the potentially

volatile subject of slavery. The propagandistic editors of the *Northern Centinel* may well have cut the reference to the slave trade to keep the issue from tainting the convention. The three late September reprintings were due to travel time. Of the seventeen reprintings, over a dozen occurred within three weeks of the original publication in the *Columbian Herald*. Counting all reprintings, the piece appeared first in N.Y., Mass., Md., N.H., Va., Conn., and then slightly later in N.J. and Pa. The New Jersey reprinting, listed as from an Albany source of August 23, not located, did not occur until September 11. The one Pennsylvania reprinting occurred in the *Carlisle Gazette*, September 12, and was listed as coming from an August 27 source. As indicated in COC1: 180, n. 1 to CC53, the letter writer basically piled error upon error. However, the comment about the slave trade, while turned around, suggests that the author may have possessed some knowledge of convention activities.

22. Compare, for example, his statement on duties with the Impost of 1781 and the Impost of 1783 as described in CDR, 140–41, 146–48 and E. James Ferguson, *The Power of the Purse: A History of American Public Finance, 1776–1790* (Chapel Hill, 1961), 116–17, 166–67, 221.

23. See n. 21 above.

24. The *Columbian Herald* item of August 2 also appeared in the *Gazette of the State of Georgia*, August 9, from which the quotations are taken. Since the letter was sent to Wilmington, the first printing probably occurred in a no longer available issue of the *Delaware Courant* or the *Delaware Gazette*. This possibility is also supported by the fact, as indicated in n. 25 below, that another August 9 *Columbian Herald* piece took two weeks to be reprinted in the *Gazette of the State of Georgia*. Certainly a reprinting time of one week for the August 2 item seems too quick. If the August 2 piece did first appear in a Delaware paper, that lessens the possibility that it was not widely reprinted because editors did not see it.

25. Given in COC1: 124–25, with the reprinting occurring in the *Gazette of the State of Georgia*, August 23.

26. This item, dated June 1 and probably written by Benjamin Rush, is given in COC1: 167–68.

27. See the *Independent Gazetteer*, June 23, for a reprinting of a Philadelphia letter first published in a Baltimore paper on June 19.

28. The *Massachusetts Centinel*, August 1, reprint carried no notation that the piece came from the *Columbian Herald*. The

Massachusetts Gazette reprinted it on August 3 and indicated it came from a Charleston source of July 16. The piece attained eleven more reprintings in the New England area by August 16. The *Georgia State Gazette* of Augusta, which reprinted it on August 11, said it came from a South Carolina source of July 5.

29. See n. 21 above.

30. See nn. 24, 25 above. Considering the availability of these items to northern publishers, in addition to the information given in n. 24 above, it is revealing that another *Columbian Herald* story from the August 2 issue was reprinted in New York on August 17. (On this reprinting, see n. 108 below.) Working on the same schedule, the August 9 *Herald* account about the delegates considering three plans could have been reprinted in New York by August 24. The Philadelphia *Evening Chronicle* of August 18 reprinted an item from a Charleston, South Carolina, source of August 6; so in that case the travel time for a reprint was just twelve days. Travel time varied, of course, but these illustrations come from the exact period in question. As indicated in n. 68 below, other examples also indicate that the normal travel time for reprints between Charleston and the major reprint centers of Philadelphia and New York was about eighteen days.

31. *Pennsylvania Herald*, August 15, given in COC1: 125, with thirty-three reprintings by September 22. Either because he did not know what the issue was, or because he did not want to suggest that the secrecy rule had been significantly breached, Dallas did not give any other details. In fact, the delegates discussed a number of issues on August 13. However, none of them was as divisive as the fight over the principle of one state, one vote. If Dallas did know what was discussed in the convention on August 13, he was probably referring to the debate about saying that only the House of Representatives could initiate bills to raise revenue. On the debates of August 13, see Farrand, *Records*, 1: 265–81.

32. See, for example, the Boston *American Herald* of August 6 (given in COC1: 185–86, and reprinted nine times by September 6) on the "national" convention producing a "new" federal constitution that would give the people "a new system"; the *Pennsylvania Gazette* of August 15 (given in COC1: 187, and reprinted twenty-four times by September 12, and then in the *Vermont Gazette*, October 15) on the convention creating "a VIGOROUS, EFFICIENT, NATIONAL GOVERNMENT"; the *Pennsylvania Gazette* of August 15 (reprinted

eleven times between August 16 and September 3) on the delegates establishing "the new government." On earlier hints about a new government, see Chapter Two, nn. 35–37, 93 and Chapter Three, n. 20.

33. The first essay, given in COC1: 189 as CC66, was reprinted twenty-nine times by September 20, and then in the *Vermont Journal*, October 22. The second essay, given in COC1: 189 as CC67, was reprinted twenty-nine times by September 11. While talking of a national government, this author also used the more common term, "federal government."

34. Reprinted fifteen times between August 25 and September 17. The commentator did not indicate what term he wanted to replace "Congress."

35. Issue of August 29, given in COC1: 191–92 as CC71, with nine reprintings by September 20; see n. 38 below for the second item.

36. See n. 32 above and n. 37 below.

37. See the August 1 *Pennsylvania Gazette* item, given in COC1: 182–83, with twenty-nine reprints by September 3, which described the need for "an efficient fœderal government" as a prerequisite for achieving America's "national glory and prosperity" (p. 183).

38. Issue of August 29, given in COC1: 191 as CC70, with thirteen reprintings by September 24; all the reprintings occurring before the relevant publication printed the Constitution.

39. See Chapter Two, n. 74.

40. Of course the failure to add the qualification did not mean a writer would endorse establishing a monarchy. As Alexander Hamilton, who liked monarchy, cogently noted, the American people would overwhelmingly oppose such a move. See Farrand, *Records*, 1: 282–93 and especially 288–89. On the general attitude toward monarchy, see Louise B. Dunbar, *A Study of "Monarchical" Tendencies in the United States from 1776 to 1801* (Urbana, 1922), especially 76–98.

41. Issue of August 16. His views were reprinted only seven times, but the reprintings occurred in five states and in Vermont. Given in COC1: 188 as CC64; the reprintings occurred in the states of Vt., N.H., Mass., N.J., Pa., and Va. by August 29.

42. Quotation from COC1: 139, and see n. 60 below.

43. The Valley Forge story appeared in both the *Pennsylvania Packet* and the *Pennsylvania Gazette* on August 1. Twenty-four papers reprinted it between August 3 and 30; the *Georgia State*

Gazette reprinted it on October 6. The *Packet* iron furnace story of August 4 was reprinted nineteen times between August 8 and September 22; all the reprintings occurred before the relevant publication printed the Constitution.

44. *Pennsylvania Gazette*, August 22, given in COC1: 189–90 as CC68, with quotation from p. 190; thirty-two reprintings occurred by September 17.

45. Alexander Hamilton self-servingly echoed Dallas's words in his unsigned piece of July 21 when Hamilton said the convention represented "the collective wisdom of the union." Quotation from COC1: 137.

46. The first quotation is from the *Independent Gazetteer*, July 28, given in COC1: 125, with seventeen reprintings by August 20; the second is from the *Pennsylvania Gazette*, August 22, given in COC1: 189, with thirty-two reprintings by September 17.

47. The first quotation is from the Springfield *Hampshire Chronicle*, August 28, with seventeen reprintings occurring from August 31 to September 14, and another appearing in the *Vermont Journal*, October 17; the second is from the *Pennsylvania Herald*, July 28, given in COC1: 125, with thirty-six reprintings by September 8; the third is from the *New Hampshire Spy*, August 7, given in COC1: 187, with fourteen reprintings by September 18.

48. Quotations from COC1: 190, and see n. 44 above.

49. Boston *American Herald*, August 6, given in COC1: 185–86, with quotations from pp. 186, 185; nine reprintings occurred by September 6.

50. Issue of July 26. On the low number of reprints, only seven between July 30 and August 9, see n. 54 below.

51. Given in COC1: 184–85, with nineteen reprintings by September 11.

52. The printer of the *Mercury* frequently lifted material silently. This item from the August 7 issue is given in COC1: 186–87, with quotation from p. 186. Eight reprintings appeared by August 30.

53. The exact statement was that the delegates "have unanimously agreed on a system for the future government of the United States, which will speedily be laid before the several legislatures, for their acceptance and ratification." This item was reprinted seventeen times by September 14, and in the *Vermont Journal* of October 17.

54. The total is based on the printings listed in the preceding notes. It is suggestive that the two July 26 stories clearly based on

the comments of convention delegates were not widely reprinted and that the two popular early August items possibly based on material supplied by delegate Strong did not indicate he may have supplied the information. The *Hampshire Chronicle* August 28 piece was the first convention piece that both openly indicated the source of information was a delegate and also gained reprint popularity. Thus, in late July and for most of August, many editors seemed to work to avoid attributing even general comments about the convention to specific delegates. Doing this continued support for the claim that the delegates were steadfastly following the secrecy rule. This pattern was only broken when it seemed that the point was no longer vital since the convention's recommendations were expected momentarily. (Although the August 18 story about the delegates never thinking of creating a monarchy was not attributed to a specific delegate, that account clearly implied that convention delegates had broken their secrecy pledge. But, as indicated in the text, this was a special case.)

55. Given in COC1: 185, with nine reprintings occurring by September 6. In addition to its initial appearance in Mass., it was reprinted in R.I., N.Y., Pa., Md., Va., and S.C.

56. *Pennsylvania Herald*, July 25, given in COC1: 98, with twenty reprintings by August 21.

57. *Pennsylvania Herald*, July 28, given in COC1: 125, with thirty-six reprintings by September 8.

58. From *Pennsylvania Herald*, August 1, given in COC1: 138, with fifteen reprintings by September 3.

59. The quotation is from COC1: 185, and see n. 51 above.

60. Given in COC1: 138–39, with quotation from p. 139; sixteen reprintings occurred by September 4.

61. *Independent Gazetteer*, August 22, given in COC1: 189 as CC67, with twenty-nine reprintings by September 11.

62. Given in COC1: 190, with thirty-two reprintings by September 17.

63. *New York Journal*, July 26, with eight reprintings between July 30 and August 20.

64. *American Herald*, August 6, given in COC1: 185–86, with quotation from p. 185; nine reprintings occurred by September 6.

65. The issue of the second week of August carried this report: "A letter from Vermont says, 'General Shays has given out, that he intends returning to his seat in Pelham the ensuing fall—*let what will*

be the consequence.' " Nine reprintings occurred between August 14 and 30.

66. *Pennsylvania Herald*, August 18, with fourteen reprintings between August 20 and September 13. The author's cheerful commentary was somewhat tempered by the observation that Shays had eluded capture despite the handsome price put on his head. This fact reminded the author of the story about a poor man whose loyalty to the Young Pretender was such that he had shunned a £30,000 reward rather than betray Prince Charles after the battle of Culloden. The illustration raised the possibility that Daniel Shays or Shaysites might threaten America in the future just as Charles and his supporters had threatened England. On the importance of the reference to the Young Pretender, see Basil Williams, *The Whig Supremacy, 1714–1760*, rev. ed. (Oxford, 1952), 238–46, 255.

67. The attribution is based on the reprinting in the *Pennsylvania Packet*, August 13. The *Palladium of Freedom*, a daily, began publication on August 1, and the only extant issue is that of August 8. The first printing probably appeared shortly before the *Packet* reprinting on August 13. Nine reprintings occurred between August 13 and September 22.

68. According to the Charleston *Columbian Herald*, August 6, the letter first appeared in the no longer available *Charleston Morning Post*, July 30. The letter began its major period of circulation once it surfaced in both Philadelphia and New York on August 17. After that, the Sullivan letter was quickly and widely reprinted; it appeared in a total of twenty-one publications by early September. The quotations come from the August 17 *Independent Gazetteer* reprinting. Nineteen reprintings occurred between August 6 and September 6; almost surely due to geographic considerations, two much later reprintings occurred in the *Vermont Journal*, October 1, and the *Kentucke Gazette*, November 10. Since the item appeared in both Philadelphia and New York papers on August 17, this example also suggests, as do those given above in nn. 24, 25, 28, and 30 above, that the normal travel time for reprints between Charleston and those major reprint centers was about eighteen days.

69. The letter was authentic. See, *The Diplomatic Correspondence of the United States of America . . . [1783 to] 1789*, 6 vols. (Washington, D.C., 1833), 6: 234–40.

70. Attribution based on *New York Morning Post*, August 21, whose publisher said it came from the Charleston paper but who did not give a date for that publication. The same information appeared

in the *Independent Gazetteer* of August 25. The dating of early August is based on a reprint travel time of about eighteen days as indicated in n. 68 above. Twelve reprintings occurred between August 21 and September 12; the *Virginia Gazette and Weekly Advertiser* reprinted it on October 11.

71. *Pennsylvania Herald*, July 28, given in COC1: 182, with twenty reprintings between July 30 and August 29; the *New Hampshire Gazette* reprinted it on October 13. Although the essay can be read as offering support for the existing government, such a reading seems to twist Dallas's intent, and he certainly did not imply that he was thinking about the convention, which was not even mentioned in the publication. Moreover, as noted, Dallas had long made it adamantly clear that he supported the convention and the stronger, more vigorous government it was expected to produce. The popularity of the piece probably reflected both hope for the future and a desire to respond to the insults of haughty Europeans. A similar kind of response to the supposed laughter of former enemies contained in Halifax papers appeared in the *New York Journal* on August 2 and was reprinted nine times between August 4 and 23.

72. *Pennsylvania Gazette*, August 1, given in COC1: 182–83, with twenty-nine reprints, in whole or in part, by September 3.

73. On the first statement, from "An American," see n. 50 above. The *American Herald* item, from the August 6 issue, is given in COC1: 185–86; it was reprinted nine times by September 6.

74. *New York Journal*, August 16. Despite its eye-catching boldness, and perhaps because of it, this piece appeared only seven times by the end of August. Still, it was printed in nearly half of the states in the Union. See n. 41 above.

75. *Independent Gazetteer*, August 8, given in COC1: 138–39, with sixteen reprintings by September 4.

76. This August 15 *Pennsylvania Gazette* item is given in COC1: 187. Twenty-five reprintings occurred, but the *Vermont Journal* did not reprint it until October 15.

77. See n. 72 above and *Pennsylvania Herald*, August 22, with seven reprintings between August and September 11; a variant from the August 28 New York *Daily Advertiser* was reprinted four times between September 3 and 6.

78. *Pennsylvania Gazette*, August 8; reprinted eighteen times by August 30, and then in the *New Hampshire Gazette*, Decem-

ber 12. Although not reproduced in COC1, this material is part of CC40D (pp. 138–39). The section of the piece given in COC1 was reprinted sixteen times by September 4, and also in the *New Hampshire Gazette*, December 12. Twelve of the reprinting papers carried both sections; in nine of the twelve cases, both sections appeared in the same issue.

79. Quotation from CC67, given in COC1: 189, and see n. 33 above. On the questionable claim, see, e.g., Chapter Two, n. 31.

80. On the importance attached to the kind of immigrants America supposedly did and did not need, see John K. Alexander, *Render Them Submissive: Responses to Poverty in Philadelphia, 1760–1800* (Amherst, 1980), 16, 27.

81. Given in COC1: 189 as CC66, and see n. 33 above.

82. Given in COC1: 191 as CC70; thirteen reprintings occurred by September 24.

83. Given in COC1: 191–92 as CC71, with quotation from p. 192. Nine full or partial reprintings occurred in a total of six states by September 20.

84. As indicated in n. 71 above, the *Pennsylvania Herald* of July 28 did produce a popular item that might be construed as questioning the need for a change in the federal government but which almost surely was not intended to convey that message.

85. "Senex," *Virginia Independent Chronicle*, August 15, given in COC1: 89; ten reprintings appeared by September 24.

86. *Maryland Journal*, August 28, with seven reprintings between September 1 and 18.

87. Issue of August 15, with eleven reprintings between August 16 and September 3.

88. The reprintings occurred in the *Massachusetts Centinel*, August 22, the Boston *Independent Chronicle*, August 23, and the *Pennsylvania Journal*, September 5.

89. For example, compare Federalist No. 51 (CC503).

90. Issue of August 20, given in COC1: 188, with the six reprintings between August 21 and 30. The Philadelphia papers were the *Evening Chronicle*, which published material defending the radical Pennsylvania Constitution of 1776, and the *Freeman's Journal*, which became a leading Antifederalist newspaper.

91. The reprinting appeared in the August 23 issue. "Meanwell" pushed what came to be seen as an Antifederalist idea because, once the Constitution was published, the call for a second convention became an important rallying cry for those who opposed the new

plan of government. See Jackson Turner Main, *The Antifederalists: Critics of the Constitution 1781–1788* (Chapel Hill, 1961), especially 178, 189, 213, 227, 239, 285.

92. "Z" was probably the same "Z" who in May in the same paper supported holding the convention, but who was for only a limited extension of powers to Congress. See Chapter Two.

93. Delegate Gouverneur Morris, who represented New York in Congress 1778–1779 and who was defeated for re-election in late 1779, did not move to Philadelphia until 1780.

94. Given in COC1: 190 as CC69; it was reprinted twenty times by September 25. The September 5 reprinting in the *Pennsylvania Gazette* was linked to a response by "A distressed original public Creditor," which is analyzed in Chapter Five. A similar item from the *Maryland Journal,* August 28, was reprinted six times between September 1 and 27.

95. See, e.g, the *Pennsylvania Herald* author, published on August 29 and reprinted sixteen times between September 4 and 27, who discussed Shays's Rebellion, a massive fire, a destructive hurricane and concluded that "however we may be touched with pity for the affliction of brethren, we cannot but perceive how much it proceeds from their own misconduct."

96. This material is analyzed in Chapter Five

97. The first quotation is from the *Massachusetts Centinel,* August 4, given in COC1: 185, with eighteen reprintings by September 11; the second is from the *Pennsylvania Herald,* August 1, given in COC1: 138, with fifteen reprintings by September 3.

98. Quotations from *Pennsylvania Gazette,* August 8, given in COC1: 138, 139, with sixteen reprintings by September 4.

99. The original printing, in the *Independent Gazetteer* of August 22, given in COC1: 189, listed the great enemies as Hutchinson and Adams. Of the twenty-nine publishers who reprinted this piece between August 22 and September 20, only six joined the *Gazetteer* in naming Hutchinson and Adams; twelve printers used Hutchinson and Arnold; ten omitted the reference to specific individuals; the *Newport Herald,* September 13, used only Hutchinson's name. (The *Vermont Journal,* which did not reprint the piece until October 22, used Hutchinson and Arnold.) Most editors obviously found it perplexing that the author called Adams an enemy. The most plausible explanation is that Adams was being attacked as a lover of an aristocratic or even monarchical form of government. Thus the author may have referred to Adams to show dislike for those

forms of government. (On the views toward Adams, see COC1: 81–90.)

100. Quotation from COC1: 190, and see n. 47 above. A hard-hitting description from the *Salem Mercury*, August 7, reprinted nine times in six states between August 14 and 30, also had strong appeal. The author, who claimed the delegates had "unanimously" agreed upon a plan of government, said those who opposed that plan would be men "of illiberal sentiments, base and selfish views, and also of weak intellects." Quotation from COC1: 186.

101. Given in COC1: 191, with nine reprintings between September 1 and the third week in September.

102. Given in COC1: 138, with fifteen reprintings by September 3. This effort reflects the basic view presented in Hamilton's July 21 attack on Clinton.

103. Quotations from COC1: 185, 186; nine reprintings occurred by September 6.

104. Quotation from COC1: 185, and see n. 51 above.

105. Given in COC1: 187, with fourteen reprintings by September 18.

106. The New York *Daily Advertiser*, July 26, published "An Admirer of Anti-Fœderal Men" which, despite the title, was an attack on New Yorkers who might oppose the work of the convention. The author praised Washington and Franklin as men who would never do anything to dishonor themselves. The people, therefore, should accept the new government they were preparing, and if that government had any defects, alterations would be made. The author then denounced the actions of several "leading" and ambitious New Yorkers—"creatures to wealth and influence"—who supposedly aimed to scuttle the convention's work. By using "mean arts," such men sought to shake the people's faith in anything that was called federal. This essay had, surprisingly at first glance, very little appeal. Only three reprintings appeared, and the first did not occur until August 21 when "An Admirer" appeared in the Baltimore *Maryland Gazette*. Then the *Pennsylvania Packet* published it on August 23, and the propaganda editors of the *Northern Centinel* printed it on September 10. The delay, like the delay in the reprinting of Hamilton's attack on Clinton, might be partially attributable to a desire to keep alive the myth that, except for Rhode Islanders, virtually everyone supported the convention's work. The delay might in time have made the piece less desirable as a reprint. In addition, the title and format may have worked against the essay

being reprinted, but it could have been run without attribution. Perhaps some editors disliked the implication of class conflict evident in the comments on the wealthy and influential.

107. This is illustrated in the approach adopted by a writer published on August 16 in the *New York Journal*. He attempted to stave off any opposition to the convention's plans by reminding the states that Rhode Island had "become a derision and a bye-word! beware of a parallel fate! should either of you once be reduced to this *vile* comparison, like her you would be *despised*—like her *lose your virtuous sons.*" This effort only got seven reprintings by August 29.

108. The first item, an extract of a letter from Philadelphia, appeared in the *Columbian Herald*. The initial reprinting occurred in the New York *Daily Advertiser* on August 17, and it was reprinted five more times by September 5. The *Independent Gazetteer* item was an extract of an undated letter described as coming from one of the southernmost states. It was reprinted twenty-two times between August 8 and 30.

109. The item appeared in the *Pennsylvania Gazette* and the *Independent Gazetteer*. The quoted material comes from the *Gazette* printing. The twenty-two reprintings occurred between August 23 and September 17. On August 25 the *Providence Gazette* published a short article from a correspondent who suggested, indirectly of course, that the majority of the Rhode Island General Assembly could go to hell. This was reprinted nine times between September 3 and 18.

110. The moral tale that ended with Rhode Island found hanging from a tree was reprinted by at least six of the eight Philadelphia newspapers, but not by Bailey of the *Freeman's Journal*. This is yet another example of how he attempted to resist the efforts to sell the Constitutional Convention.

111. Bryan had long been a justice of the Pennsylvania Supreme Court. Smith held a judicial position in the Court of Common Pleas of the city and county of Philadelphia. See Merrill Jensen, ed., *Ratification of the Constitution by the States: Pennsylvania* (Madison, 1976), 727, 733.

112. The reprinting occurred on September 9. The suggestion that "Tar and Feathers" and "Halter" may have been the same person is based on the fact that both pieces were reportedly produced by someone living in the Northern Liberties section of Philadelphia.

5

"An Opposition Will Shew Itself":

Anticipating the Constitution

Although news media commentaries on the convention reached a peak in late August, straight news accounts of the delegates' actions were noticeably absent. The *Pennsylvania Herald* report of August 15 on a long debate held two days before was the last account of the convention published during August. As Americans waited, they grew testy. A Connecticut resident's observations, published in early September, seemed appropriate and became popular. He lamented that 1787 could accurately be called the year of discontent and apprehension, when every man played the politician and everyone became so cross that one could scarcely laugh without hurting someone's feelings. Concerns about Shays and the Union's commerce joined with an impatience to know what the grand convention was doing. That impatience, which had been building for more than two months, made citizens "no less snappish to each other."[1]

With few exceptions, the news media had over the months urged support—even blind support—for the convention. At least in public, however, publishers and editors would have rejected any suggestion that they were less than impartial.

They would have readily agreed with the sentiments of William Spotswood, publisher of the *Pennsylvania Herald*.[2] On September 5, when announcing that his paper would become a triweekly, Spotswood proclaimed his desire "to preserve an honest impartiality upon all controversial questions that have been offered for publication." He also tried to absolve himself and his editor, Alexander Dallas, of responsibility for printing the ideas expressed by correspondents and essayists; he pleaded: "FREEDOM OF THE PRESS OUGHT NOT TO BE RESTRAINED; and consequently, that the responsibility of an author, ought not to be transferred to the Editor."[3] In reality, when it came to the convention, most publishers had cast aside impartiality long before September arrived. In many cases, even the veneer of impartiality was stripped away in September 1787. Many publishers moved past their normal cheerleading for the convention and engaged in a new form of news management. The ever more aggressive press coverage, and the realization that the delegates would soon complete their work, forced dissenters into trying to halt the proconvention momentum the press had been building for months. That was a formidable task, but the critics knew they must act or the battle might be lost before the convention's recommendations even appeared in public. So, in September, "antifederalists" finally made a concerted effort to combat the media hype for the convention.

• • •

On September 5 the editors of the *Pennsylvania Gazette* told the anxious citizenry that the delegates would adjourn the following week. Three days later, however, the *Massachusetts Centinel* carried an August 24 letter from a supposedly well informed New Yorker who said the convention would sit until mid-October. The delegates would then, he claimed, uncloak a plan of government including a governor general, a legislative council, and a senate. Benjamin Russell, publisher of the *Centinel*, declared that would be "better than at present, but not as good as could be wished." The New Yorker's observations were intrinsically more interesting than the bland *Gazette* item, but the latter got reprinted almost twenty times while the New Yorker's letter gained only eight reprintings.[4] The disparity in appearances could have sprung from the continuing effort to avoid reproducing items that might undermine the convention or the media hype for it. If people believed the delegates planned to plod along for another month, it would become easier to doubt their unity and the urgent need to erect a stronger central government. Moreover, the New Yorker's claims were soon contradicted by the *Pennsylvania Herald*, a source with a reputation for knowing about the convention's inner workings.[5]

On September 13, editor Dallas claimed to have reliable information that the convention had finished its work except for determining the best way to issue its report. He informed his readers that the convention would break up on the fourteenth or the fifteenth. By September 18, only four papers had reprinted this *Herald* piece. Perhaps publishers were wary of printing more erroneous reports on when the convention would finish. Perhaps they believed the delegates would soon complete their work and so just waited.[6] That course of action was rewarded on the 18th when the *Pennsylvania Packet* announced the convention had broken up the previous day and that its secretary was taking the results to Congress.[7]

Editors often used "news" announcements of the anticipated completion of the convention as propaganda tools. The report in Hall and Sellers's *Pennsylvania Gazette*, which proved most popular with other publishers, certainly sounded like a paid political announcement. "We hear," they said, "that the CONVENTION propose to adjourn next week, after laying America under such obligations to them for their long, painful and disinterested labours, to establish her liberty upon a permanent basis, as no time will ever cancel."[8] Although using news reports to praise the delegates was not new, the way the press covered reports of violence was.[9] In September, the press ventured into the realm of news management of stories about internal disorder in the land.

Reports of internal violence and possible rebellion were,

of course, important news and typically judged worthy of reprinting. Throughout the spring and summer of 1787, the press had often used such accounts to champion the convention. Nevertheless, one such story that appeared in an openly proconvention paper enjoyed extraordinary popularity. On September 3, Oswald of the *Independent Gazetteer* reported learning from residents of Wyoming, Pennsylvania, that violence might explode in their area. "A dangerous combination of villains, composed of runaway debtors, criminals, and adherents of Shays, &c." was gathering near Tioga Point on the Susquehanna River. These ruffians opposed the introduction of law and order into their settlements and threatened anyone who did not do as they wished. It was said they wanted to create a new state. Their numbers increased rapidly, so they could soon become most dangerous if not expeditiously restrained. Yet government seemed paralyzed. "It is for want of energy in this respect," said Oswald, "that we see *banditties* rising up against law and good order in all the quarters of our country." The report that internal insurrection might soon erupt in Pennsylvania spread like wildfire. Thirty-four publishers promptly reprinted it.[10]

On September 14, to his journalistic credit, Oswald printed an extract of a letter from Wyoming, dated September 6, in which the author noted that "affairs wear a much better aspect here than they did a short time ago."[11] Nothing had been learned about the gathering at Tioga except that it was less well attended than expected. This account suggested that Oswald's earlier widely reprinted tale of woe exaggerated the potential danger. Based on news value, and in the interest of accuracy, those publishers who reprinted the first news story should have reprinted this one. However, it was not reprinted even once.

The same kind of apparent news management occurred with accounts of internal violence in Virginia. On September 7, the New York *Daily Advertiser* claimed that Edmund Randolph, Virginia's governor and a convention delegate, had received the alarming news that inhabitants of several Virginia back counties had shut down the courts. Ten papers reproduced this news, which suggested that the horrors of Shaysism loomed once again.[12] On September 11, the *Daily Advertiser* reported it was happy to inform its readers that the revolt was confined to Green Brier County. Yet only three papers reprinted this good news.[13] Once again the reprinting pattern smacked of news management aimed at promoting the idea that the convention's plan must be adopted. By handling the stories as they did, many publishers abandoned their avowed role as sources of news.

The proconvention view evident in the management of news in early September was matched by partisan commentary that reflected the growing intensity of feelings about the convention's work.[14] When Hall and Sellers reported about the expected conclusion of the convention, they also offered the pronouncements of a decidedly proconvention correspondent. In two marvelously crafted paragraphs, he touched on many themes in a few words. In a short first paragraph of just the right length for easy reprinting, he proclaimed that "the impatience with which all classes of people (a few officers of government only excepted) wait to receive the new federal constitution, can only be equalled by their zealous determination to support it." He prophesied that 1787 would be celebrated as a year of revolution in favor of government just as 1776 was celebrated as a revolution in favor of liberty. This clever bit of political advertising and prognostication quickly became an immensely popular reprint.[15]

The correspondent's lengthy second paragraph proved decidedly harsher in tone and much less appealing to publishers. He asserted that each state had "its SHAYS, who either with their pens—or tongues—or offices—are endeavouring to effect what Shays attempted in vain with his sword." The analyst ridiculed various arguments that might be used against the delegates' proposals and denounced an unnamed New Yorker, surely Governor Clinton, as a Shaysite demagogue. Only such a person, the correspondent asserted, would proclaim it dangerous to give Congress more power. Any person who said the states would not adopt the new frame of government coming from the convention was one who "whispers distrust." Those who might say the convention lacked the power to redress the problems the Union faced were, of course, also Shaysite demagogues. In a clear reference to the liberally reprinted essay about it being "laughable" to think a few strokes of the pen could cure America's ills, the correspondent denounced anyone who made such pronouncements as an opponent of all attempts to restore order and government to the United States.[16] He branded virtually all the criticisms of the convention that might be articulated as embodying "the spirit and wickedness of SHAYS." The author closed with the pungent warning: "Let Americans be wise. Toryism and Shayism are nearly allied. They both lead to slavery, poverty, and misery."[17] These comments, although reprinted only six times, revealed that the August escalation in rhetoric continued into September. They formed part of the increasingly strident attempt to convince "antifederalists" that they should not, dare not, oppose the convention's recommendations.

A popular Northampton, Massachusetts, *Hampshire Gazette* essayist, also published on September 5, struck similar themes and warnings to those voiced by the Philadelphian. "Numa" proclaimed it a vital time when those who could do good should do it and when those who could exert influence should exert it. Since America's prosperity should be in all citizens' thoughts, "what shall we think and say then of him who disobeys her voice and disregards her interest?" The answer was clear: "Shun, my countrymen, the sham patriot, however dignified, who bids you distrust the Convention, and reject the collective wisdom of these states. Mark him as a dangerous member to society. Brand him as hostile to the commerce, respectability and independency of America."[18] Although many of the reprintings occurred after they had published the Constitution, publishers made Numa a popular author.

In the *Independent Gazetteer* of September 7, the Reverend Nicholas Collin, writing as "Foreign Spectator," also used the image of the Union dismembered to issue a warning.[19] Asserting that every part of the federal empire had been won by the sword, Collin evoked memories of the great War for Independence as he proclaimed: "What American can without horror, indignation and grief, reflect that a fatal disunion may basely throw under foreign domination *the plains of Saratoga, York Town, or the Cowpens.*" There could be but one response: "Here methinks I see every sordid wretch hang his head, and *every brave American clap his hand to his sword, and swear by the ashes of all their* fellow soldiers, and by their own noble hearts, *it shall not be.*" More than a score of publishers found these sentiments worth reprinting.[20]

Although authors had employed increasingly acerbic language in August when they discussed those who might oppose the convention's work, publishers generally had shied away from reprinting material that charged potential "antifederalists" with treason. Perhaps because he wanted to get reprinted, Collin, like the *Gazette* correspondent and Numa, danced around but did not use the words "traitor" or "treason." On September 12, in a short paragraph that gained popularity, another *Pennsylvania Gazette* correspondent moved closer to employing those terms. The older distinction that marked Americans as Whigs or Tories, he counseled, should be replaced. Now the important distinction was between federal and antifederal men. Federal men, "the friends of liberty and independence," supported giving the central government greater powers. The antifederal men, those who opposed granting the government more power, were "the enemies of liberty, and the secret abettors of the interests of Great-Britain."[21]

Widely reprinted articles aimed at the "antifederal" types were thus typically harsher than similar popular reprints published before September. However, save for Collin's patriotic hyperbole, essayists who advocated violent action remained unlikely candidates for popular-reprint status. Still, two points are vital. In September, hot rhetoric and threats of violence to thwart any possible opposition to the convention and its work appeared routinely in press commentary. And, as the month progressed, these inflammatory pieces, while not widely reprinted, were more likely to be reprinted than ever before.

"Rough Carver," published in installments on September 3 and 4 in the unabashedly partisan New York *Daily Advertiser,* displayed the increasingly tough language. Many New York legislators who had voted against the impost and thus against strengthening the Confederation government were, Rough Carver charged, "mere machines." "Creatures to Jacobitish intrigue," they were "controlled in their sentiments by menial sycophants to British influence." Accordingly, they stood ready to oppose the absolutely necessary strengthening of the federal government that the convention would surely recommend. Although no names were used, Rough Carver clearly intimated that Governor Clinton must be cast out of office because he controlled the mere machines. Whether his ousting should be accomplished via the ballot box or other means was left to the reader's imagination. Even given the admittedly heated world of New York politics, editors found Rough Carver too rough for reprinting.[22]

Writing in the stridently proconvention *Independent Gazetteer* of September 8, "A Friend to Liberty and a good Government" did more than denounce the author of the "laughable" essay. Calling him "an *antifederal* writer," A Friend cautioned the author about the dangers of opposing the new constitution being styled by the glorious Washingtons, Franklins, and Madisons. A moral tale illustrated how hazardous dissent could be. A tenant, noticing that leaks in the roof had made his rented house unsafe, asked the landlord to make repairs. The landlord refused to believe the building was in danger and even laughed when the tenant, fearful for his safety, moved out. Soon thereafter the roof collapsed and killed the landlord. Despite its violent implications, A Friend gained a reprinting in the *Massachusetts Centinel.*[23]

The limited yet increasing willingness to reprint items that contained implicit or explicit threats is well illustrated by another piece carried by the *Independent Gazetteer.* The thoughts of "Senex," allegedly penned in Virginia in late August, appeared in the September 10 issue. Senex explained how horrified he had become upon reading the news that "the phlegmatic Dutch in Amsterdam" had hung a dozen respectable citizens just because of their political principles. But ruminating on what might happen if the American people did not embrace the government being formed by the "Grand Convention" had caused him to reach a more sympathetic understanding of what had happened in Holland. Senex then bluntly suggested that, if tar and feathers failed to deter those who opposed the new government, the best course would involve "amputation of the rotten limb" to stop the gangrene from spreading. He proposed that associations of individuals should force acceptance of the new governmental system the convention would recommend. Given its outrageous endorsement of deadly force, Senex was understandably not a favorite with editors. Still, it achieved two reprintings.[24]

Even though authors who advocated violence did not get widely reprinted in September, their denunciations of "antifederalists" had never been so uniformly hostile and threatening. For months the press had said it would be selfish, ignorant, and wrong to oppose the work of the convention. Now opposition meant more. The opponents would be playing, perhaps willingly so, into the hands of America's enemies. In sum, "antifederalists" were embracing treason.

The convention boosters of September who expended considerable energy attacking "antifederalists" and who did gain popularity often laced their pieces with established proconvention arguments, particularly with warnings about the possible destruction of the Union. On September 5, a date when many proconvention items appeared, Eleazer Oswald presented an economic variant of the dismemberment theme. The account told of a correspondent's visit to the Philadelphia harbor where he watched the loading and unloading of ships. He counted sixteen ships flying British colors and only a solitary vessel sporting the Stars and Stripes, and it was merely loading lumber bound for the West Indies. The central government *had* to do something, the correspondent argued, to regulate American trade and help it compete in the world market. If things remained as they were, he foresaw shipwrights parading the wharves and using their broad axes to chop up American ships that had become mere junk. This graphic illustration of America's commercial impotence achieved wide circulation, and the *Massachusetts Centinel* reprinting added the comment that the same situation existed in Boston.[25]

On September 12 the *Pennsylvania Gazette* carried an inventive piece that worked all the basic proconvention themes developed over the summer. Editors Hall and Sellers strategically placed it under the paragraph about the fundamental division among Americans now being the one between federal and antifederal people. The author anxiously looked into the future and beheld a wonderful world if the convention's recommendations were adopted and a horrible world if rejected. Because it was quite long, his commentary normally would be an unlikely candidate for popular-reprint status. However, in sweep of argument and stress on major points developed over time, his essay provided a fitting capstone to press efforts to convince Americans that they had to support the convention's recommendations. Perhaps because of that, it did become a popular reprint.[26] Hall and Sellers stated their own position clearly when they introduced the piece by declaring that even to speak of a possible rejection of the convention's soon-to-be-revealed government was to utter "AWFUL WORDS." Their correspondent cleverly demonstrated why this was the case. Looking into the future to June 1789, he supplied the paragraphs a correspondent would submit if the awful words proved true. Shays, the new governor of Massachusetts, was about to have the deposed governor hanged. A mob thirsting for the creation of paper money had burned the statehouse in Richmond, Virginia. New Jersey had entered into negotiations to be placed under the protection of the English Crown. Ship carpenters were emigrating to Halifax in search of work. Crops rotted because American ships were being shut out of the ports of Europe and the West Indies. Pennsylvania farms were worth less than the taxes due on them. Formerly valuable government certificates had no value. Great Britain and the Emperor of Morocco had signed a treaty dividing the various states between them. When asked to head what would be the British government of Rhode Island, Benedict Arnold refused because he feared being corrupted by living among speculators and traitors.

That horrifying future need not occur. If the convention's federal government were adopted, the correspondent foresaw marvelous news on many fronts in June of 1789. A solicitous British emissary had just arrived to negotiate a commercial treaty with the United States that would open all British ports to Americans, duty free. The British, moreover,were contracting to have two hundred ships built every year in the ports of Boston, New York, Philadelphia, and Charleston. America was receiving thousands of immigrants from all parts of Europe. Why, just the day before, a hundred reputable immigrant families, each carrying an average of £4,500 sterling, had landed. They were eager to purchase farms. The value of land near Carlisle, Pennsylvania, had doubled since 1787. That was logical since roads had been improved; the state's exports had nearly doubled in a year; the price of wheat had also nearly doubled, in no small part because Spain had confirmed that the United States had the right of navigation on the Mississippi. When insurgents tried to stage a rebellion at Tioga, the new federal militia quelled them. Because of all this and because of the new successful taxation system adopted by the United States, public securities had risen to par with specie. It was easy to understand why September 15, "the birth-day of our present free and glorious fœderal constitution," was as dear to all Americans as the Fourth of July. Independence Day gave Americans liberty, and the 15th of September 1787 "gave us, under the smiles of a benignant Providence, a *Government*, which alone could have rendered that liberty *safe* and *perpetual*."[27]

The *Gazette* correspondent, who brilliantly touched upon so many basic issues, clearly expected the convention to announce its plans on September 15.[28] Oswald of the *Independent Gazetteer* probably shared that view and acted accordingly. On September 14, the day he printed the letter that revealed the reports of violence at Tioga Point had been exaggerated, he published a partisan item that smelled of invention. Oswald offered an extract of a letter allegedly written on July 6 by a Londoner who longed to hear about "your Grand Convention." As a friend to America, he warned that the country would never prosper until it had a government composed of three independent branches chosen by the people or their representatives. Only "UNION" could save America and disappoint its enemies. Conveying the mixture of hope and fear often expressed in newspapers and magazines, he asserted: "If your convention gives you a strong government, and if you have the wisdom enough to adopt it, you will half depopulate this country by emigration, for thousands are waiting only to see whether a *Shays* will seize your Supreme power by force, or whether you will as an enlightened and free people chuse a *Washington*—a *Hancock*—or a *Franklin*, to be the legal head of your country." More than mere chance caused this letter to appear at the opportune moment. The writer's comments fit too neatly with the Constitution made public three days later. The list of possible candidates too conveniently mentioned a leader from each section of America. Not surprising given the press's record, this veritable political advertisement, despite its apparent fabrication, proved quite popular as a reprint.[29]

The *Gazetteer* writer surely expected applause to greet his suggestion that Washington might lead the new government. Indeed, if Oswald invented the letter, he did so knowing it was supported by an accurate news story just published in the *Packet*. On September 12, Dunlap and Claypoole reported that Don Diego de Gardoqui, the Spanish minister, had traveled from New York to Philadelphia to visit his "excellency" General Washington. The minister, it seemed, wanted to talk with the general before he left for Mount Vernon. In this widely reprinted story, Washington was treated as if he already were the head of state.[30]

The September press hype in favor of the still unknown new government thus refined themes popularized since the convention opened. Now, however, commentators who worked those themes more routinely used them to threaten.

Their pronouncements warned potential "antifederalists" that they too could expect to be skewered if they dared venture into print. Facing September's increasingly vicious assault and the impending release of the convention's recommendations, critics of the press hype supporting the convention finally responded in force. It is revealing that, even as they attacked, some writers employed gentle and indirect language to avoid the appearance of challenging the convention.

The most successful "antifederal" piece materialized, as usual, in the *Freeman's Journal.* Publisher Francis Bailey's September 12 issue carried a letter from Baltimore designed to undercut the idea of accepting whatever the convention produced. The writer claimed that John Adams's view that one must be "well born" to be of consequence gained ground in America as evidenced by the fact that newspaper advertisements of all kinds used the terms "good families" and "gentility." But such distinctions mattered little to American republicans. Indeed, "we accomplished the late Revolution without being *Well Born* (that is, we are descended only from plain laborious ancestors), we have sense enough to become legislators, merchants, farmers and manufacturers without being *Well Born.*" Playing upon the image of the humble citizen-soldier, he recalled that no one asked if a man was a noble or wellborn when war broke out. They only asked if he could and would fight in heat and cold, from Canada to Georgia, to repel the invaders of his rights and country.

Although the author did not spell them out, two important points flowed from his examples. Since John Adams had purportedly turned aristocratic, one should be suspicious of any governmental system he would endorse. Thus, if the convention produced such a government, it might not be a good one. The crucial second point invited average citizens to trust their own judgment and to reject the principle of deferring to their supposed betters. In these ways, as he hammered Adams, the Marylander also pummeled those who called upon the people to accept uncritically what the delegates decided. By making his challenge subtle, the writer increased his chances of garnering reprints. Considering its message, the missive proved moderately successful as four papers reprinted it.[31]

A *New Jersey Journal* essayist of September 12, who also raised questions about the convention, was less successful. While ostensibly talking about raising sheep, "A Zealous Columbian" echoed sentiments expressed by the author of the "laughable" essay. Observing that people seemed to expect the convention to cure all the Union's political ills and also to make people rich and happy, he reminded them that riches and happiness would have to be earned by hard work. A Zealous Columbian went unreprinted.[32]

The *Norwich Packet* of September 13 also carried comments that could be perceived as "antifederal." The author observed that "at present it appears to be the *Vox Populi*, that the decisions of the federal convention be agreed to in every punctilio." Without even implying that he challenged the notion of accepting those decisions, the writer warned against boasting too soon. Those well versed in politics predicted, he said, that when the convention's plan went to the states for ratification, "an opposition will shew itself, either on the right hand or the left." Press commentary had routinely said that only a few deluded people, especially officeholders and their cronies, would oppose the convention's proposals. In contrast, this author argued, and logically so, that the opposition would espouse various perspectives. His essay thus went against the grain of most press coverage. It also went unreprinted.

Similar circumspect efforts that seemed to question the convention or the notion of accepting whatever the delegates recommended had appeared sporadically in the press. By September, however, defending the right to evaluate the convention's recommendations before accepting them required more than sporadic forays against the convention boosters. Ideally, the potential dissidents needed to mount their own sustained press campaign. Such an endeavor got underway in New York on September 6 when the *New York Journal* published two tough essayists who, finally, responded to the July 21 attack on Governor Clinton. Clinton and his supporters had probably hoped that silence could defang the piece or that the convention would fail. By early September, silence no longer seemed a viable tactic. The convention was assuredly about to reveal its plan for a new government. The press beat the drum for the convention with even greater force. Dissenters such as Clinton had to choose: they could stand and fight or quit the field.

The major problem confronting the dissenters was that few publishers would print their thoughts. It was not mere chance that the pro-Clinton essays appeared in the *New York Journal*, one of the few papers that became Antifederalist once the Constitution appeared. Despite the difficulty of their task, the *Journal* authors could console themselves on one point: by focusing on the anti-Clinton essay, they could question the convention's work under the guise of responding to an attack launched by someone else.

"Adrastus," who offered the more general analysis, opened the counterattack with a plea for civility in the public prints that, not so subtly, branded the press as unfair. The fact was that "the management of the press, unfortunately for the public, like many other useful institutions, often falls into improper hands." Quite simply, some newspapers were controlled by weak-minded editors who lacked discernment. Because of this, newspapers, traditionally valuable for instruction and entertainment, had been turned into "the instruments of scandal, calumny, and abuse." "We frequently, of late," he said, "have had examples of a slander sheltered under the cover of the press, and the name of a calumniator held sacred by a printer."[33] Declaring that he wrote because he opposed using newspapers merely to abuse, Adrastus claimed that he could name one of the offending authors. For the time being, he would keep that information to himself in the hope that those who produced abusive items would stop. As he wrapped himself in the garb of an advocate of fair play, Adrastus adopted a ploy used by proconvention writers: he threatened to savage opponents if they refused to keep quiet.

By questioning the abilities and judgments of various

unnamed publishers, Adrastus surely did not endear himself to them as a group. Also, despite its comments on general issues, the essay clearly reflected New York political wranglings. These facts may explain why the essay was not reprinted. Nevertheless, Adrastus did not openly question the need for a strong government or challenge the convention in any way. Therefore, the fact that Adrastus went unreprinted boded ill for those who sought to stem the increasingly vicious attacks on persons who might question the delegates' handiwork.

The second pro-Clinton essay of September 6 had a veneer of civility, but "A Republican" was more direct and challenging than Adrastus. Tackling the question of why the Governor had not responded to the July 21 essay, he speculated that the governor of a great state did not want to enter into an unseemly newspaper controversy with an anonymous scribbler. Clinton had treated the scurrilous attack with the silence and contempt it merited. A private citizen interested in protecting the welfare of his state was not, A Republican noted, under the same kind of obligations as the Governor.

A Republican worked to avoid being labeled a Clinton stooge. He pointedly claimed that he knew neither Clinton nor if the Governor held the views attributed to him. This essayist also observed that the July account was circulating and being accepted, but he claimed that Clinton most certainly had not publicly expressed the sentiments ascribed to him. A Republican then took the offensive by pointing out that no hint of the Governor holding such views had surfaced in public *until* the scribbler's piece appeared. This line of argument cleverly implied that the July piece was written by a liar or a political hack supporting "a certain lordly faction" that aimed to "establish a system more favorable to their aristocratic views."

Having adroitly asserted that Clinton had not publicly expressed the views attributed to him, A Republican pointed out the inconsistency of claiming those views had influence. How, pray tell, could unexpressed views influence people? Here A Republican emphasized that the July author had admitted having no direct knowledge of the veracity of what he attributed to Clinton. This allowed A Republican to observe that the July piece was a rude attack aimed solely at influencing prejudiced and unthinking people. The July scribbler's essay was, in sum, "not the offspring of patriotism." In venturing his comments, A Republican used a literary allusion to imply that Alexander Hamilton authored the outrageous July essay.[34]

A Republican was disseminated more than might have been expected. Three newspapers reprinted his essay in full or in part. The reprintings are suggestive. A full reprinting appeared in the *Hudson Weekly Gazette* of September 13, a newspaper that tried to give balanced coverage to the New York combatants.[35] The Charleston *Columbian Herald*, which had also long demonstrated a willingness to offer balanced coverage on issues related to the convention, printed an extract. This printing occurred two days after the *Herald* published the Constitution.[36] An extract also appeared in the Philadelphia *Freeman's Journal*, the paper that had most consistently printed items that could be branded "antifederal" or labeled as less than enthusiastic about simply trusting the delegates.[37]

Four days after A Republican appeared, "An Old Soldier," yet another New York author, joined the effort to discredit anti-Clinton press pieces. He wrote in response to a September 3 *Northern Centinel* publication, "Impromptu," which had charged Governor Clinton with the "Treason" of wanting to "wreck" the Union.[38] An Old Soldier found the charge absurd. Clinton had, he asserted, steadfastly defended the United States and its government from the start of the Revolution to that very day. An Old Soldier, whose pen name was itself a nice touch, supported his claims by saying of Clinton's war record: "In the most gloomy hours of our warfare, who more readily drew his sword in our defense?—Who was more unwearied in his endeavours to defeat the vain attempts of our enemies to subdue us." Clinton's record in civil life shone as brightly.

The description of the Governor's noble character and

achievements emulated the praise routinely lavished on the delegates. An Old Soldier, obviously angered, charged that it was "the height of ingratitude to vilify a character, which ought to be esteemed, and even revered, for his services." He then pressed the counterattack. If the author of "Impromptu" had proof of Clinton's alleged treason, let him produce it. If the Governor was guilty, he should suffer. But "for God's sake let us not traduce a character so valuable to us, but by every means in our power, support him in all measures tending to the general good of our country."

An Old Soldier turned the tables on Impromptu by depicting *him* as the dangerous anti-Union villain, as the secret enemy of Americans such as George Clinton who had resisted British tyranny and helped establish the independence, freedom, and liberties of the rising empire that was America. An Old Soldier charged that Impromptu's essay, obviously an illogical and inflammatory piece, seemed designed to aid British agents who tried to play on America's troubles. The public should, of course, "ever detest those vile incendiaries, who (under British influence) secretly endeavour to sow the seeds of division, discontent and distrust among us." This approach skillfully mirrored the increasingly bold style the proconvention press had been using. Nevertheless, only one editor reprinted the essay, and, predictably, it was Thomas Greenleaf of the *New York Journal*.[39]

Much of the defense of Governor Clinton applied as well to others charged with "antifederalism." One point with general application was the claim that the press had foresaken impartiality. Adrastus indicted the press on that count and so did others. The most thoughtful and incisive analysis came from "Rusticus," whose work, as one might have guessed, originated in Greenleaf's *New York Journal* on September 13.[40] Rusticus evinced anger and frustration as he spoke of his "indignation at the many illiberal publications" on political matters that "constantly crowd our newspapers" in a campaign to sell the work of the convention at any cost. Various of the illiberal publications made it seem highly criminal, especially now, for anyone to differ in opinion from "a certain

Aristocratic junto." Those aristocrats "appear determined, by their writings, to silence, and traduce every person who will not subscribe to every part of their political creed."[41] To push their political creed, the junto and its adherents frequently told the people that the convention was surely doing what was "wisest and best" for the United States. In fact, it was depicted as akin to treason to suggest that the noble convention could possibly recommend a measure or system inconsistent with liberty or good government.

Rusticus had to concede that the propagandizing was being done skillfully. Most of the offending political publications were artfully calculated "to prepare the minds of the people, implicitly to receive *any form* of government that may be offered them." Why else, he asked, would authors anticipate the convention's results? If the delegates' recommendations proved consistent with the Union, promoted the general interest, and secured the people's essential rights, then "every good and virtuous citizen will not only subscribe to them, but use all his influence; nay, strain every nerve to carry them into effect." It did not need to be said, nor was it, that if the delegates' plans failed to meet those criteria then the people could and should reject them.

Rusticus also offered what he considered proof of the attempt to use the press to indoctrinate the people. He cited a paragraph published in the *Daily Advertiser* and other New York papers that suggested the good people of a Pennsylvania county wanted to accept any government recommended by the convention.[42] Rusticus rejected these claims. He had, he said, too much respect for the people to assume that they would supinely accept a potentially tyrannical government "let it be recommended by any man, or body of men, however wise, learned, or dignified." He dutifully noted that many delegates were indeed fine, liberty-loving men. Rusticus stressed that some, however, would gladly trample on the rights of the people. These delegates considered the people no better than slaves and vassals who should serve those of superior genius, high birth, and fortune. Rusticus's acerbic remarks reflected the growing intensity of the debate. Except for the news story carried by the *Pennsylvania Herald* on June 13, once the convention started, no press commentator had dared to imply that any of the delegates might be less than committed to preserving the rights of the people. Rusticus did.

Despite such boldness, an important restraint bound "antifederal" authors such as Rusticus. Even while attacking some unnamed delegates, he had to concede that most were fine men. Still, his trenchant arguments that the people should use the protection of their rights as a measuring stick to accept or reject any proposed form of government were sound. It would require fancy philosophical footwork to reject his emphasis on the basic tenet: free people in a free society have a right to speak their minds on great political issues. Challenging that basic right opened one to the damning charge of rejecting the ideals of the Declaration of Independence. In addition, Rusticus's complaints about the general press coverage of the convention were accurate. As with much of the proconvention material, his effort was undeniably adroit propaganda, but it appeared rather late to have much effect before the convention's results were known. It also shared the fate of most antihype essays: just one newspaper, the *American Herald* of Boston, reprinted Rusticus.[43]

It was only in September that sustained efforts were mounted to counter the press campaign to sell the constitutional convention. Those dubbed "antifederal" developed three principal lines of attack. First, they challenged the patriotism of their opponents and pilloried as aristocrats and possible traitors those who did not heartily embrace the principle that the people, including Governor Clinton, had the right to pass judgment on any proposed government. Second, emulating what had been done for the convention delegates, "antifederal" authors wrapped Governor Clinton, one of their potential leaders, in the mantle of Revolutionary Hero. Finally, by demonstrating that such a campaign existed, they undertook to counter the press campaign to sell the results of the convention before they were known.

The September effort to combat the selling of the convention, despite its ardor, began from a weak position. It is essential to remember that the dissenters' efforts were actually a counterattack—a defensive response—to what proconvention forces had printed and reprinted time and again. The proconvention press writers had effectively controlled what would be emphasized in any discussion of the convention. "Antifederal" thinkers had for months been trapped in part because it seemed unreasonable to question the convention's activities until its work appeared in public. Given the constant portrayal of George Washington as savior of the Union and of the delegates as the collective wisdom of the continent, such a premature challenge would have seemed petty. Moreover, the essays that savaged persons considered "antifederal" had been extensively reprinted over the months. An especially important example is Alexander Hamilton's July 21 cannonade against George Clinton, which was, for the time it was printed, an extraordinarily vicious piece. His essay was reprinted in whole or part eighteen times in eight states and in Vermont.[44] A far different fate befell the five essays written in September to defend Clinton not just from Hamilton's attack, but from various attacks. Each of the essays originated in a New York publication; and, between them, the five authors could garner only six reprintings in four states.[45]

The essays the New York "antifederal" writers got published in the weeks following September 6 could not possibly counterbalance the massive press effort to sell the convention. The New Yorkers nevertheless gained some minor victories. A Republican could claim three reprintings. His essay, aided quite possibly by the Adrastus piece, was yet more impressively successful in that the specific arguments advanced against Hamilton prompted two responses, including one by Hamilton himself. That was a new development. "Federal" authors had been used to bombarding their foes with impunity, not defending themselves. Proconvention authors had launched preemptive strikes against their suspected foes. They had produced damage-control pieces after the potentially dangerous *Pennsylvania Herald* story appeared on June 13. Some had deemed it necessary to discredit the "laughable" essay. But A Republican was the first author to force a proconvention writer to defend himself.

A Republican's September 6 essay so disturbed "Aristides" that he quickly dashed off a response, published in the partisan *Daily Advertiser* on September 10. Aristides conceded, as A Republican had implied, that Hamilton wrote the July attack on Governor Clinton. However, adopting the style of a campaign manager, Aristides suggested that Hamilton's authorship gave the publication greater merit because no New Yorker merited more praise than Hamilton. Having played campaign manager, Aristides imitated his opponent. A Republican claimed he did not know Clinton; Aristides claimed he did not know Hamilton. The important point was, said Aristides, that no one could deny Clinton had long opposed measures absolutely necessary to support "a substantial Federal Government." Accordingly, Clinton had a responsibility to prove he supported the federal government. Until the governor demonstrated such support, one could rightfully assume he was "openly opposed to any change which the wisdom of the present Convention may recommend." Once again Clinton and anyone else who might question the delegates' work were whipsawed. Lest they be called political slanderers, the dissenters had little choice but to withhold negative comment until the results of the convention became known. Yet, at the same time, they had to struggle to uphold their right to reject the convention's recommendations, if that proved necessary.

Moving to counterattack the counterattack, Aristides maintained that he was not trying to guess what motivated the governor; rather, he was merely stating the obvious facts and logic of the case. In so doing, he stressed that, if the charges leveled in the July 21 essay were false, all the governor need do was declare them false. Clinton had not done so because he could not. The charge that Clinton embraced "antifederalism" was true. To support this claim, Aristides maintained that New York, like the other states, had two distinct political groups, the "Federal and Anti-Federal." The meaning of these terms seemed so obvious that Aristides did not bother to define them when he spoke about the membership of each group. New York's federal group included, he claimed, the clergy, "the respectable body of Merchants—the intelligent, independent Country Gentlemen—and about every citizen of discernment and public spirit." As for those who were antifederal, Aristides said he would leave it to A Republican to describe them since he knew who they were. In his discussion, Aristides made it clear that Alexander Hamilton should be ranked as one of the truly noble political figures of the day.

Aristides closed his lengthy essay by saying he thought most people would find A Republican's attack on Hamilton unfair in part because Hamilton was not in New York to defend himself. He was, without any special thanks, working with the other great men at the convention in Philadelphia. Perhaps in part because it would have given greater circulation to the views of A Republican, Aristides gained only one reprinting.[46] The significant point is that such an essay had to be written. Its very existence shows that "antifederal" authors were finally, if belatedly, fighting back aggressively.

Once it became an open secret that Alexander Hamilton authored the anti-Clinton essay, he entered the newspaper combat in his own defense. The essay published by the *Daily Advertiser* on September 15, although unsigned and although Hamilton was referred to in the third person, clearly pointed to Hamilton as the author.[47] The writer acknowledged that Hamilton undoubtedly wrote the July 21 essay. Indeed, Hamilton had never meant to conceal his name. He had told the printer to release it to Governor Clinton or his agents if requested.

Hamilton contended that the people would surely see the July essay as an honorable attempt to warn the people about the governor's determination to oppose the convention's measures. The goal was to unmask "the pernicious intrigues of a man, high in office, to preserve power and emolument to himself, at the expence of the Union, the peace, and happiness of America." The assertion by A Republican that the governor had not responded to the July essay because he objected to entering into a newspaper war with an anonymous scribbler was a miserable subterfuge. Clinton could have issued a terse public statement denying he held the views attributed to him; or, he could have obtained the name of the essay's author and had "a personal explanation on the subject with the writer." Still, Hamilton asserted that neither action would have saved Clinton: if he publicly denied the charges leveled in the July 21 essay, Hamilton would then have been forced to produce his evidence. The proof was certainly available, said Hamilton, since he regarded his own reputation too highly to level charges he could not substantiate. Having stuck the knife in, Hamilton twisted it by adding that he was still ready to provide that evidence if a public denial ever appeared. Finally, Hamilton unpersuasively claimed that his tender regard for Clinton had caused him to avoid saying in the July essay that he had first-hand knowledge of Clinton's views.[48]

Perhaps nettled by A Republican's form of attack, Hamilton used a similar argument. He charged that A Republican was a political hack who supported a party that sought to strip citizens of the invaluable right of questioning their rulers. The technique being used was to malign any independent man. This kind of unfair action, Hamilton maintained, was used routinely to keep the deceiving politicians in power.

Hamilton's defense went unreprinted, quite possibly because the quick subsequent publication of the Constitution rendered continuing commentary on the July essay less important than discussing the now public document. Still, the essay is important because it shows that the "antifederalist" authors were able to put Hamilton on the defensive. However, this one minor victory did little to deflate the general press hype for accepting the delegates' recommendations.

The images each side tried to project onto its opponents during the infighting over Hamilton's July 21 piece are revealing. Those dubbed as "antifederal" were depicted as selfish demagogues who had, as Hamilton put it, *"consummate talents for popularity"* but little love and sense of the Union. The

forces calling for deferentially accepting the convention's recommendations were depicted as aristocrats longing to crush
the people's liberties. These arguments foreshadowed basic
lines of attack used once the Constitution was made public.

For the "antifederalists" of mid-September, the crucial
issue was not Alexander Hamilton's essay. They needed, as
Rusticus said, to counter the press campaign to sell the work
of the convention sight unseen. Their effort concluded with
an essay by "Anti-Defamationis" that was ready for publication
on September 13 but did not appear in the *New York Journal*
until September 20.[49] The author's pseudonym struck a basic
theme being developed by those seeking to protect the right
to question the convention's recommendations. Following the
other combatants, Anti-Defamationis attempted to establish
his supposed neutrality by saying he did not know or support
either Clinton or Hamilton. He chose to write, he claimed, out
of an honest concern over issues raised in recent publications.
He expressed anger over the many illiberal publications that
pilloried Governor Clinton for some "accidental expressions"
about the convention. The arguments of Aristides especially
disturbed him. Nevertheless, Anti-Defamationis's defense of
Clinton and of the right to challenge the results of the
convention seemed to concede that Clinton held "antifederal"
views. Surely, said Anti-Defamationis, any free man, including
the governor, had a right to scrutinize all public measures.
Moreover, just because a person stood with the minority
on such an issue, by what right or necessity was he to
be reprobated for that stand? If Governor Clinton or any
man believed the work of the convention posed a danger,
he should express that view.

Infusing his ideals with hope, Anti-Defamationis boldly
proclaimed: "The free citizens of this continent will never
consent to have a constitution crammed down their throats.
They have an undoubted right to examine before they accede,
and to deny if they do not approve." Firm in his faith in the
rights and abilities of the people, he confidently asserted
that the obvious ploys of Aristides and his colleagues—their
unjust stigmas and innuendoes—would not work. "The people

are not so easily gulled." Most certainly New Yorkers possessed "too much wisdom and spirit to be imposed upon, or browbeaten." Only the *Hudson Weekly Gazette*, which tried to print both sides in the debate, reproduced this piece.[50]

By the time Anti-Defamationis penned his arguments, the opportunity to judge the work of the convention was, as Dunlap and Claypoole of the *Pennsylvania Packet* reported, nearly at hand. On September 18, they used extra large type to announce: "We have the heart-felt pleasure to inform our fellow citizens that the Fœderal Convention adjourned yesterday, having completed the object of their deliberations— And we hear that Major W. Jackson, the secretary of that honorable body, leaves this city for New York, this morning, in order to lay the great result of their proceedings before the United States in Congress." Augustine Davis, publisher of the *Virginia Independent Chronicle*, also employed extra-large print to proclaim he had learned upon good authority that the Constitution had passed unanimously. He also praised the document he promised to publish in the next issue as "the Boon" coming to Virginia. Once again news stories sounded like paid political announcements.[51]

Confirmation of the *Pennsylvania Packet* report quickly followed. The *Evening Chronicle* may well have printed the Constitution on September 18, and five other Philadelphia papers did publish it on September 19.[52] Two days later, New York City papers carried the Constitution. It was published in New Jersey and Maryland on September 25. A day later, the Boston *Massachusetts Centinel* printed it. Two Connecticut and two Virginia newspapers presented the Constitution to their readers on the 27th.[53] It appeared in print in New Hampshire by September 29, in South Carolina by October 2, and in North Carolina on October 4. The Constitution did not get printed in Georgia for another week, and a fair amount of time elapsed before the few frontier presses could obtain and print the document. The *Pittsburgh Gazette* published it on October 6; the *Kentucke Gazette*, which got its copy from the *Pittsburgh Gazette*, printed a first installment on October 20 and did not complete publication until November 3.

• • •

In September, as in the months before and after, news media coverage of the convention essentially belonged to those who came to be called Federalists. They mounted ever more strident attacks on anyone who would challenge the new government produced by the convention. Graphic examples were printed in support of well-established themes. The promise of greatness for the Union if the people would deferentially accept the work of the noble men of the Grand Convention was also trumpeted ever more loudly. Only rather belatedly did essayists such as Adrastus, Anti-Defamationis, and Rusticus strongly try to alert the citizens to the press campaign to sell the convention.

There is no effective way to assess the degree to which people were moved or possibly even controlled by the news media. Nevertheless, with one crucial exception, Rusticus was right when he charged that much of the coverage of the convention had been artfully calculated to prepare the minds of the people to receive any form of government the delegates offered. If pushed, even Rusticus would have had to admit that the press, in essays and commentary, had adamantly opposed creating an American monarchy.

Many editors completed their selling of the Constitutional Convention and made the transition to the championing of the Constitution by following the lead of the editors of the *Pennsylvania Gazette*. When Hall and Sellers printed the Constitution on September 19, they also published what was the first commentary on the proposed document. Reflecting their already established open support for the delegates' effort, Hall and Sellers offered their readers this analysis: "The division of power of the United States into three branches gives the sincerest satisfaction to a great majority of our citizens, who have long suffered many inconveniencies from being governed by a *single* legislature. All *single* governments are tyrannies—whether they be lodged in *one* man—A *few* men—or a *large* body of the people." That endorsement of the just-released Constitution eventually appeared in print twenty times.[54]

The commentary published by the *Pennsylvania Gazette* on September 19 was the opening salvo in a print campaign to support adoption of the Constitution. Perhaps buoyed by the media's coverage as well as their own hope, some analysts who commented immediately after the Constitution appeared expressed the belief that the document would win approval—perhaps even easily. In a September 20 dispatch, Phineas Bond, a Loyalist who had returned to America as a British consul, reported to London that "as far as I can judge, the sober and discreet Part of the Community approve of the Plan in its present Form."[55] Writing at the same time to a Federalist, Robert Milligan, a Philadelphia lawyer, confidently proclaimed that "the convention is at last risen—their plan of Foederal government is applauded here for its moderation, & we have no doubt of its being adopted."[56] There did, in fact, seem to be real enthusiasm for the Constitution at the time.[57] Benjamin Franklin, who also offered his analysis on the 20th, was less sure of success than was Milligan. Franklin observed that the Constitution might "not be receiv'd with the same Unanimity in the different States that the Convention have given the Example of in delivering it out from their Consideration."[58]

Franklin proved the more perceptive analyst. Working to delay the ratification votes on the Constitution, pushing the idea of a second convention, and hammering at the fact that the Constitution lacked a Bill of Rights, Antifederalists turned the ratification process into a protracted conflict. Contemporaries considered the allegiance of the press important in that struggle. Indeed, although few publishers supported the Antifederalist cause, those who did faced attacks ranging from cancelled subscriptions to crowd violence. Reflecting their efforts to sell the Constitutional Convention, the overwhelming majority of publishers championed the Federalist cause during the battle over ratification in 1787–1788.[59] By the time the Constitution was made public, many publishers, in essence, had already served a kind of apprenticeship for what became the campaign to market the Constitution. They had served it by spending the summer and early fall of 1787 selling the Constitutional Convention.

Notes to Chapter Five

1. Extract of a letter from Connecticut dated August 25, *Freeman's Journal*, September 5; reprinted thirteen times between September 6 and 27. Except for the *Worcester Magazine*, which reprinted it in the same issue that carried the Constitution, the reprintings appeared in newspapers before they printed the Constitution.

2. See, e.g., the masthead statements or mottos of the *Freeman's Journal*, the *Massachusetts Centinel*, and the *Newport Mercury*, and note also that many papers included the word "independent" in their titles. See also William F. Steirer, "Riding 'Everyman's Hobby Horse': Journalists in Philadelphia, 1764–1794," in *Newsletters to Newspapers: Eighteenth-Century Journalism*, ed. Donovan H. Bond and W. Reynolds McLeod (Morgantown, 1977), 263–75, and especially 270–72.

3. Although publisher Spotswood issued the statement and although the name of editor Dallas was not used, part of the article supposedly gave the views of the editor. It may be that the publisher and editor felt they had to be more restrained. That would explain why, in contrast to the normal praise for convention activities, the September 13 *Herald* report on the convention, discussed later in this chapter, was phrased in neutral language. In the September 18 issue, where it was noted that the Constitution had been completed and would soon appear, the editor observed: "We trust every friend to the peace and prosperity of America, is prepared to receive with respect and to consider with candour the propositions which will then be divulged."

4. *Pennsylvania Gazette*, September 5, given in COC1: 125, with nineteen reprintings by September 24. The September 8 *Massachusetts Centinel* item was reprinted eight times between September 10 and 18, and only three of the reprintings appeared outside of Massachusetts. The reprintings appeared in Mass. (5), N.H. (2), R.I. (1).

5. The expectation that the convention would soon complete

its work may explain why a September 12 *New Jersey Journal* story that would normally be widely reprinted received no reprints. This newsworthy item, an extract of a letter purportedly written by a member of the convention and dated at Philadelphia on September 9, reported that the convention had finished its business. Indeed, as soon as the delegates gave what they had produced "the final polish," it would be made public. The lack of reprints is especially hard to understand as the *Journal* should have quickly arrived in the major reprint areas of Philadelphia, New York, and Boston. It is possible that the September 13 *Pennsylvania Herald* story cited in the text supplanted the place the *Journal* report normally would have taken on the reprint circuit. In addition, some publishers might still have wanted to support the claim that secrecy ruled in the convention. Date of publication combined with distance and what can be called low visibility probably explains why a newsworthy September 12 *Carlisle Gazette* item went unreprinted. In an extract of a letter from a "gentleman in Philadelphia," the writer praised the work of the convention and said at least some parts of its work would be made public in about two weeks. Items from the *Carlisle Gazette* typically did not get reprinted even if they were impressive productions.

6. Thomas B. Wait, publisher of the *Cumberland Gazette* (in which the Constitution did not appear until October 4), showed this kind of attitude when in his September 27 issue he said: "It is needless to mention the reports we hear relative to the Report of the Federal Convention to Congress, as we expect in our next [issue] to give our readers an exact copy of it; when they can make their own comments."

7. In a different report that focused on what would happen in Pennsylvania, the September 18 *Pennsylvania Herald* also indicated that the convention had broken up the day before.

8. See n. 4 above.

9. The vital announcement in the *Pennsylvania Herald* was phrased in a neutral way, and the publisher of the paper, William Spotswood, claimed, as cited in COC1: xxxix, that he was trying to be neutral. However, as indicated in the text and in n. 3 above, this neutrality may have been a forced neutrality.

10. Three basic versions were reprinted. Between September 5 and 25, full reprintings occurred in twenty-one papers. The second most popular version ended with the section that reported that those opposed to law and order wanted to create a new state. This

version appeared in ten papers between September 13 and October 15. A version that ended with the description of how people were forced to agree and thus excluded the reference to creating a new state, appeared in four papers between September 15 and 27. The *Columbian Herald*, October 15, which reprinted the version that ended with the new state notation, was the only paper to reprint the report after having reprinted the Constitution. The story was, in all, reprinted thirty-five times between September 5 and October 15. On September 12 Oswald published another story that told of the "banditti" getting ready for action and that sounded his call to action. This story, which in milder form was a complement to the first Tioga report, got reprinted only four times. The four reprinting papers were: the *Pennsylvania Herald*, the *Maryland Journal*, the *New York Journal*, and the *Middlesex Gazette*, September 13, 18, 20, 24, respectively.

11. Despite his honest news reporting in this case, Oswald was probably still willing to invent items to sell the convention's work. See the discussion in this chapter of his probably invented piece, also published on September 14, that purportedly came from London.

12. In each case the reprinting occurred before the individual papers had published the Constitution. None of the reprintings occurred in a newspaper published outside New England. That might in part be due to the fact that a Petersburg *Virginia Gazette* item of September 6, reprinted in the *Pennsylvania Packet* on September 15, and in six other papers by October 11, said the violence in Green Brier County had been quickly and effectively confronted by the "civil authority." See COC1: 96 and 96n.

13. Once again the newspapers were located in New England, and the three reprintings occurred between September 20 and 27. None of the other seven papers carried the *Virginia Gazette* item, described in the preceding note, that would also have alerted readers to the fact that the original *Daily Advertiser* report was overly alarmist. Nor did any of the other seven papers reprint an article from the *Virginia Independent Chronicle*, September 20, that carried the news that things were not as bad in Green Brier County as had been suggested. This item was reprinted four times between September 27 and October 8, with all of these reprintings occurring after the papers had printed the Constitution.

14. In addition to the examples given in the text, see: the Boston *Independent Chronicle*, September 13, reprinting a Sep-

tember 8 account from Portsmouth, New Hampshire; extract of a Philadelphia letter, *Carlisle Gazette*, September 12; "Observator," *New Haven Gazette*, September 20. The last two items were not reprinted. Counting the Boston reprinting, the report from New Hampshire, which described how the people of New Hampshire and the other states seemed to be strongly in favor of receiving the "new federal government," was reprinted five times between September 13 and 27. The one Pennsylvania reprinting occurred in the *Packet*, September 22, after the paper had printed the Constitution. There were, in total, three reprintings in Massachusetts, New York, and Virginia, and all of them occurred before each paper had printed the Constitution.

15. *Pennsylvania Gazette*, September 5, given in COC1: 125, with twenty-five reprintings appearing between September 6 and 25.

16. Other writers joined in the effort to savage the author of the "laughable" essay. "A distressed original public Creditor" (*Pennsylvania Packet*, September 4, reprinted in *Pennsylvania Gazette* and *Pennsylvania Herald*, September 5) depicted the author as a heartless wretch and "an officer of government." "A Friend to Liberty and a good Government" (see n. 23 below) was more vicious. Together, the attacks on the "laughable" essay appeared in print a total of twelve times.

17. The New York *Daily Advertiser* of September 8 reprinted all of the essay except the last line about Toryism. Its reprinting is accordingly included as one of the six reprints.

18. As originally published, this "Numa" was cited as being Number VII in his continuing series entitled "Political *and* Moral Entertainment." Only the Boston *Independent Chronicle* of September 20, which labeled the piece as No. 5 in the "Numa" series, reprinted this lengthy piece in its entirety. Probably because the author's general praise of the delegates was, by then, rather typical, that part of the essay got reprinted less than his comments on the possible opponents of the convention's work. The sections cited in the text were certainly the most popular; they appeared in every newspaper that reprinted any part of "Numa," and partial reprints of this essay appeared in a total of fifteen papers between September 11 and October 12. However, only three papers reprinted "Numa" before they had printed the Constitution. The delayed reprinting of this piece probably occurred because it was not reprinted in Boston until September 11 and not in Philadelphia until September 24.

19. Collin, a Swedish immigrant and pastor of Philadelphia's Old Swedes Church, was the author of the general series "An Essay on the Means of Promoting Federal Sentiments in the United States," which originated in the staunchly proconvention *Independent Gazetteer*. For this identification, see COC1: 290n.

20. Seventeen of the total of twenty-seven reprintings occurred before the reprinting newspaper had carried the Constitution.

21. Given in COC1: 193; eleven reprintings occurred by October 11. Four papers, including the *Evening Chronicle* of September 8, reprinted this before they printed the Constitution; one reprinted it the day it carried the Constitution.

22. All quotations come from the September 3 New York *Daily Advertiser*.

23. *Independent Gazetteer*, September 8. As with other such letters Oswald printed, the piece might have been invented. The reprinting occurred in the September 22 issue of the *Centinel* and thus appeared before that paper published the Constitution. The reference to Madison suggests that the author, whoever he was, may have had a source inside the convention: Madison's public standing at that time hardly pointed to placing him anywhere near the level of Washington and Franklin.

24. The reprinting in the *Massachusetts Gazette*, September 21, occurred before that paper printed the Constitution; the printing in the *Newport Herald*, October 4, occurred after the paper printed the Constitution.

25. Thirteen newspapers published this *Independent Gazetteer* item in full, and another five printed the first section about the dominance of British shipping. With one exception, the reprintings occurred between September 6 and 22, before the reprinting publication had printed the Constitution. The *Maryland Chronicle* reprinted it on October 3, the day the paper's final installment of the Constitution was printed. The comment on Boston is from the *Massachusetts Centinel*, September 17.

26. It was reprinted fifteen times between September 15 and October 15. Most editors used it to support the Constitution they had already printed; only two papers reprinted the piece before printing the Constitution.

27. Given in COC1: 193–95, with quotations taken passim. For another proconvention anticipation piece that looked forward to May 1788, see the *Newport Herald*, September 13, which was reprinted five times between September 17 and 27.

28. Since he talked about a federal assembly and senate in 1789, he may well have had a source of information inside the convention. The September 15 date probably stemmed from the *Herald* report, as indicated above at n. 6, about the delegates completing their work on the 15th.

29. Thirteen reprintings appeared between September 15 and October 11. Four occurred before the reprinting paper published the Constitution; four reprinted it when they published the Constitution or the first installment of the Constitution; five publishers reprinted the piece after they had published the Constitution.

30. *Pennsylvania Packet*, September 12, with twelve reprintings by October 3. Nine occurred before the paper in question printed the Constitution; two reprintings occurred in the same issue of the reprinting paper that carried the Constitution; the *Maryland Chronicle* reprinted it and the paper's second and last installment of the Constitution on October 3.

31. This extract of a letter is given in COC1: 89–90; the four reprintings, which occurred before the reprinting papers published the Constitution, appeared between September 18 and 25.

32. The logic that made three authors attack the "laughable" essay marked "A Zealous Columbian" as a target. However, perhaps because his essay appeared so late and went unreprinted, he escaped direct assault.

33. As noted later in the text, Hamilton thought this essay referred to his July 21 essay. It may also have referred to "Rough Carver" and the poem by "j——r" (see n. 41 below).

34. An extract of "A Republican" is given in COC1: 139–40. Quotations are taken from p. 139 and the unreprinted portion of the original. As the editors indicate (p. 141, n. 5), it is possible that "A Republican" was Clinton himself.

35. For example, the *Gazette*, September 6, carried the "j——r" political poem (see n. 41 below) and on September 20 reprinted "Aristides," an essay opposed to the views of "A Republican."

36. The reprint of "A Republican" appeared in the issue of October 4, and the Constitution was published in an extra edition on October 2.

37. Reprinting in issue of September 12.

38. "An Old Soldier," which was dated September 7, was published by the *Northern Centinel* on September 10. Given their open effort to support the convention and correspondingly to attack "anti-federalists," Babcock and Claxton surely did not want to publish

"An Old Soldier." Having published "Impromptu," however, they may have felt compelled or in some way been forced to allow a response to be printed. "Impromptu" was originally published in the *Massachusetts Centinel*, August 18, and the *Northern Centinel* was the only newspaper to reprint it.

39. Issue of September 20.

40. According to the *New York Journal*, which published it on September 13, "Rusticus" was written in Queens County on September 10. "Rusticus" was probably aware of "Rough Carver" and quite possibly of "Impromptu." It is also possible, but unlikely, that he had seen "Aristides," published on September 10, which is discussed later in this chapter.

41. A useful example that fits in with the New York newspaper war described in this chapter is "Political Fox Craft, An original Fable: Written, April, 1787" signed "j——r." This political poem described Clinton and his followers as dirty foxes who had monopolized the offices of the state since the Revolution and, "monarch-like," ridden the backs of the people. Given the notation in one reprinting newspaper, it is possible that the item originated in the no longer extant *Albany Gazette* of August 30. The first printing discovered is the *Hudson Weekly Gazette*, September 6, with reprintings in the proconvention New York *Daily Advertiser*, September 14, and the propagandistic *Northern Centinel*, September 17. It also appeared in the November issue of the Philadelphia *Columbian Magazine*.

42. Despite his reference to one county, "Rusticus" was probably referring to an item that originated in the August 22 *Independent Gazetteer*, given in COC1: 189, that said: "By letters and private accounts from most of the counties in Pennsylvania, we learn that the good people of this state, of all parties, are alike prepared and disposed to receive the new federal government." This item was reprinted in the New York *Daily Advertiser*, August 29, and in three other New York City newspapers between August 29 and 31. It also appeared in Babcock and Claxton's *Northern Centinel*, September 10.

43. Issue of September 24.

44. For fuller analysis and documentation, see Chapter Four, n. 14.

45. The states were N.Y., S.C., Mass., and Pa. See the discussion of "Adrastus" above; nn. 34–39 above; the discussion of "Anti-Defamationis," the fifth essay, is at nn. 49–50 below.

46. The reprinting occurred in the *Hudson Weekly Gazette*, September 20.

47. For the identification of Hamilton as the author, see Harold C. Syrett, ed., *The Papers of Alexander Hamilton*, 27 vols. (New York, 1961–1987), 4: 248–49, n. 1.

48. In a less than clear comment, Hamilton also claimed that he hesitated to admit he had first-hand knowledge of Clinton's remarks because he was at the convention when the July essay was written.

49. Assuming the work was in editor Greenleaf's hands in time to have been printed on September 13, the author wrote without having seen "Rusticus" or Hamilton's response to "A Republican." The September 13 *New York Journal* carried the note that, for want of space, "Anti-Defamationis" would appear in the next issue. Such an occurrence was normal in the eighteenth-century press. Nevertheless, Greenleaf published "Rusticus" on September 13, and he might have wanted to increase the impact of the essays, which expressed similar views, by having them appear in separate issues.

50. Reprinted in issue of September 27.

51. *Virginia Independent Chronicle*, September 26. Davis printed the Constitution as a pamphlet before the next issue of the *Chronicle* appeared. Here and elsewhere, dates of first printings of the Constitution are based on the sources and information given in Introduction, n. 9. See also n. 14 above for examples of news stories that resemble political advertising.

52. Two more Philadelphia papers published it on September 21.

53. It is possible that one Connecticut paper, the Litchfield *Weekly Monitor*, first printed and circulated the Constitution as a handbill on September 24.

54. Given in COC1: 217; nineteen reprintings occurred by October 11.

55. Given in ibid.

56. Milligan was writing to William Tilghman, who voted for ratification of the Constitution as a delegate to the Maryland ratifying convention. For the quotation, see COC1: 219.

57. Robert A. Rutland, *The Ordeal of the Constitution: The Antifederalists and the Ratification Struggle of 1787–1788* (Boston, 1983; originally published 1966), 1–2 and Andrew C. McLaughlin, *The Confederation and the Constitution 1783–1789* (New York, 1905), 278.

58. Given in COC1: 218.

59. For contemporary analysis from the Antifederalist perspective, see Herbert J. Storing, with the assistance of Murray Day, ed., *The Complete Anti-Federalist*, 7 vols. (Chicago, 1981), 3: 111–13, 132, 192–93; 4: 24–25; 5: 74–75. Although the media's Federalist stance in the period after September 17 is well known, the actual story of the media and the selling of the Constitution awaits a detailed history. The best general analysis is woven into Robert A. Rutland's *The Ordeal of the Constitution*, passim and especially 21–24, 37–38, 51–54, 59, 62, 72–74, 98–99, 128–39, 148–49, 165–66, 200–201, 204, 211, 265–67, 308–9. Representative notations of the news media's Federalism are offered in John B. McMaster and Frederick D. Stone, eds., *Pennsylvania and the Federal Constitution, 1787–1788* (Philadelphia, 1888), 15; Evarts B. Greene, *The Revolutionary Generation: 1763–1790* (New York, 1943), 388–91; Edmund S. Morgan, *The Birth of the Republic, 1763–89* (Chicago, 1956), 151–52; Jackson Turner Main, *The Antifederalists: Critics of the Constitution, 1781–1788* (Chapel Hill, 1961), 201, 210, 214, 215–16, 217, 221; Donald H. Stewart, *The Opposition Press of the Federalist Period* (Albany, 1969), 4–5. The general view is summed up briefly in COC1: xvii–xx, and the editors of the *DHROC* offer valuable analyses along with their transcriptions of various items the media published during the ratification fight. In addition, Linda G. De Pauw and John P. Kaminski, in separate works, offer valuable discussions of the situation in New York. See De Pauw's *Eleventh Pillar: New York State and the Federal Constitution* (Ithaca, 1966), especially 91–105, and Kaminski's "New York: The Reluctant Pillar," in *The Reluctant Pillar: New York and the Adoption of the Federal Constitution*, ed. Stephen L. Schechter (Troy, 1985), 48–117 passim, and especially 65–72.

Conclusion

America's eighteenth-century news media enjoyed depicting itself as an evenhanded and vital force for good in the land. The word "independent" often appeared in newspaper titles, and more than one masthead announced that the paper was open to all but influenced by none. Publishers argued, with special vehemence in 1787, that the Union's well-being depended upon the dissemination of news and information by a free press. Reflecting this ideal, the press was expected to display impartiality when dealing with important public questions, and publishers, even partisan ones, strove to give at least the appearance of being fair.[1] When covering the Constitutional Convention, very few publishers lived up to the expressed ideal. Francis Bailey of the *Freeman's Journal* and Thomas Greenleaf of the *New York Journal* supported the convention, but they also opened their pages to authors who rejected the notion of deferentially accepting the delegates' recommendations. Some other publishers, such as those of the *Columbian Herald*, the *Gazette of the State of Georgia*, and the *Hudson Weekly Gazette*, displayed evenhandedness. But most publishers did not. Indeed, they moved past applauding Congress's authorization of the convention to strengthen the Union and even past ballyhooing for the delegates. As Anti-Defamationis charged, many in the press worked to convince citizens they should relinquish the right to scrutinize the delegates' proposals. The general press coverage unquestionably was designed to make it difficult for anyone to challenge the delegates' handiwork.

Although their complaints rarely were reprinted, some writers tried to blow the whistle on the news management campaign. In mid-August, as the media bristled with propagandistic material, a Rhode Islander approached the issue in a roundabout way. He maintained that newspapers throughout the land, for more than two years, had routinely printed articles that grossly exaggerated the Union's problems. Without mentioning the convention, he charged that the aim was to undercut America's republican governments. By mid-September some exasperated New York authors bluntly charged that much of the press ruthlessly sought to convince Americans that they must accept the convention's still unannounced recommendations.

Some publishers conceded that they attempted to induce Americans to follow the convention delegates unquestioningly. David Humphreys boasted of it in a private letter sent to George Washington shortly after the convention adjourned. John Babcock and Thomas Claxton, editors of the *Northern Centinel*, publicly admitted it well after the fact. Mathew Carey did not acknowledge trying to sell the convention but did concede that he wanted to publish only pro-Constitution material once it appeared. Analysis of press coverage demonstrates that propaganda publishers such as Babcock and Claxton were more typical than Bowen, Vandle, and Andrews, the publishers of the *Columbian Herald*, who did open their press to all sides.

The essential evidence that reveals the effort to sell the convention comes from reprinting patterns. Authors who praised the convention and said the delegates must be followed had good reason to expect their comments would be widely circulated. Benjamin Rush's "Harrington" essay is the classic example. Writers who urged that the public should not accept uncritically whatever the convention produced could garner some reprintings if they employed proconvention rhetoric, but those authors rarely produced a popular item. The observations "Z" published in May provide the best example of this. Authors, like Sidney or Cornelius, who questioned the necessity of the convention or who questioned the delegates' nobleness, had virtually no chance of getting reprinted.

The news media routinely carried items denouncing any American who did not accept the view that the convention was absolutely necessary and that its recommendations should be approved. "Rogue's Island" was offered as a ready symbol of the opposition, and Rhode Island bashing occurred regularly during most of the convention period. One technique often used in proconvention commentary shows the press's bias. Editors routinely published writers who savaged the idea of using mere conjecture about the delegates' activities to question the convention. Yet month after month, convention boosters engaged in a riot of conjecture about the great things expected from the delegates' work. Month after month, those thoughts got reprinted. Few publishers appeared willing to acknowledge the inconsistency of publishing proconvention speculation while castigating speculation that was not so flattering to the delegates.

Considering their own vaunted ideals, the most damning evidence of publishers abandoning impartiality comes from their news coverage. The events of late 1786 through the early fall of 1787 certainly demonstrated that the convention had serious problems to tackle. Publishers, however, were not always willing to settle for news as it actually occurred. In 1787, some in the news media occasionally fabricated letters that championed the convention. Here again the vital consideration is the general pattern of reprintings. Just as publishers engaged in selective reprinting of commentary, they also engaged in selective reprinting of news and, at times, in outright news management. The handling of the story about the Connecticut legislative debate over sending delegates to the convention offered a hint of things to come. The full press report of the May 1787 debate devoted significantly more space to the proconvention representatives than their numbers warranted, but it was not completely misleading. However, truncated versions of the original story gave even less coverage to anticonvention views, and one version actually neglected to mention that any representatives opposed sending delegates to the convention. Such omissions were minor occurrences compared with how the media engaged in outright news management.

One significant example of news management occurred as the convention was ending. In September, stories about violence in Pennsylvania and Virginia that called up images of Shays's Rebellion were widely reprinted. In each case, reports published just days later corrected the overly alarmist picture drawn by the earlier press accounts. These corrective stories were either totally ignored or reprinted only rarely. That kind of coverage made it seem that the time of troubles had returned; it reinforced the proconvention message that the central government must be strengthened. Such manipulation of the news illustrates the degree to which many publishers had abandoned the press's avowed responsibility to disseminate news.

The other major example of news manipulation comes from the way the press handled reports about convention activities. In spite of the delegates' secrecy rule, leaks occurred. In addition, some writers who lacked convention sources nevertheless implied that they had inside information. So publishers had numerous opportunities to print stories about the delegates' actions. Once again a clear proconvention pattern emerged from what was reprinted and what was not. If a piece seemed less than laudatory or conveyed possibly undesirable news about the convention, it was invariably underreported. Thus, the article from early June about the delegates sitting for months and producing a totally new government gained few reprintings. Later very newsworthy stories from the *Columbian Herald* that raised potentially troublesome points also rarely got reprinted. On the other hand, *Columbian Herald* reports that tended to applaud the delegates proved popular.

The prime illustration of manipulative coverage comes from the press response to the *Pennsylvania Herald* account of June 13 about the delegates being divided and about some holding antidemocratic ideas. In accordance with the standard proconvention coverage, this most newsworthy piece was underreported. Moreover, many publishers, including the editor of the *Herald*, acted quickly in ways that undermined or discredited the June 13 story. Authors rushed into print to stress that the secrecy rule was being followed, and a new word—"unanimity"—came into vogue in widely reprinted commentary about the delegates. Then, except for talking about unity, publishers stopped printing convention stories based on alleged insider information. Doing that silently but forcefully suggested that the people should not trust any stories of the June 13 variety. Even into September, many publishers remained wary of printing items that suggested information had leaked from the convention. There was one important exception. The press gave prominent play to a quotation that reportedly came directly from the delegates. It said the delegates had never once thought of a king and thereby served to squelch the rumor that they might be creating a monarchy.

To a significant degree, the nationalistic proconvention forces had a monopoly on the message the news media presented. That message reflected a pragmatic or nontheoretical approach. When Alexander Dallas praised the delegates for not getting mired down in philosophical discussions about political principles, he could just as well have been talking about press coverage of the convention. Publishers showed little inclination to reprint essays that offered abstract philosophical analysis. Authors who attained popularity usually kept their message simple as they commented upon the dangers inherent in weak governments and argued that the central government must have more power. Although analysts rarely delved into theoretical intricacies, popular commentators did suggest limits on how much power the central government should have. Monarchy would not do for America, and an "aristocratical" or other "anti-democratic" government would also be unpalatable. The government of the Union had to be "republican." A number of popular authors also stressed that the excesses of democracy could and were ruining at least some of America's governments.

The commentary on all these points typically was offered in short pronouncements about seemingly established truisms. No systematic effort was undertaken to define the various political terms.

The same pragmatism was evident in the press's favorite proconvention theme. It held that America faced a time of troubles that could only be cured by strengthening the central government. The evidence cited most often to buttress that claim concerned threats that could destroy the nation. Fear of Shays-style bloodshed, fear of the Union breaking apart, and fear of foreign invasion were cited repeatedly to prove the necessity of accepting the convention and its recommendations. Correspondingly, the most frequently reprinted appeals to support the convention's efforts raised the specter of the nation crumbling if that support were withheld.

The pragmatic approach was also evident in articles about economic issues. Authors spoke of a variety of pressing problems rather than offering theoretical discussions. They held, for example, that steps should be taken to assist farmers and manufacturers, to improve commerce, to create a fair tax system, to pay government debts, and to stop the emission of paper money. Almost invariably, those points were made in the context of saying the central government required augmented powers to deal with noneconomic as well as economic problems. At times the message was varied to say that economic problems somehow would fade away and a glorious future would come forth—*if* the central government had more power. However, except for making the general point that government had to have more power, even popular authors who focused on economics tended to be descriptive rather than analytical and prescriptive.

For much of the convention period, the press gave economic issues less play than one might expect. Through July, discussions about economics usually appeared as part of general commentary on the Union's feeble political situation. Economic points received more attention once it was assumed the delegates would soon unveil their recommendations. In August, more than ever before, popular authors made unabashed pocketbook appeals often phrased with emphasis on the potential economic greatness of the Union. Although the increased interest in economic matters continued into September, the emphasis on pocketbook considerations faded slightly. Once again economic analysis usually appeared in general commentaries about accepting the convention's work in order to save the Union by strengthening its government.

The basic proconvention message on the necessity of strengthening the government was linked to the idea that the people could and should trust the convention delegates to repair the ship of state. George Washington became a vital ingredient in the effort to build trust. The press depicted Washington as a true savior and also tried to transfer some of the people's love and respect for him to all the delegates. When the convention started, and routinely thereafter, the people read variations on the theme that the delegates represented the collective wisdom of the Union, of the continent, of the world—past and present. As the weeks passed, praise for the patriotic delegates increased, which made it harder to question their efforts. Thus, a fundamental theme hammered at with increasing intensity over time was that the patriotic delegates were so noble, so honest, so talented—in sum so like George Washington—that the people should trust and support them resolutely.

Unfolding events, including what the press published, naturally caused publishers to adjust their coverage. Pieces about the convention or related issues understandably increased in May when the delegates were expected to commence work. The June 13 story caused a publishing flurry. Then as accounts about the convention stopped, little new material appeared in print. Another spurt of publication occurred in August, when it was expected the delegates would soon make their recommendations public. Despite such fluctuations, the intensity of feeling exhibited in the press escalated over time. There was, for example, always a bite to items that discussed persons who might oppose the convention or its results. But as time progressed, authors became more vicious. The potential dissidents were, in preconvention days, described as misguided, selfish politicians. By July, penmen regularly charged that the potential dissidents, perhaps unintentionally, were aiding the country's enemies. By late August, when the convention's results were expected almost daily, writers were more likely to describe dissenters as actually being in league with those enemies. By mid-September, convention boosters had slipped almost comfortably into using the term traitor, or its equivalent, in commentary about those who might reject the convention's recommendations. The prescription for dealing with potential dissidents also hardened over time. It went from saying they should be shunned, to saying they should be treated as the Loyalists, to saying they should be, if necessary, exterminated. Virtually all editors refused to reprint authors who said persons should be killed if they opposed the delegates' recommendations. As a group, the publishers' actions suggest that they disliked blatant threats to use physical violence against political enemies. Nevertheless, as the convention period progressed, publishers showed less hesitancy about publishing allusions to employing violence.

What prompted publishers to champion the Constitutional Convention, and then the Constitution, so ardently? In their public declaration of March 1788, Babcock and Claxton said they became propaganda editors out of a patriotic sense of duty to the Union. They claimed to believe that the central government had to be strengthened for the good of the Union. In their minds, patriotism moved them. Other propaganda editors probably used the same reasoning to justify their own actions. There is good reason to give credence to the claim that publishers acted because they thought the Union must be reformed. As best it can be discovered, Babcock and Claxton's view was the popular one in America. The central government obviously needed more power. Although the imposts of 1781 and 1783 failed to garner the necessary unanimous approval, every state in the Union had, at one time or another, voted to increase Congress's power. The year 1787 *was* marked by dangers and anxiety. Some Americans exaggerated the extent of popular involvement in Shays's Rebellion, but it occurred. It was not the invention of the news media. Congress had become moribund. Neither the congressional requisitions nor the public debt were being paid. The British still maintained forts on American soil. Westerners screamed about the drastic steps they would take if denied use of the Mississippi River. So it is understandable that most publishers, like most Americans, supported holding the convention and strengthening the central government.[2]

Even accepting patriotic motives at face value, there were other logical reasons for the press to champion the convention and, when it appeared, the Constitution. Newspapers and magazines were, overwhelmingly, urban entities. Publishers, especially those who lived in the largest cities, could see the need for strong government because of the problems so endemic to the urban environment. Like urbanites generally, they, along with their subscribers and advertisers, were part of the commercial network that ultimately produced the most ardor and votes for the Constitution. In addition, publishers were attuned to issues and problems that extended past their immediate locale. They were likely to have a cosmopolitan outlook and, as Alexander Hamilton put it, to think continentally. That was natural. They depended on the central government's post office to bring papers from the rest of America. Their duties as publishers made them consider the news of the world as well as from the Union as they selected what to reprint or not reprint.[3] Publishers who participated in the selling of the Constitutional Convention therefore probably acted from intertwining motives. Happily for them, and perhaps not coincidentally, their patriotic position and their urban, commercial view of the world happened to mesh conveniently. But when editors attempted to sell the Constitutional Convention, they demonstrated a willingness to overlook expressed journalistic ideals in the service of what they maintained was a good cause.

Notes to Conclusion

1. For a particularly useful example that shows how the ideal of balance existed and how it could be broached even as it was

proclaimed, see "A Plain Man," *Connecticut Courant*, March 19. See also Chapter Five, n. 2.

2. Totally discounting "Rogue's Island," there was, as the debate in the Connecticut legislature reveals, some responsible opposition to holding the convention and to altering the Confederation government significantly. Moreover, the voice of the people expressed in the elections for representatives to the state ratifying conventions shows that there was strong sentiment against the Constitution. However, it would be an error to read that degree of division back into the convention period. People who might well have opposed the Constitution proposed in 1787 did not necessarily oppose the idea of holding the convention or of strengthening the Confederation government. See COC1: 11–40, 259–60, and the works by Main cited in the following note.

3. On these points generally, see Jackson Turner Main, *Political Parties before the Constitution* (Chapel Hill, 1973) and *The Antifederalists: Critics of the Constitution, 1781–1788* (Chapel Hill, 1961). On the newspaper network, newspaper distribution, and who subscribed to media publications, see COC4: 540–42; Edwin Emery and Michael Emery, *The Press and America: An Interpretative History of the Mass Media*, 4th ed. (Englewood Cliffs, 1978), 97; Frank L. Mott, *A History of American Magazines 1741–1850* (New York, 1930), 100–101. On the possible influence of living in a large urban environment, see John K. Alexander, *Render Them Submissive: Responses to Poverty in Philadelphia, 1760–1800* (Amherst, 1980), 43, 61–63, 73–74, 86–88, 91–92, 130–31.

Appendix 1

Short Title List for Newspapers and Magazines, 1787

The following list of short titles is for newspapers and magazines published in 1787. Place of publication is given if it is not contained in the title. Frequency of publication is indicated using the following symbols: M for monthly; BW for biweekly; W for weekly; SW for semiweekly; TW for triweekly; D for daily. All notations on missing or extant issues refer only to 1787. If a few issues for the March–September period are missing, that is indicated by the statement "some missing." If significant numbers of issues for that period are missing, that is clearly indicated. Where no comment on missing issues is given, a full file exists for at least the vital period from the start of March through the end of September 1787. Where relevant, other pertinent information is appended. All information on newspapers given here is based on Clarence S. Brigham, *History and Bibliography of American Newspapers, 1690–1820*, 2 vols. (Worcester, 1947) and on his *"Additions and Corrections to* History and Bibliography of American Newspapers, 1690–1820," *Proceedings* of the American Antiquarian Society 71 (1961, Part I): 15–62. Full titles and indications of title changes are given in Brigham, *History and Bibliography*. The information on magazines is from Frank Luther Mott, *A History of American Magazines, 1741–1850* (New York, 1930).

CONNECTICUT
American Mercury, Hartford. w.
Connecticut Courant, Hartford. w.
Connecticut Gazette, New London. w.
Connecticut Journal, New Haven. w.
Fairfield Gazette. W; 21 of 31 issues March–September missing
Middlesex Gazette, Middletown. w.
New Haven Chronicle. w: some missing
New Haven Gazette. w.
Norwich Packet. w.
Weekly Monitor, Litchfield. w.

DELAWARE
Delaware Courant, Wilmington. w: 21 of 31 issues March–September missing
Delaware Gazette, Wilmington. w: 25 of 30 issues March–September missing

GEORGIA
Gazette of the State of Georgia, Savannah. w.
Georgia State Gazette, Augusta. w.

MARYLAND
Bartgis's Marylandische Zeitung, Fredericktown. BW: no 1787 issues extant
Maryland Chronicle, Fredericktown. w: some missing
Maryland Gazette, Annapolis. w.
Maryland Gazette, Baltimore. sw.
Maryland Journal, Baltimore. sw.
Palladium of Freedom, Baltimore. D: started August 1; only issue extant August 8

MASSACHUSETTS
American Herald, Boston. W.

American Recorder, Charlestown. w: paper discontinued
  May 25
Boston Gazette. w.
Continental Journal, Boston. w: discontinued June 21
Cumberland Gazette, Portland, Maine. w.
Essex Journal, Newburyport. w.
Hampshire Chronicle, Springfield. w: started March 6; 11 of
  30 March–September issues missing
Hampshire Gazette, Northampton. w.
Independent Chronicle, Boston. w.
Massachusetts Centinel, Boston. sw.
Massachusetts Gazette, Boston. sw.
Salem Mercury. w.
Worcester Magazine. w.

NEW HAMPSHIRE
Freeman's Oracle, Exeter. w: some missing
New Hampshire Gazette, Portsmouth. w.
New Hampshire Mercury, Portsmouth. w.
New Hampshire Recorder, Keene. w: started August 7
New Hampshire Spy, Portsmouth. sw.

NEW JERSEY
Brunswick Gazette, New Brunswick. w: 1787 issues to July 3
  missing
New Jersey Journal, Elizabeth Town. w.
Trenton Mercury. w: started May 12

NEW YORK
Albany Gazette. w: 10 of 31 March–September issues missing
American Magazine, New York. M: started December
Country Journal, Poughkeepsie. w: some missing
Daily Advertiser, New York. D.
Hudson Weekly Gazette. w: some missing
Independent Journal, New York. sw.
New York Gazetteer. sw.
New York Journal. w: became a daily November 19

New York Morning Post. D: just under 50 percent March–
September issues missing
New York Packet. SW.
Northern Centinel, Lansingburgh. W: started May 21

NORTH CAROLINA
North Carolina Gazette, Edenton. W: started October 24; only
December 12 extant
North Carolina Gazette, New Bern. W: only three 1787 issues
extant
State Gazette of North Carolina, New Bern. W: only three 1787
issues extant

PENNSYLVANIA
American Museum, Philadelphia. M.
Carlisle Gazette. W.
Columbian Magazine, Philadelphia. M.
Evening Chronicle, Philadelphia. TW to August 7 then SW: 24
of 84 March–September issues missing
Freeman's Journal, Philadelphia. W.
Germantauner Zeitung. BW: some missing
Independent Gazetteer, Philadelphia. D.
Lancaster Zeitung. W: started August 8
Pennsylvania Chronicle, York. W: started October 24; only
two 1787 issues extant
Pennsylvania Gazette, Philadelphia. W.
Pennsylvania Herald, Philadelphia. SW to September 11 then
TW to October 10
Pennsylvania Journal, Philadelphia. SW.
Pennsylvania Mercury, Philadelphia. W.
Pennsylvania Packet, Philadelphia. D.
Philadelphische Correspondenz. W: some missing
Pittsburgh Gazette, W.

RHODE ISLAND
Newport Herald. W.
Newport Mercury. W: some missing

Providence Gazette. W.
United States Chronicle, Providence. W.

SOUTH CAROLINA
Charleston Morning Post. D.
Columbian Herald, Charleston. SW.
South Carolina Weekly Chronicle, Charleston. W: started
    May 22 [?];only extant issue October 9
State Gazette of South Carolina, Charleston. SW: some mis-
    sing

VERMONT
Vermont Gazette, Bennington. W.
Vermont Journal, Windsor. W.

VIRGINIA
Kentucke Gazette, Lexington. W: started August 11
Norfolk and Portsmouth Journal, Norfolk. W: only September
    28 supplement and November 2 extant
Virginia Gazette, Petersburg. W: 26 of 31 March–September
    issues missing
Virginia Gazette, Winchester. W: started July 11
Virginia Gazette and Independent Chronicle, Richmond. W:
    only October 6 extant
Virginia Gazette and Weekly Advertiser, Richmond. W.
Virginia Herald, Fredericksburg. W: started June 7; only four
    1787 issues extant
Virginia Independent Chronicle, Richmond. W.
Virginia Journal, Alexandria. W

Appendix 2

Note on Methodology

Unless otherwise noted, all information on the number, kind, and status of newspapers and magazines was derived from the works of Brigham and Mott cited in the headnote to Appendix 1.

A basic problem with determining number of reprintings stems from the effort required to obtain and go through the various media publications. After reading several files of newspapers fairly readily available on microfilms and microcards, it became obvious that gathering copies of the extant papers and magazines and reading them required the financial and human resources of a team rather than the efforts of a single scholar. Fortunately, a research team had compiled some of the necessary information for the sources printed in the *Commentaries on the Constitution* volumes. However, for the current study, it was necessary to use many items not printed in *Commentaries*. John P. Kaminski, believing that the most that can be obtained from the raw research files should be obtained, kindly allowed me to augment my own research by using the files of The Documentary History of the Ratification of the Constitution Project to obtain exact dates and other information on reprintings both for material published in *Commentaries* and for other items important to this study. Given the way reprinting occurred and given the complexity and scope of the task, reprintings of some items have surely been missed. All statements on numbers of reprints must thus be viewed as subject to some slight revision. The few reprintings that may have been missed would not, however, alter the basic findings about press coverage of the Constitutional Convention.

For the few items cited from COC1 where the reprint total used in this study differs from that given in COC1, the reason invariably is that an additional reprinting was discovered. Because a file of the newspaper was not then available to the Project research team, in virtually all cases the additional reprinting occurred in the Philadelphia *Evening Chronicle*. Where the reprint total of a COC1 item is increased by one in this study, it is, unless otherwise noted, because a reprinting occurred in the *Evening Chronicle*.

The maximum number of reprintings discovered for items cited in this study was used to establish ten or more appearances as the standard for being classified as a "popular" or a "widely" reprinted item. The sample used was based on the reprinting information for 114 items, given in COC1, published from late February through mid-September. This includes the COC1 reproduction of the items published or reprinted in a newspaper or magazine from the time of Congress's February 21 resolution through the reprintings of the last major item that appeared before the Constitution was published. The 114 thus includes the CC1-CC74 items with the exception of the following CC numbers: 2A, 2B ,47A, 47B, 55. The total of 114 follows the editors in counting both CC18A and CC46A as two items based on different reprintings of different parts of the publication. The champion reprint item from the 114, with a total of forty-six appearances, was the first "news" report on what the delegates were supposedly planning to do (CC35A). The next two most widely circulated items were a letter from Dr. Richard Price (CC22, with forty-two appearances) and Congress's resolution authorizing the Constitutional Convention (CC1, with thirty-nine appearances). Only four of the 114 items appeared thirty-five times or more. If an item was printed at least ten times, the piece had received between twenty and twenty-five percent of the appearances it was possible to attain. Based on the ten appearances standard, eighty of the 114 COC1 items would be classified as "popular."

Certain other points of terminology and procedures followed require comment. The use of the term "correspondent," or "writer," should not be understood as referring to an employee. Moreover, in the press of that time, commentary and news were often provided by publishing extracts of letters provided to publishers by their recipients. When editors printed such extracts, the letters typically were quoted literally. If the editor described a letter as an extract, that is indicated in the text or a footnote of this study. Although publishers were not hesitant about printing their own words and opinions, newspapers did not have separate editorial sections. Something labeled as coming from a "correspondent" could in reality be an editorial in disguise. Moreover, editors or publishers usually did not acknowledge authorship of the items they produced. Where the context strongly suggests that material was written either by the editor or publisher, this has been noted.

Anonymous essays, usually signed with a pen name, were a staple of the press in 1787. While it is possible that some essays not identified as being written by a woman were, in fact, so authored, none of the pen names of the items cited in this study suggests, as some pseudonyms do, that a woman authored the item.[1] Similarly, although some women assisted husbands or brothers in publishing, only one woman was a publisher of a newspaper or magazine in 1787, and it is not clear if she actually directed the paper. The *State Gazette of South Carolina* was, in 1787, described as being published "for" Ann Timothy. The normal statement would have been published or printed "by [name of editor]."[2] Because of these points, when publishers in general are being discussed, the male pronoun is used.

Where an article has been reprinted in the COC1 volume, that source is always cited. Finally, the transcription policy adopted by the editors of the *Commentaries* volumes is followed in this work. (See COC1: xxv.)

Notes to Appendix 2

1. See, e.g., "A Female," May 10, and "A Distressed Widow," April 5, in the *Newport Herald* and also the reference to "a female correspondent" in the *Pennsylvania Packet*, May 24.

2. Cf. Evans 20724 with 20638, 20639, 20718, 20719, 20723. Leona M. Hudak's description of the work of Ann Timothy shows that Timothy's role in publishing the *State Gazette of South Carolina* in 1787 is not clear. See Hudak's *Early American Women Printers and Publishers 1639-1820* (Metuchen, 1978), 471-72, 479-80.

Index